Lifeguarding

by Cary Epstein &
Cameron DeGuzman

Lifeguarding For Dummies®

Published by
John Wiley & Sons, Inc.
111 River St.
Hoboken, NJ 07030-5774
www.wiley.com

For general information on our other products and services, please contact our Customer Care Department within the U.S. at 877-762-2974, outside the U.S. at 317-572-3993, or fax 317-572-4002. For technical support, please visit https://hub.wiley.com/community/support/dummies.

Wiley publishes in a variety of print and electronic formats and by print-on-demand. Some material included with standard print versions of this book may not be included in e-books or in print-on-demand. If this book refers to media such as a CD or DVD that is not included in the version you purchased, you may download this material at http://booksupport.wiley.com. For more information about Wiley products, visit www.wiley.com.

Library of Congress Control Number: 2023934628

ISBN: 978-1-119-98619-5 (pbk); 978-1-119-98621-8 (ebk); 978-1-119-98620-1 (ebk)

SKY10045332_041123

Contents at a Glance

Table of Contents

Introduction

Welcome to *Lifeguarding for Dummies*! You have this book in your hands, so we imagine it must be for one of several reasons. You're in the market for a new job and this is the hundredth book you've picked up. Perhaps you've earned your lifeguard certification and don't quite know what to do with it. Maybe the colder months are winding down, and you're looking for a fun and exciting way to keep busy in the summer. Look no further!

The lifeguarding career is perfect for anyone in search of a job with flexibility to work full-time, part-time, or even seasonally. You learn how to act as a first responder to various emergency scenarios and serve your greater community. It is a career with no age bias, teaching you skills that you can apply in any situation. And you become part of an elite team of lifesavers (see Figure I-1).

Cary Epstein (Author)

FIGURE I-1: A LIFEGUARDS ONLY sign closes off the designated lifeguard area from the general public.

WARNING

At the time of writing this, lifeguard shortages are affecting pools, beaches, and parks around the United States. Empty lifeguard stands and towers are forcing communities and municipalities to shorten their hours and scale down their staffing, putting the general public at risk. There is no better time to become a lifeguard and ease this situation!

So you think you can swim?

About This Book

If you've decided on a career in lifeguarding, you are in luck! This book is all encompassing, and there is very little we don't cover surrounding this topic. We can't think of any other publication that shares so many different angles of the profession. This isn't a manual or a brochure telling you how to join your country club as a lifeguard, nor is it a lifeguard cheat sheet for those currently employed. *Lifeguarding for Dummies* gives you a full 360-degree perspective on one of the most beloved and respected professions in the world.

You can learn every aspect of what it takes and means to be a lifeguard by reading this book. We dive into the various career opportunities that exist once you become certified. We explain how lifeguarding has grown into a worldwide community that goes back over 100 years, rich in history and lifesaving tradition. We throw in tips for becoming a lifeguard as well as workouts to help you kickstart your swimming and running training.

TECHNICAL STUFF

Note that web addresses and programming code appear in mono-font. If you're reading a digital version of this book on a device connected to the Internet, note that you can click the web address to visit that website, like this: www.dummies.com.

To make the content more digestible, we divided it into five parts:

>> Part 1: Getting Started with Lifeguarding

>> Part 2: Lifeguarding in the Different Facilities

>> Part 3: Training and Preparation

>> Part 4: Exploring Other Lifeguarding Activities

>> Part 5: Part of Tens

Foolish Assumptions

People in general have a natural tendency to make assumptions about others. As lifeguards, we (Cary and Cameron) make assumptions every second we are on the stand or in the tower. In this book, we also make a few about you, dear reader:

>> We assume you know what lifeguarding is and you have seen lifeguards at work or in action at some point in your life. If not . . . let's just say you've been swimming in all the wrong places!

>> We assume you know how to swim, or at least you *think* you know how to swim. Everyone's definition of swimming is different; if you have a competitive swimming background, you know what we are talking about. However, not all lifeguards have a competitive swimming background (nor do you need one!). If you're not sure where you stand, try one of our swimming workouts in Chapter 8 to assess your strengths and weaknesses.

>> We assume that you are physically, mentally, and emotionally fit to face some of the most extreme health emergency situations and are aware and ready to tackle this fast-paced environment.

>> We assume you are willing to enter that same, and potentially dangerous, water that almost took the life of a victim.

Icons Used in This Book

Throughout this book, icons in the margins highlight certain types of valuable information that call out for your attention. Here are the icons you'll encounter and a brief description of each.

TIP

The Tip icon marks tips and shortcuts that you can use to make your day-to-day duties on the job run smoothly.

REMEMBER

Remember icons mark the information that's especially important to know. To siphon off the most important information in each chapter, skim through these icons.

The Technical Stuff icon marks information of a technical nature that you can skip over if you're in a hurry.

TECHNICAL STUFF

The Warning icon tells you to watch out! It marks important information that may save you headaches, especially because it is entirely possible you will run into these types of situations on a day-to-day basis.

WARNING

Beyond the Book

In addition to the material in the print or e-book you're reading right now, this product also comes with some goodies you can access on the web. Check out the free access-anywhere Cheat Sheet that includes tips and advice. To get this Cheat Sheet, simply go to www.dummies.com and type **Lifeguarding For Dummies Cheat Sheet** in the Search box.

Where to Go from Here

The best part about this book is that you do not need to read the whole thing cover to cover if you don't want to (although we think you should!). Depending on the stage of the lifeguard search you're in, or if you are already a certified, employed lifeguard, you will likely approach this text in a different way.

The book is broken into 19 easy reading chapters and five main parts. Simply open the Table of Contents and find the area you are interested in. From there, the world is your oyster! You want a macro-perspective on the career, turn to Part 1. Want to know your employment options, look at Part 2! You can read this book sequentially or jump around as you see fit without feeling lost about any one particular topic. It's meant to be a fun, easy — but informative — read. (Cary and Cameron, shown in Figure I-2, hope you enjoy the journey!)

Cary Epstein (Author)

FIGURE I-2: Authors Cary Epstein and Cameron DeGuzman at Jones Beach State Park.

1

Getting Started with Lifeguarding

Understand what it takes to be a lifeguard and take a deeper look at what goes on day-to-day in this profession.

Become familiar with the lifeguard's encounters with nature, the science of drowning, various first aid techniques, and the different kinds of equipment you'll use.

Learn about the rich history of lifeguarding as well as how the original lifesavers have evolved into the aquatic rescuers and watermen we know today.

Chapter 1

Lifeguarding 101

Welcome to the world of lifeguarding, "the best job you will ever have." While we admit that is a pretty bold statement to start off with, ask anyone you know who has spent any amount of time lifeguarding and see what they have to say. This lifeguard world is filled with culture and tradition that goes back decades, and we are very excited to share it all with you in this book.

While stereotypically you might think of lifeguarding as a teenager's job, across the United States and around the world, there are dedicated people (including some who have given their lives to save others) who are proud to call themselves professional lifeguards. Think of Aquaman . . . but a realistic day-to-day version! We cordially invite you to kick off your shoes, grab your most appropriate bathing suit, and dive right in!

The Importance of Lifeguarding

Drowning is one of the leading causes of death across the United States and around the world. It is considered one of the most avoidable ways to die. How is it avoidable, you might ask? By simply swimming and recreating in waters protected by lifeguards, swimmers greatly reduce their risk. The majority of drownings are avoidable, but human nature just can't resist the temptation of getting wet. Did you know that 74 percent of fatal pool drownings happen residentially? When no lifeguards are present, public pools and beaches post signs that read "Swim at your own risk," yet people ignore the posted warnings and tragedies happen. Everyone thinks bad things can't happen to them. If that were the case, then bad things wouldn't happen to anyone. Frankly, this attitude can get you in a lot of trouble!

At the end of the day, if there are no lifeguards on duty, you really shouldn't be swimming . . . and yes that goes for people who are good swimmers too!

The Perks of Lifeguarding

Although there are waaaaay too many perks of the job to list in one chapter, we figured we would share some of our favorites!

>> **The beach, pool, or park is your office.** When you are told to report to work, this is where you are going! This couldn't be any more atypical. Your views of the sunset (if you're not working indoors) will be way better than your friends' who work typical 9-5 jobs at their desks, guaranteed!

>> **You have the best seat in the house.** People actually pay to come to your job, but you get paid *and* get the best seat in the house! Everyone wants to sit up on the lifeguard stand, chair, or tower . . . but they don't get to visit the Royal Palace and sit on the throne! Being high above the ground looking down on all brings both pride and power.

>> **No shoes, no shirt . . . no problem!** Try showing up to a traditional office and stripping down to a speedo or your favorite bathing suit. You'll never have a problem deciding what to wear either, since as a lifeguard you need to be in uniform at all times (no heels, no laces, no ties, no briefcases, no belts . . . no problem!).

>> **Being outdoors (unless you're indoors!)** While there most certainly are indoor lifeguarding jobs, we think that one of the best perks is getting to work outside. The warm blanket of sun covering you from head to toe, the gentle breeze that slightly blows your hair, the sweet scent of sunscreen infiltrating your nose, ending with a gorgeous sunset. And yes . . . you get paid for all of that!

>> **When the ocean is closed to the public for big surf, it is open to you.** This is a great opportunity for you and the lifeguard team to train. While we recognize the hazards of getting in the water during a high surf advisory, this is how ocean lifeguards fully prepare for the worst! Each agency has its own rules and regulations when it comes to putting guards in the water on these hazardous training days.

>> **Use of all the fancy equipment.** All the toys! Each specialized piece of equipment has a purpose and the only way to get proficient with them is to take them out. Grab a kayak, surfski, or rescue board! Get trained to row or operate the jet ski or motorized lifeguard boat!

>> **You get paid to work out!** Staying in shape is an important part of this job, as we will discuss in Part 3, but not many jobs pay you to work out. Yes, you read that correctly. Go to the gym on your own time or work out on the clock! In many cases, lifeguard shacks and areas have a variety of workout equipment to help you maintain your lifeguard physique.

>> **You develop lasting friendships.** It is not uncommon to make lifelong friends on the job. Due to the close-knit nature of the work, coupled with trainings and teamwork, you will quickly find yourself developing friendships with fellow lifeguards that can last a lifetime. These may be the people in your wedding party and at your children's first birthdays. Crazy as it sounds, you might even meet your future partner on the job (trust us, it has happened on more than one occasion)! P.S. Lifeguard weddings get wild!

Developing skills that will benefit you beyond the water

Being a lifeguard, you get much more than just a lifesaving skill set. There are many, many benefits that you develop from working as a lifeguard that transition into other jobs and industries.

Increased self confidence

Self-confidence and self-esteem take time to build up, especially for teenagers. Some of us never get our self-confidence up to a level we are happy with, even into our adult lives. Lifeguarding is an extremely serious job that requires making life and death decisions. At the end of the day, knowing that the decisions and actions you made helped keep people safe will absolutely lead to a boost in your own self-confidence!

Communication skills

Working in this role requires you to speak to all kinds of people, including your fellow coworkers, and adult and juvenile patrons visiting your facility. You need to be able to clearly express your thoughts and communicate with the public. Sometimes people just want to walk up to your lifeguard stand or chair to chat or ask a question. But in more serious situations, being able to delegate tasks with clarity and efficiency goes a long way when the clock is ticking.

Leadership qualities

Leaders are made, not born! Let's face it . . . some of us are better at leading than others. That doesn't mean that you can't learn to be a good leader. Leadership qualities take time to develop. As a lifeguard, there is no doubt you will find yourself in situations where you need to use these skills! Lifeguards who possess this skill set may find themselves being offered leadership positions or administrative titles, such as aquatics director, coordinator, captain, lieutenant, boatswain, and so on. These positions not only earn you more responsibility but also more money.

TIP

You do not need to be in an administrative or leadership position to be a leader. Some of the best lifeguards we know display incredible leadership skills. They are not bosses or administrators . . . just plain old salty lifeguards. Be the best version of yourself, and, in time, your leadership qualities will grow.

Teamwork

In almost all circumstances in this job, you need the rest of your crew to help you out. Whether you find yourself in a multi-person rescue or simply need backup to cover your chair when you jump in, you must be able to rely on your coworkers. You also need to be reliable in any situation that arises. Lifeguards often work closely together with the common goal of executing a rescue and saving someone's life. Without the ability to work as a team, the likelihood of a successful outcome significantly decreases.

REMEMBER

Teamwork makes the dream work!

Problem-solving skills

Some lifeguards might say that no two rescues are the same. Many certainly are similar, but when it comes down to it, you were tasked with a situation at hand and it was ultimately you who had to make the decision. This builds off the point about self-confidence. As you become more comfortable making autonomous decisions for the safety of others, you will realize that all this time you were dissecting the problem and coming up with the most efficient and sensible way to bring a swimmer or patron out of danger.

Handling stress

Stress is part of everyday life. However, as a first responder, levels of stress can be elevated, based on what you saw or actions you took while administering medical aid or performing a water rescue. Professional lifeguards learn that it is healthy and okay to feel stressed. You will learn not to compartmentalize your feelings and learn that there are ways you can express how you feel without being afraid of looking weak. Learning how to handle and recognize post-traumatic stress disorder will help you tremendously — not just as a lifeguard, but in everyday life as well. *Critical incident stress debriefings* (CISDs) are common practices after a serious rescue, especially when there is loss of life.

TECHNICAL
STUFF

A critical incident stress debriefing, or *CISD,* is a process that occurs soon after a traumatic incident, typically 24 to 72 hours after the event. It is led by a designated facilitator and designed to support recovery to those exposed to high levels of stress or trauma. It may link employees to counseling and treatment services if needed.

REMEMBER

You should never feel ashamed to talk about your stress or anxiety. In most jobs, services exist should you need or want to talk to a professional.

Meeting all types of people

We touch on this in far more depth in Chapter 7, but you will meet people from all walks of life in this career, providing a massive network arguably more diverse than any other profession.

While lifeguarding is typically thought of as a young person's job, the reality is that you can't have 20, 30, or even 40 years of experience and still be a teenager! One of the unique parts of this job is the age difference between the younger and older guards. Unlike a traditional "office," where friendships are formed in a more structured setting, it is not uncommon for professional yet more casual friendships to form between guards of different ages. It's not rare to get dinner after work with a table of lifeguards in their 20s, 30s, 40s, 50s, and 60s.

Most people's closest friends are within a few years of their age. As a lifeguard, true friendships are formed despite differences in age, based on their shared commonalities and love for lifesaving!

The love of the water and saving lives attracts people from all walks of life. Some choose this as a full-time job and others as part-time work. In later chapters, we go into more detail about the varying options you have as a lifeguard. Regardless, you could be working with people from different careers and backgrounds. One second you could be listening to someone's experiences working on Wall Street, and the next moment you could be talking to someone working in public safety, medicine, or education, to name just a few. They each have their own story and journey to share with you, as long as you are willing to listen. The common denominator that brings all lifeguards back to the lifeguard chair is their passion for water safety.

Maintaining a healthy lifestyle

Generally speaking, maintaining a healthy lifestyle is something that goes hand in hand with being a lifeguard. Since this job is extremely physical at times and requires a certain level of fitness, it is not uncommon for people who care about their health and fitness to be drawn to it. There are many ways to maintain a healthy lifestyle and we hope you follow some of our suggestions in the following sections.

Practice healthy eating habits

You are what you eat! What you put into your body not only affects how you look, but also how you feel. You don't necessarily have to feel 100 percent all the time, but you should always be ready to exert a lot of energy at any given moment. Emergencies can go down in the blink of an eye. Eating healthy means maintaining a balanced diet that is comprised of all the major food groups and nutrients.

Get in your cardio and don't forget to lift!

The job calls for you to be physically fit, and what better way to maintain fitness than intense cardio and lifting? The daily duties of the job help you maintain physical fitness without even realizing it. Swimming and running on rescues, treading water, and pulling victims to safety are all workouts in and of themselves. Call this a perk of lifeguarding; as mentioned earlier, you are getting paid to work out!

Get an appropriate amount of sleep

Most people have a hard time in this category, but getting the right amount of sleep each night can make or break you . . . especially as a lifeguard. Your work requires you to focus and concentrate. It's not a good idea to be tired, sluggish, or sleepy while on the job. On average, you should be getting a minimum of eight hours of sleep a night. So many great things happen while you are sleeping, so you are cutting yourself short if you aren't getting enough. If you want to feel your best and function at peak performance, consider setting yourself a bedtime and sticking to it. We promise you won't regret it.

Take care of yourself and your body

As a lifeguard, the first step in any situation is to make sure that the scene is safe. You are in no state to help others if you are not in the proper shape. Be sure to take care of yourself to avoid injury and illness. When in doubt, err on the side of caution and rest or take the day off. The job relies on you being healthy in order to make the facility safe for everyone else — and that means attending to your physical, mental, and emotional health.

Being a lifeguard fosters the perfect environment for your mental health. You are surrounded by a fun group of coworkers in a fast-paced, exciting environment. There will be times when the job gets stressful, of course, but if you do not allow negative feelings to overtake you, you will become stronger and more prepared for all types of situations.

REMEMBER

Don't be afraid to put yourself first! As the 1940's fitness pioneer Dan Lurie always said, "Health is your greatest wealth!"

The Tough Side of Being a Lifeguard

While lifeguarding most certainly has its perks, don't be fooled
... the job can and will be difficult at times. We don't often talk
about the tough side of being a lifeguard, but the reality is, it does
exist. Dealing with the public does present its challenges. In the
following sections, we address some of the more common difficulties about the job and offer our best advice on how to handle
them.

Being the bad cop

While lifeguards are known for their ability to make rescues, they
spend the majority of their days trying to prevent them! They do
that by enforcing a list of predetermined rules, which are set up
by the facility. All of the rules are in place for safety reasons, but
some seem more apparent than others. Being the bad cop isn't
always easy, but it comes with the job and you must own it!

Some of the most common "bad cop" rules you will have to
enforce include:

>> NO running

>> NO lifejackets or flotation devices in the water

>> NO glass bottles on the pool deck

>> NO ball playing in the water

>> NO roughhousing (chicken fights, dunking, and so on)

>> NO loud music (or music at all)

>> NO diving

>> NO sitting directly in front of the lifeguard stand or tower

>> NO swimming in unprotected waters

>> NO surfing

>> NO fishing

>> NO swimming while fully clothed

While these are just some of the more common rules you will
most likely need to enforce, it is important to think about how
you will deliver the message. Just because you need to be the "bad
cop" doesn't mean you need to be nasty. You know the old saying,

"You can catch more flies with honey than you can with vinegar."
That applies here. The rules should be posted somewhere obvious
in the facility too, as shown in Figure 1-1.

NO DIVING
NO SITTING,
NO STANDING,
NO JUMPING,
FROM THE
INFINITY POOL
EDGE/LEDGE

Jazmine / Adobe Stock

FIGURE 1-1: A sign at the edge of a resort pool designates the swimming rules.

You should act professional at all times. There are very few reasons to yell at anyone. In a stern, loud, and commanding voice, you should enforce the rule and explain why. It's better to kindly but firmly explain the situation, including why they can't continue doing whatever they are doing, and describe the implications of their actions. This is better than just barking orders. Taking that extra moment to explain goes a long way.

TIP

If a patron is giving you a hard time, simply remind them that you are doing your job, which is to keep all the swimmers safe. Starting a sentence with, "For your safety . . ." goes a long way. When in doubt, follow your facility's emergency action plan, which in most cases involves contacting a supervising lifeguard. For more serious circumstances, be sure you know who the next party is in the chain of command. Oftentimes, it is law enforcement.

WARNING

There is never a reason to get confrontational! Keep your cool at all times, because you never know what type of person you are dealing with or what they are capable of. We speak from personal experiences!

It's not always waves, saves, and babes

When you think of lifeguarding in general, you probably can't help but think of the most picturesque, beautiful summer day. However, the harsh reality of the job includes nasty weather conditions, which lifeguards deal with on a daily basis.

Harsh work environments (hot and cold)

Lifeguards work on hot days, cold days, rainy days, stormy days, and everything in between! Each facility has its own set of guidelines for how lifeguards should perform their duties in harsh weather environments. During the hottest heat waves and the coolest cold fronts, lifeguards need to be fully prepared to spend the entire day outside. This means having the appropriate clothing and gear. Any given day's weather can quickly turn on a dime. It can be 95 degrees and sunny all afternoon and then pouring rain and cold with heavy winds an hour later. Umbrella forts, as shown in Figure 1-2, can provide the protection you need.

Cary Epstein (Author)

FIGURE 1-2: Lifeguards on the East Coast take shelter beneath a strategically placed array of umbrellas, otherwise known as an umbrella fort.

REMEMBER

Pack your bag appropriately! This means you should have clothing and gear for all weather types. Don't just rely on the forecast, as conditions can change and develop quickly.

You might assume that lifeguards don't sit in the rain. Well, that may be the case in some places, but not everywhere! We can tell you from personal experience that we have most definitely sat on the lifeguard stand during the coldest, most rain-driven days with only a few umbrellas tied up with rope to protect us. As long as it is not lightning, we sit on the stand (and get soaked if necessary) in torrential downpours. While you might think this is terrible (and to a certain extent it is), it is way better than the alternative of getting sent home with no pay.

Lifeguards who have towers (as opposed to stands) can protect themselves from the harsh environments, like wind and rain, by going inside and watching the water.

When thunder roars, stay indoors!

One of the harshest environments you may experience are thunderstorms. While they are fascinating to watch and at times even fun to be caught in, they can be very dangerous and you should take them seriously.

As a lifeguard, it is part of your job to monitor the weather and know when thunderstorms are forthcoming. It is also your responsibility to safely and efficiently remove swimmers from the water, close down your operation, and seek shelter. Swimmers put themselves at serious risk if they wait until the last minute to pack up and get moving. Swimmers need to do better at listening to the instructions of lifeguards when they are telling them it is time to get going.

WARNING

Getting struck by lighting is not as uncommon as you might think. In recent years, lifeguards have been killed on the job during lightning storms. Is it worth your life?

TECHNICAL STUFF

According to the National Weather Service, lightning strikes the United States about 25 million times a year (for more, see weather.gov). Although most lightning occurs in the summer, people can be struck at any time of year. Lightning kills about 20 people in the United States each year, and hundreds more are severely injured.

Facility maintenance

As nice as it is to feel that the facility is yours, since you and the other lifeguards are the ones running the show, with that comes other responsibilities. Just like with your own home, you have to take care of it and maintain it. That means cleaning up your lifeguard area and, if it falls on your list of responsibilities, the bathrooms. You might be in charge of hosing down the locker rooms or disinfecting parts of the facility related to the pool area.

During the peak of the COVID-19 pandemic, many recreational facilities remained open and required extra care for keeping them clean. At the end of the day, many changing areas resembled pigsties. The responsibility for cleaning them often fell on the lifeguards. Piles of hair, empty bottles of shampoo, and used toiletries might litter the floor awaiting your clean up and removal. Lifeguards at pools and waterparks may be called upon to test pool chemicals and balance the chlorine or pH levels all throughout the workday to ensure a safe environment for swimming.

These types of maintenance might not be glamorous, but they are certainly responsibilities you could be tasked with.

Decision making (am I making the right decision?)

This job has a lot of autonomy. That's mostly good, but sometimes making so many decisions can take its toll. You will always have hard decisions to make, starting with whether you should or shouldn't go in for the rescue.

TIP

You should always go in for the rescue. "When in doubt, go out!" All lifeguards know the feeling of teetering on the edge of their seats and not knowing whether someone needs help, is just fooling around, or is just chilling. It's worth saying again: You should always go in for the rescue.

On another front, you might sometimes struggle when dealing with coworkers. How do you respectfully express a different opinion than your colleague? Than your superior? These internal battles are commonplace in all careers, and lifeguarding has no shortage of these situations.

Making mistakes and learning from them

You'll mess up, you'll slip, you'll make mistakes. Just like any other job! And just like any other job, there will be consequences.

Sometimes the consequences are small. You show up late to work, maybe you'll get a slap on the wrist and docked a few minutes.

But other times, your mistakes could put someone's life in danger or, even worse, lead to their death. For example, you miss a rescue or are delayed in getting off the stand. Thankfully, lifeguarding has a built-in system where fellow lifeguards watch over each other's waters and share responsibilities. You might be told or directed to make a rescue that you otherwise might have waited on. Senior guards, officers, and supervisors play a big role in helping you learn from your mistakes and good ones will ultimately make you a better lifeguard. The common goal of safety should always be top of mind.

Illness/injury

People get hurt on this job. There is no hiding that. Think about it: At any given moment you will go from sitting on the stand to engaging every muscle in your body from the second you stand up, jump off your perch, run into the water, and swim to your victim. If you aren't properly stretched and ready to go, you could injure yourself. We have seen it time and time again — lifeguards pulling a muscle and ending their season. During morning workouts or mid-rescue, you must be careful when employing full exertion of your body.

Stress

Lifeguarding comes with a good amount of stress. Whether it is directly related to a rescue or not, there are many types of scenarios that you will be involved in that will activate your general adaptation syndrome for responding to stress. It may be something as simple as dealing with an unruly patron who is giving you a hard time, or something more serious and life threatening. Either way, as a lifeguard you will learn how to best deal with stress. This can most certainly help you outside of the job in your everyday life.

Death

Although this is something we hope you never have to deal with on the job, we would be lying if we said that it doesn't happen. It is most definitely a possibility; you may encounter death if you work as a lifeguard long enough. Our job is saving lives and the thought of losing someone is the worst possible thing that can happen. A harsh reality of the job is that no matter how good you are, it can still happen despite your best efforts. The most important thing to remember — just because someone dies, doesn't mean you did something wrong. As long as you did everything you were taught and trained to do, you can at least rest knowing you did your best.

Every facility has its own way of dealing with an on-duty death, and you should use your facility's employee assistance program or whatever they have in place to seek out professionals such as counseling and support services. You should never feel ashamed to talk about something that might be bothering you, especially after losing someone. Deaths in aquatic facilities don't have to occur just from drownings or water-related incidents. Sudden cardiac arrest can happen anywhere, at any time, and that includes your pool deck, waterpark, or beach front.

WARNING

Regardless of the cause, premature death is shocking and difficult for all of us to deal with. Add to that any feelings of responsibility you feel as a lifeguard, and that's a heavy burden to carry. Don't carry it alone. Go talk to someone about your grief. Your feelings are valid and normal. Not dealing with them can lead to depression and even thoughts of suicide.

While others run out, lifeguards dive in

If most people were asked to come up with a list of public service/ first responder heroes, they most likely would say firefighter, police officer, or EMT. When people think of these amazing heroic professionals, they can't help but think of:

>> Firefighters, coming out of a burning building carrying a lifeless child in their arms.

>> Police officers, responding to a 911 call for help.

>> EMTs and paramedics, pulling up lights and sirens in the ambulance, ready to care for the sick, dying, and injured.

But people don't often think of *lifeguards*, who are the first ones to risk their lives diving into dangerous waters to assist a swimmer in distress.

When the building is on fire and everyone is running out, firefighters run in. When a mass shooting happens or a terrorist attacks and the public runs away, the police run toward them.

When the world was in complete shutdown, EMS providers showed up for work to provide the most important job in the middle of a healthcare crisis, barely ever going home and putting their own lives at risk.

Yes, these people serve heroic duties. But lifeguards never seem to get the same notoriety as their fellow first responders. Maybe it's because their services are not equally used or provided in every part of the country, or simply it is just being overlooked.

You don't dial 911 to get a lifeguard to respond. The lifeguard is just there, sees the problem, and responds. A true *first* responder. With fire and police responses, the media has a chance to arrive on the scene and cover the event. Unless there's a news crew at your facility, media coverage of lifesaving efforts go unreported to the public.

When the surf is pounding and the waves are crashing well over-head, who are you going to call? The lifeguards who respond to these calls for help will do whatever it takes to get that victim back to shore, safe and sound. Whether that be diving through the surf, jumping off a boat, or launching the jet ski . . . these professionals risk their lives to save others.

While it doesn't happen often, lifeguards do occasionally lose their lives on the job. May we never forget them, their actions, and all they sacrificed to save another human life.

TIP

Next time you find yourself at your local pool, beach, or lake, per-haps take a second to thank the lifeguards for their service!

Considering What It Takes to Be a Lifeguard

So, you've picked up this book and are probably wondering what are the next steps to kickstarting your career. Whether you are in search of a full-time career, something to do for extra cash, or a job to keep you occupied during the summer, we hope we can help you navigate this path.

Getting into and staying in shape

It likely comes as no surprise that performing the duties of this job is physically demanding and is not a good fit for everyone. We go in far more depth about this in the coming chapters, but it is important that you recognize the importance of being physically fit in order to perform this job well. The qualifying procedures prior to starting a lifeguarding career test your ability to run, swim, and ultimately bring a struggling victim back to safety.

REMEMBER

Note that being in physical shape does not end after you land the lifeguard job. It is important that you maintain a high level of fitness throughout your lifesaving career, in order to properly perform the daily duties of a lifeguard.

Training and classroom work

Just like with any other job, you need to undergo training to learn the ins and outs of lifeguarding. There are many technical things to learn and a required number of hours in the classroom. You have to become certified as a professional rescuer in first aid, CPR, and AED. You'll develop an extensive lifeguarding skill set, learning how to make rescues in all different scenarios and situations. The lifeguarding career and what you learn varies depending on which route you take: pool, waterpark, open water, or ocean. However, the fundamentals are the same. Whichever destination you choose and wherever you go, you'll learn in far more depth the specifics of the job and the role you play.

It all begins in the classroom, transitioning into hands-on skills in the water with your classmates and instructors. This will fully prepare you to be a functioning lifeguard, ready to save lives on the job.

Taking the required certification exams

In order to be a certified lifeguard, you must pass a series of physical and written exams. While we would love to share with you the specifics of exactly what you need, this is complicated because it depends on where you work. In fact, the type of environment you guard and the state or area you live in together play a role in the lifeguard requirements.

What we can definitely say is that all lifeguard tests require some sort of physical activity that includes swimming and performing rescues. When you are trying out for open water positions, there will most likely be a run portion as well. Also expect a written exam in some capacity. Just as an example, if your facility requires an American Red Cross Lifeguard Certification, you will be required to get an 80 percent or higher on the American Red Cross Lifeguard Training final examination. No matter how you slice it, your knowledge and skills will be tested and you should be ready to give it your all!

TIP

Inquire about the lifeguard qualifications at your local pool, beach, or waterpark ahead of time. Know what is expected so you can prepare yourself to be successful! Every lifeguarding park and facility has different expectations.

Considering Where Lifeguards Put Their Skills to Use

You might be wondering what your options are for working as a lifeguard. The truth is that we can say with confidence that there is no shortage of opportunities. Employers everywhere are looking for certified lifeguards to staff their facilities. Wherever there is water designated for swimming, a lifeguard is needed!

At pools and waterparks

Few things are more nostalgic than the memories of going to your neighborhood pool or waterpark with your friends and family to cool off during a hot and sweaty day. I think everyone at one point wanted to be the lifeguard sitting atop the chair, with a bird's eye view of the entire pool. Get certified and you can now have this opportunity!

You might be surprised by the number of pools in your area, all of which need lifeguards to function. Here are different settings for lifeguards:

>> Neighborhood pools

>> Aquatic centers

>> Gyms

>> Apartment complexes

- » Hotels and resorts
- » College and high school campuses
- » Country clubs
- » Camps

In big and small bodies of water

Visiting the beach is often a childhood favorite for many. Watching the lifeguards up on the stand and in the water, we thought they always seemed so cool. Little did we know that with a bit of determination and talent, we could be just like them . . . all we had to do was take the test! There are lifeguard jobs available at all open bodies of water, big and small — from the sleepaway camp lake, to the ocean beach, to the bayside park. Get certified, take the tests, and you can have this opportunity!

TIP

Qualifying procedures for open bodies of water typically occur a number of times during the year (or sometimes only once at the start of the season). You can't just jump on board at any time, like you might be able to as a pool lifeguard. Find out when your beach is hiring, make sure your certification is valid, and mark it on your calendar!

A DAY IN THE LIFE OF A JONES BEACH LIFEGUARD

We recognize that every lifeguard job is different, so it is impossible to describe a generic day in the life of a typical lifeguard. We can, however, share a day in the life of a Jones Beach lifeguard, which is located on Long Island, New York, where we work. There will certainly be some parallels with other lifeguarding agencies, but I think you'll find that the differences outnumber the similarities. We live and die by *The JBLC Golden Rule of Hour UP/Hour DOWN*, as described here:

Shift Time: **0930-1730**

0925: Sign in at designed location and report to your designated lifeguard area.

0930-0955: This is your own time to get ready for the day. Stow your personal belongings in the locker room. Put on your uniform. Apply your sunscreen. Throw your lunch in the fridge. Refill your water bottle and get mentally prepared for the day!

0955-1000: Report to the main lifeguard stand (the *mainstand*) for your assignment and first sit. They tell you what stand you are sitting on or opening for the day.

1000-1100 1 Hour UP: You lifeguard for one hour in the stand (in most cases, you will be sitting with another lifeguard), scanning the water, taking preventative actions, and if necessary, performing water rescues.

1100-1200 1 Hour DOWN: The most important thing to know about this is that your hour down is not a break . . . it's an hour off the stand. You are expected to respond to any and all emergencies. In most cases, this means backing up the primary guards on the opposite hour who are currently in the stands. On your hour down, you may choose to go for a swim, run, or work out in any capacity. This is also a great time to get hands-on and practice with different types of lifeguard-related equipment. Drills and in-service trainings often occur on your hours down. Regardless of what you choose to do, and especially if you opt to leave the lifeguard area, you must receive permission from your field's lifeguard officer on duty. As long as you are poised to respond to emergencies, you may sit behind the mainstand and read a book, relax, and take in some shade. This is your time to recharge and relax, as you will be going back up to lifeguard stand at the top of the hour.

1200-1300: 1 Hour UP

1300-1400: 1 Hour DOWN

1400-1500: 1 Hour UP

1500-1600: 1 Hour DOWN

1600-1700: 1 Hour UP

1700-1730: This is your own time at the end of the day to get your belongings together and unwind before signing out. Head on back to the designated lifeguard area, grab an outdoor shower (optional), get a snack from the fridge, and call it a day!

(continued)

(continued)

Cary Epstein (Author)

A lifeguard on a crowded afternoon at Jones Beach, NY gets on his feet for a better view of the patrons swimming.

SUMMER SCHEDULE FOR A LOS ANGELES COUNTY LIFEGUARD

By Joel Gitelson

Based on your seniority, compiled by the number of hours you have worked over the years, you can choose which section you want to work in (Southern, Central or Northern). Within that section, you choose the area where you want to work and then choose the 40-hour work week schedule for that area. This could be Hermosa in Southern, Venice or Santa Monica in Central, or Zuma and Malibu in Northern. You accrue hours during the rating period from September 1st to August 31st. Once you're put into that schedule, there's an area meeting where you get to meet your supervisors and go over the rules of the road. At the end of the meeting there might be a group buoy swim, or a pier jump, or maybe just bagels and coffee.

Generally, that's the last time you will all get together as one unit until the first weekend in August for the International Surf Festival. That's the weekend for Intracrew night competition (LA County areas only) and Taplin night competition (open to all beaches). After that, it may not be until the end of season area party in late August when you see almost everyone again in one place.

When your schedule starts, you directly go to your assigned tower, ready for a full eight hours (or more) of lifeguarding. Opening and closing the tower can be the most distracting part of the day and diligence in keeping your eyes on the water while setting up the tower and the area around it is critical. Checking in with headquarters to let someone know you are there is obviously important. Some specifics:

- You get a half hour workout during the weekdays and 20 minutes on the weekend. There is some flexibility to these times as it depends on the level of activity in your area. Sometimes it's longer; other times there's no time for a workout at all.

- At all times, you are responsible for *your* water, and you need to be aware of what is going on at the towers adjacent to you as well. Like all beaches across the country, some areas are busier than others, but the rules are the same: WATCH THE WATER/STAY IN SHAPE/DO THE RIGHT THING.

- You bring to the tower everything you need for the day. Fins, lunch, fluids, radio, binoculars, workout gear, and so on. There is no lunch break. There are no breaks. If you need to use a toilet, the permanent (guard) will come to your tower and give you the truck to take to the main station or the nearest public restrooms. As a permanent lifeguard, I can tell you that this was done infrequently. Lifeguards just adjust their habits to avoid this from happening.

- The towers have a phone or radio, high director's chair, first aid box, rescue can, and boat tow line. The boat tow line is used for exactly what its name implies. If you see a disabled boat that is slowly being pushed into the surfline, you immediately notify headquarters, who will the alert your area permanent and Baywatch. You then swim out to the vessel in distress, hook the tow line to the boat and, with the help of backup, tow the boat out of danger. This is one of the most intense aspects of tower lifeguarding. Attaching the line to a boat, and the line to your rescue can, and then the rescue can strap across your torso is just plain gnarly. You must keep your wits about you so as not to get jerked by a wave as it hits the boat you are now attached to! You might be alone for a few minutes until back up arrives. The safety of the persons aboard the vessel in distress comes first. If they need to come off the boat you take care of that. Lives come first, property second, and safety for all, always.

(continued)

(continued)

- When in the tower, your gaze is constant. You are responsible for the area in front of you and to the towers adjacent to you. If the can is hanging from the tower, you're in it. When you leave the tower, the can ALWAYS goes with you. When on the sand it's important to keep the can in motion so that the guards in the adjacent towers can keep track of you. You do the same when you see a tower without a rescue can hanging. If a guard in an adjacent tower goes down to the beach, you need to know where they are in case they need backup. Generally there should be some gesture with the rescue can that you see each other.

- If you get to work out, the permanent in charge of the area needs to approve it and then the towers adjacent to you need to know. Placing your can in the sand at the base of the tower is the sign that you are on a workout. If the can is resting on the railing in a horizontal position, it means you are treating someone for minor first aid. Any treatment that goes beyond what you have in your first aid box requires the permanent to respond with the rescue truck. They will handle it and you return to the tower to watch the water.

- As the day progresses, activity in some areas may decrease while in other areas it may increase.

- At the end of your shift, you call in your activity for the day. Rescues, prevents, first aids performed, boat warnings, and so on. Beaches with large parking areas will always be busier than beaches in residential areas, but people always manage to find that one parking spot after driving an hour from their inland home and show up just as you're about to close. This is why it's so important to constantly be on your toes. As you leave the tower to walk off the beach, ALWAYS look back.

Chapter **2**
The Elements of Lifeguarding

A s a lifeguard, you will constantly be faced with an ever-changing environment that will ultimately influence your decision-making process. You'll quickly grow familiar with the elements that an average person might not associate with lifeguarding. Over time, you will become a mini expert in various areas. In addition to learning how to read body language, you might also learn to understand weather patterns, cloud formations, wind, waves, and oceanography. You might even become an expert in understanding the correct balance of pH and chlorine in your local pool. If you work outdoors, you'll develop a love-hate relationship with the sun.

In this chapter, we even touch upon the science of drowning and what physiologically happens in this process. You will learn how quickly a good day can become a tragic one and how knowing the proper first aid techniques can help when a situation suddenly takes a turn for the worse!

There's More to Lifeguarding than Just Sitting in the Sun

Who knew?! While it might look like they are just sitting in their stands and towers taking in all that vitamin D, lifeguards are doing so much more! Lifeguards eventually become experts at reading the water, even though to many swimmers it may seem as if they are simply having a conversation with another lifeguard or staring into the abyss!

The reality is that there are many organized thoughts going on in their heads as lifeguards process what they see in and around the aquatic environments that they patrol. They just might be the professional people watchers of the world. That means the best lifeguards are trained to be on the lookout for certain characteristics that indicate someone needs help, well before their toes even hit the water!

Look left, look right: Constant surveillance

One of the first lessons you learn when becoming a lifeguard is how to effectively scan. *Scanning* refers to the practice of looking over the water in a particular pattern or way to ensure that you can see everyone and everything.

There are many different methods to scanning, but the goals are always the same:

>> Leave no area uncovered

>> Make sure to overlap your zone with the other lifeguards' zones (assuming there is more than one lifeguard on duty)

>> Know and check your blind spots!

>> Watch the water

You should be providing constant surveillance, never taking your eyes off the water for a prolonged period of time.

Watching the water

Lifeguards often use the most common scanning patterns, called the side-to-side or top-to-bottom techniques. Both of these scanning techniques require you to move your gaze side to side and top to bottom. It is often suggested that lifeguards move their heads and not just their eyes. That's because sitting still in one position for a prolonged period can make you tired and compromise your ability to focus. For this reason, numerous lifeguard organizations have rotating schedules that allow the lifeguards to change stations. This helps them maintain their mental focus.

TIP

During the scanning process, if you identify someone you consider to potentially be a problem, you should get out of your tower and make precautionary contact with that person. Don't wait for something to go sour, when you can prevent it. Trust your instincts.

For a situation that appears less concerning, note the swimmer in your mind ("keep an eye on the young girl in the pink bathing suit") and when scanning back, be sure to identify the person again and take stock of their situation.

Staying focused while on duty is by far the most important part of the job. Anyone with the proper training can make a rescue, but a good lifeguard might be able to prevent one if they recognize and respond to a potentially dangerous situation.

Here are few tips for staying focused while scanning:

>> Stay hydrated! This will help keep your mind sharp. Dehydration is a real obstacle, especially in outdoor settings under the sun.

>> Every few minutes, switch positions! Sitting or standing in one spot for too long is never a good thing.

>> Do a self-check! Every so often, ask yourself . . . am I fully focused? Am I watching or just looking? Anyone can look . . . but lifeguards *watch*.

>> Seek shade! Sit under an umbrella. Wear a hat and a pair of polarized sunglasses. You will be surprised how much all of this helps you stay focused while guarding.

It's much easier to stay focused in a busy, crowded area than one that is relatively deserted. Your focus should be on your area and the areas adjacent to you. You may need to back up a rescue in a different area and, conversely, you may need backup in your area.

TIP

If you happen to be on the lifeguard stand or tower scanning the water alongside another crew member, it is very beneficial to be talking through the things you are seeing. For one thing, it keeps you and your coworker more focused and on your toes. More importantly, there is a slimmer chance you will miss anything, as two sets of eyes working together will limit the things that go unnoticed. See Figure 2-1.

Photograph by Patrick Campbell

FIGURE 2-1: Two lifeguards on duty scan the ocean and point out characteristics of patrons in the water.

Getting paid to be professional people watchers

While someone yelling for help is an overt sign of a struggling swimmer, more often than not, there are many other, more subtle signs that professional lifeguards need to watch for.

Did you know that many drownings are silent? One of the biggest misconceptions is that all drowning victims yell and scream for help. However, many victims don't have the energy or where-withal to yell. If they can't breathe, they can't yell for help.

WARNING

Remember this frightening fact: The majority of drowning victims slip right under the water without making a sound! This is another reason that paying super close attention is so important.

There are many things a lifeguard can see that they should take note of when looking at the swimmers in the water. As professional people watchers, some of the things they should note include:

>> Swimmer attire. How are the swimmers dressed — is their attire beach appropriate? Do they look like they are frequent beach goers?

>> Overall body language before and after they get in the water.

>> Swimming ability — do they swim with strokes?

>> Boogie boards, flotation devices, lifejackets, and so on. Do they have them?

>> Facial expressions in the water.

Each of the items says *a lot* about any one particular swimmer. Lifeguards are not just sitting in their lifeguard chairs and towers; they are taking it all in and piecing it all together before anything ever happens. It should not come as a surprise that the people who end up needing help are most often one of the swimmers you previously identified.

Understanding the Effects of Water

The composition of the water makes a big difference in the way you feel and float! Most people don't realize that there is a real difference between freshwater pools, lakes, rivers, saltwater pools, and other open bodies of water.

REMEMBER

Taking all of this into consideration, remember that the way that you lifeguard will change as the conditions shift, minute by minute, hour by hour.

Swimming in salt water vs. freshwater

The Dead Sea, located between Jordan and Israel, is the lowest body of water on the surface of the Earth. Because of this, the amount of salt in the Dead Sea is many times higher than the average ocean. In fact, about 25 percent of the Dead Sea is salt! On the contrary, only about 5 percent of the world's oceans' composition is salt.

It is because of this high salinity that swimmers easily float in the Dead Sea. Although this is not the case for all other oceans, it is important to recognize the difference when recreationally bathing in freshwater versus salt water (you can still drown in the Dead Sea, and they do have lifeguards!). The bottom line is that swimmers are less buoyant in swimming pools and freshwater lakes than they are in salty oceans and seas.

TECHNICAL STUFF

There is also a difference in buoyancy when it comes to water composition, and this is attributed to the density of water. Density, in the simplest terms, is a measure of how packed together the individual molecules of something are. Salty water has more molecules! Freshwater is just H_2O (okay, unless you are swimming in distilled water, freshwater is composed of a lot more than just H_2O, but what matters for this discussion is the H_2O). Salt water, on the other hand, has all those salt, or NaCl, molecules floating around with it. All those molecules create a significant difference in density, meaning it's harder for objects to sink.

Gauging warm water vs. cold water

Do you consider yourself a warm water person or a cold water person? Open bodies of water tend to vary in temperature and there are many reasons as to why. Location, of course, plays a huge role, and other things like the time of year and which way the wind blows might add or drop a few degrees to your favorite swimming hole!

While there may be some benefits to warm Caribbean water, we also argue that swimming in cold water has its own benefits! As a matter of fact, did you know that the likelihood of surviving a drowning is better in cold water than in warm? This is because of something called the *Mammalian Diving Reflex* (MDR). Essentially, this is a survival instinct that takes place in colder water, typically below 70 degrees. When the MDR kicks in, it slows down the heart to allow the person to stay underwater for an extended period of time. In addition, their blood vessels constrict and reduce blood flow, redirecting blood to their vital organs. There have been many documented cases where people have been fully resuscitated after being underwater in frigid waters for over 15 minutes!

For this reason, cold water victims aren't pronounced dead until their bodies have been rewarmed in the emergency department and methods of resuscitation continue to fail.

Guess what? We're not quite done talking about density. Can you guess which water temperature has a higher density? You might have to brainstorm back to your physics or chemistry class. If you remember that warmer molecules move around faster, you may realize that colder waters are more dense, making floating in cold water just a tad easier. The molecules in warm water spread and bounce around at a faster rate. At about 40 degrees Fahrenheit, water reaches its maximum density. Once you drop a couple degrees colder, water turns to ice. There's no argument that you can float better on ice (float is clearly not the right word, but you're getting the picture here) than in the waters of a tropical beach somewhere. Just not nearly as long or as comfortably.

Navigating in calm water vs. turbulent water

No two bodies of water are the same. Conditions on open bodies of water change by the second. Many times, judging a book by its cover can be misleading. Underwater currents and even rip currents may not be visible to the average swimmer.

Just because the water looks calm, doesn't necessarily mean it is safe to swim in.

Turbulent bodies of water are a lot harder to swim in than calm water. Even great swimmers have a more challenging time swimming through choppy waters. Lifeguards should be much more vigilant when watching swimmers in moving, turbulent water.

If you have ever seen the ocean during a storm and compared it to the ocean on a more average day, you have noticed larger-sized waves, faster flowing moving water, and a lot more "white water." White water is the water you see at the surface of a breaking wave. On these turbulent water days, it wouldn't be uncommon for you to get in the water in one location and be swept down the beach within seconds. Swimming in this kind of environment has been likened to swimming in a washing machine.

Understanding the Effects of the Sun

While we all love the vitamin D we get from the sun, we need to be aware that too much sun can cause significant and permanent health problems. While basking in mother nature's glow might be your favorite part of the day, we should all take in the sun's rays in moderation. Skin cancer is one of the most common types of cancers around the world. As a matter of fact, according to the Skin Cancer Foundation, 1 in 5 Americans will develop skin cancer by the age of 70.

Sun protection

When was the last time you visited your dermatologist? Do you even have one? Lifeguards should visit a dermatologist annually. Believe it or not, this simple appointment could save your life. While most skin cancers are not deadly and can be treated when caught early, that's not the case with melanoma.

Melanoma is the most dangerous type of skin cancer. When it develops, it can spread to other parts of your body and kill you. The best way to protect yourself from all types of skin cancers is by wearing protective sunscreen and avoiding the sun for pro-longed periods of time. This is a serious issue for lifeguards, an on-the-job hazard that they need to take seriously to mitigate.

TECHNICAL STUFF

SPF stands for Sun Protection Factor and is the measurement of how well a sunscreen protects your skin from UVB rays. A lotion rated SPF 30 will protect you from burning 30 times longer than without any protection. UVA and UVB rays both contribute to skin cancer. UVB rays are typically associated with sunburns, while UVA rays are typically associated with skin aging. Understanding the dangers of the sun and the best ways to protect yourself can help you choose the appropriate lotion to block these dangerous rays.

Another (and better) way to protect your skin from excessive sun damage is to sit under an umbrella or wear sun-protective clothing. There are many long-sleeve, lightweight sun shirts that provide breathability on the hottest of days, yet maintain the same protection (or better) from the sun. The rating system for sun-protective clothing is Ultraviolet Protective Factor (UPF). It protects you from both types of sun rays.

A shirt with a UPF rating of 30 signifies that the fabric only allows 1/30th of the radiation from the sun to penetrate the material and make it onto your skin. A UPF of 50 allows 1/50th of the UV radiation to pass through it. For comparison, a typical cotton T-shirt offers a UPF rating of about 5.

Facts about skin cancer

Consider these important points about skin cancer. If you think it can't happen to you, you're wrong. Figure 2-2 shows a chart graphic that can help you keep an eye on those ABCDE moles.

>> Skin cancer is the most common type of cancer in the United States.

>> It only takes 15 minutes for the sun's UV rays to cause damage to unprotected skin.

>> You need to wear protection even when it's cloudy.

>> It is not the temperature, but the UV rays that cause skin damage.

>> The five-year survival rate of melanoma is 99 percent when it's detected early.

>> Having five or more sunburns doubles your risk of developing melanoma.

Sources: `skincancer.org` and `cdc.org`.

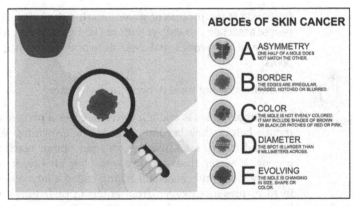

Alena / Adobe Stock

FIGURE 2-2: Knowing what to look for: the ABCDEs of skin cancer screening.

Understanding the Science of Drowning

Although many people think about drowning as a process of not being able to breathe, in fact it is a lot more than that. The science of drowning is both simple and complex. We briefly touch on the process, broken into a few stages.

According to the Centers for Disease Control and Prevention, *drowning* is the process of experiencing respiratory impairment from submersion or immersion in liquid. Not all drownings are fatal. *Fatal drowning* happens when the drowning results in death. *Nonfatal drowning* happens when a person survives a drowning incident with a range of outcomes, from no injuries to very serious injuries or permanent disability. See www.cdc.gov/drowning/facts/ for more information.

WARNING

We want to preface this section by acknowledging that the following discussion may be sensitive for many readers. Part of being a lifeguard, or any type of professional rescuer, is being able to accept that these unfortunate situations exist. You may not be able to save everyone. You must be able to spring to action when your help is needed, regardless of the gravity of the situation. During these high-stress encounters, it is very important to remain collected and professional.

Understanding what happens when someone drowns

Drowning is the process of water entering the lungs. While many people associate drownings with big bodies of water, a large percentage of drownings and near drownings happen in backyard pools.

REMEMBER

Drownings do not need to occur in deep water.

All it simply takes is enough water to cover a person's nose and mouth before they become a victim of drowning. When their nose and mouth take in water, oxygen cannot reach their vital organs. If water finds its way into your airway, it will involuntarily close and cause something called a *laryngospasm*. This, in turn, prevents oxygen from entering their lungs. Once they become unconscious, the water fills their lungs and the process of drowning begins.

Here's a breakdown of the stages of drowning:

1. As the victim fights to stay above water, they enter a state of fight-or-flight and struggle to breathe. It is at this point that they begin to swallow or take in excess water.

2. To prevent water from entering, the victim's airway begins to close. For up to two minutes, the victim may involuntarily hold their breath, causing them to lose consciousness.

3. When the victim becomes unconscious, they can still be revived through resuscitation efforts such as CPR and/or rescue breathing. If this issue is addressed within the appropriate time frame, they can have a good chance of a positive outcome. This stage can last for several minutes.

4. Not long after a drowning victim stops breathing or their heart stops beating, the body will enter a state called *hypoxic convulsion*. This often resembles a seizure. Without oxygen, the person may turn blue and jerk around erratically. In most cases, you need to use an AED (automated external defibrillator) in order to get them to *ROSC*, or return of spontaneous circulation.

5. The brain, heart, and lungs reach a state beyond where they can be revived. This final stage of drowning is called *cerebral hypoxia*, where the brain has been depleted of oxygen for an extended period of time. The victim passes away shortly thereafter.

Secondary drowning vs. dry drowning

When most people think about a drowning episode, they envision the typical scenario in a pool or open body of water where someone is submerged and eventually gets pulled out by the lifeguards or first responders.

While this may be true in many circumstances, there are a few rare instances where drownings can occur *after* a near drowning incident, several hours later. This process is known as *secondary drowning*. Secondary drownings occur when water enters the lungs and irritates the lining, causing something called *pulmonary edema*. It wouldn't be uncommon for a victim suffering from secondary drowning to have symptoms of difficulty breathing, lethargy, and a persistent cough up to 24 hours after a near drowning incident. These circumstances only account for 1-2 percent of all drowning cases, but it is important for the general public to know the signs and symptoms of secondary drowning.

The term *dry drowning* is one that you might find as controversial among healthcare and medical professionals, as it is not an official term/diagnosis. During a dry drowning, no water makes its way into the lungs. Rather, dry drowning occurs when water makes its way into the larynx (voice box), causing it to constrict and seize. This blocks the flow of air to the lungs, often resulting in respiratory arrest.

Knowing how fast someone can go under

A person can drown in less than 60 seconds. It has been reported that it only takes 20 seconds for a child to drown and roughly 40 seconds for an adult. In some cases, only as little as a half cup of water needs to enter the lungs for the drowning process to be underway. While the process of active drowning in most cases keeps the victim struggling at the surface of the water and able to gasp for air before fully submerging, there are times when some victims will not have the strength or ability to keep themselves even slightly above water. Panic is a huge factor. We have seen adults and children sink like rocks, closing the window for making an appropriate rescue before the victim becomes unconscious and starts to take in water.

WARNING

Hollywood often portrays drowning as a dramatic process where swimmers are screaming for help and slapping down on the water. While some active drowning victims may do that, the majority may just simply slip under water.

It is not uncommon for a drowning victim to not even be able to call out for help! Drowning can happen in the blink of an eye, which is why the number one rule of lifeguards is never take your eyes off the water!

Bottom line: *Watch the water!*

Getting to Know the Equipment You'll Use

In the world of lifesaving, there are a plethora of toys at your disposal. Over the years, new pieces of lifesaving equipment have been developed and implemented in the field, but at the same time some things are exactly the same. This section briefly covers some of the most common lifesaving equipment you will use while working as a lifeguard at various facilities.

Suiting up sensibly

Not many jobs require you to wear a bathing suit. But let's not be confused — your uniform and how you wear it is extremely important! Being a lifeguard in any capacity qualifies you as a professional rescuer. Therefore, you should dress and act as such!

Lifeguard uniforms of course vary from agency to agency. Regardless, your uniform — even if it consists of a bathing suit, T-shirt, shorts, and sweatshirt/outerwear — should be worn professionally and with pride. Uniforms should be consistent across the lifeguard crew, and your employer should have very clear rules of what is acceptable. Not being in uniform while on duty poses a problem at many levels and can get you into hot water!

REMEMBER

Patrons visiting your facility should be able to easily identify the employees and lifeguards.

The way you present yourself says a lot about who you are and how seriously you take your job; this all plays into what it means to be a professional. Being out of uniform and/or wearing tattered uniforms with holes does not convey the sense of professionalism that employers and patrons are looking for. Being a professional rescuer means acting like one and dressing like one. Take pride in your lifeguard uniform and always put your best foot forward.

On a side note, don't give away your lifeguard sweatshirts, because your exes will probably not give them back! Worse yet, they'll be mistaken for a lifeguard and expected to act like one, perhaps in an emergency when no "real" lifeguard is around.

The way you present yourself on the lifeguard stand and in the lifeguard area makes a difference in the way that swimmers, patrons, and parents perceive you. I mention parents because as much as they are (or should be) watching their kids, they also rely on the lifeguards to provide an extra set of eyes and act accordingly if something goes wrong.

Looking unprofessional will cause swimmers to feel a bit uneasy. Sometimes that small feeling of discomfort may be enough for them to lose confidence and start to slip underwater. Appearing unprofessional can cause people to not take you seriously. Just like in any situation, an unprofessional lifeguard may not be afforded the proper respect. This makes communicating with the public much more difficult.

A lifeguard without a whistle is like a firefighter without a hose!

When people traditionally think of a lifeguard, oftentimes one of the first symbols that comes to mind is the good old-fashioned whistle!

TECHNICAL STUFF

Lifeguards have been using whistles since the early 1900s. The traditional metal whistle with a ball on the inside has been replaced for a more modern plastic one with no ball. These 21st century whistles produce a louder, higher-pitched sound that turns heads from every direction!

The lifeguard whistle plays a crucial role in this profession. As a matter of fact, for the majority of agencies that still use whistle systems (and most of them are), some might argue that it is the most important piece of equipment. The lifeguard whistle is a communication system between you and the public to help enforce rules and/or actions.

It also serves as an internal way to communicate with other lifeguards. Most importantly, lifeguards use their whistles to help communicate preventative actions, which ultimately save lives! When water rescues or other emergencies arise, the lifeguard's whistle is the most important way they can communicate with fellow first responders who are going to provide backup during that rescue!

Every lifeguard agency and patrol has its own set of whistle signals. There is no national or worldwide universal system. That may cause some confusion, if you finally understand what the whistles mean at your local pool, ocean, or other recreational bathing facility. When in doubt, don't be shy and ask your local lifeguards what all their whistling activity means!

The power of perching on a lifeguard stand/tower

Try playing this scene out in your head: You're walking down the beach to catch an early morning sunrise or late afternoon sunset. The lifeguard tower or stand is empty and there is just something that draws you closer to it. You walk or climb up it, grab a few photos, maybe even a selfie, and just stare out at the ocean, enjoying all of what mother nature has in store for you in that exact moment.

There is some kind of attraction that draws people to want to sit atop the lifeguards' perch and look over the water. When perched in your lifeguard stand or tower, you have the ability to oversee the entire bathing area. This bird's-eye view allows you to take in everything that is going on, both in and out of the water. It also allows the public to be able to quickly and easily identify the lifeguards if they need assistance. For ocean lifeguards, this high elevation also helps them identify rip currents more easily.

You may have noticed that there are several different styles of lifeguard stands and towers. Let's compare them:

» On most ocean-facing beaches on the West Coast and in the southeast, you will typically find lifeguard towers (see Figure 2-3). This is primarily because lifeguards work all year round and are more concerned about excessive sun exposure, which can lead to skin cancer. These lifeguard towers allow the lifeguards to watch the water from inside the tower through glass windows or from the elevated deck outside surrounding the tower.

Sebastian / Adobe Stock

FIGURE 2-3: A silhouette West Coast lifeguard tower overlooking the water in Los Angeles County.

>> On the other hand, most East Coast ocean lifeguards use an elevated lifeguard stand, as pictured in Figure 2-4. It looks more like a giant chair that can seat multiple people. There is no enclosure. To protect themselves from the sun, these lifeguards typically secure umbrellas to create shade. Others may have a hard-top roof or canopy over them to keep the sun away.

Photograph by Lee Weissman

FIGURE 2-4: A typical lifeguard stand found on many East Coast beaches.

Next time you are at your favorite beach, check out the lifeguard stands and see what they have!

Lookin' cool in polarized sunglasses

Looking the part is at least half the battle, and we know that when it comes to lifeguard equipment, a solid pair of sunglasses can make the difference between life and death. The mid/late afternoon glare on the surface of the water is more than just an obstruction from seeing your swimmers; you can also be damaging your eyes!

Polarized sunglasses help you see all of your swimmers and cut down on that nasty glare from the water. This prevents you from squinting (creating more wrinkles around your eyes) and getting those late afternoon headaches from staring into the sun's relentless rays.

On the East Coast, the glare happens in the morning. On the West Coast, the glare happens all afternoon until the sun sets. On the south shore of Long Island, NY, where the authors work, and on the beaches facing south along the Gulf Coast, the sun sets to the right with a glare through the late afternoon.

Polarized sunglasses tend to be a bit more expensive, although many companies now make middle-of-the-line polarized lenses so you don't have to rob a bank to protect your eyes!

We know that polarized glasses reduce glare, but how? To start, we must understand what glare is in the first place. Light coming from the sun strikes the Earth in a disorganized, erratic motion. When light reflects off a flat surface such as glass, asphalt, or water, it bounces off and travels in one concentrated, organized beam. Light that reflects off a horizontal surface such as the surface of a pool, lake, or ocean takes on this horizontal orientation, called glare.

Polarized lenses have a chemical film that allows only vertical light to pass through. Glare, which is obstructive horizontal light from the water, is absorbed by the polarized film embedded in the lenses. Another way to think of polarized lenses is like a filter. Polarized lenses match the orientation or alignment of horizontal light, allowing it to be absorbed. Only vertical light enters your eyes.

Knowing your rescue equipment (all about buoys)

Becoming familiar with your rescue equipment is key! In the world of lifesaving, however, it comes down to one key piece of equipment: your lifeguard buoy. There are many types of lifeguard buoys on the market. Some are designed for still-water operations, such as pools, lakes, and bays, while others are designed for open water and the oceanfront.

The *buoy* is designed to float the lifeguard and the victim to safety. There are two main kinds:

>> *Peterson tube:* This is a traditional lifeguard buoy. It's a long, soft Styrofoam tube that can be easily handed to a struggling victim.

Peterson tubes can also be used on unconscious victims who are unable to hold on and in large surf where even a strong swimmer might not be able to hold on. In these cases, it is clipped under the arms of the victim. Should the rescuer lose contact with the victim in large pounding waves, the Peterson tube keeps them afloat more easily than the Burnside buoy.

The original Peterson tube was invented by Preston "Pete" Peterson, who was a championship surfer and lifesaver on the Santa Monica, California lifeguard patrol. A renowned craftsman when it came to shaping surfboards and paddleboards, he applied his thrifty ability in 1935 by inventing the first rescue buoy. This Peterson Belt was an inflatable buoy that came equipped with a snap hook and harness to secure the struggling swimmer. Modern day rescue tubes came about from this invention.

>> *Burnside buoy:* This is the harder plastic, more oval buoy you might have seen on the beach.

There are pros and cons to using both of these types of buoys, but when it comes to equipment, the bottom line is that your buoy is your best friend! Figure 2-5 shows both types of buoys.

Michael O'Neill / Adobe Stock   Sirena Designs / Adobe Stock

FIGURE 2-5: The lifeguard to the left stands (a) with a Peterson tube across her waist, while the Burnside buoy to the right (b) is set up in the sand, ready to be deployed at any time.

TIP

The best way to become familiar with your flotation device is to practice with it. Run mock rescues with your crew to familiarize yourself with how the buoy feels in your hand and bobbing behind you while you're swimming.

There are many other types of lifeguard equipment you will come in contact with. Some of the more common items you might find around an aquatic facility in both still and open water are backboards, ring buoys, shepherd's crooks, medical bags/first aid kits, AEDs, line buckets, rescue boards, and kayaks. We dive deeper into each of these as we investigate the different types of lifeguards in Chapters 4-6.

First Aid Techniques You Need to Know

Lifeguard or not, everyone should be trained in basic first aid. These skills can make a difference in life and death situations. If you haven't already learned the lifesaving measures covered in this section, contact your local American Red Cross or American Heart Association chapters and get to training.

REMEMBER

An important lifeguard duty is to prevent accidents by correcting certain behaviors and actions that can lead to injury. However, we always say it's not a matter of if, but a matter of when!

Performing CPR

Knowing when to perform CPR on someone can be the difference between life and death. Having the knowledge and confidence to step up and take action in an emergency is just one attribute of a professional lifeguard. CPR stands for cardiopulmonary resuscitation. Simply put, when someone suffers a condition called cardiac arrest, for one reason or another, their heart has stopped beating and they have stopped breathing. By performing this lifesaving technique, you are providing lifesaving measures by artificially circulating blood and providing oxygen to the brain.

WARNING

It only takes a few minutes for brain damage to occur when oxygen is not flowing to the brain. After ten minutes without oxygen, brain death occurs.

Chest compressions are part of CPR. These compressions push oxygenated blood around the body to all the major organs. By providing ventilation (either by mouth to mouth or via pocket mask/bag valve mask), you are providing oxygen to the brain for survival. There is no question that a person's chances at surviving sudden cardiac arrest or drowning increase when CPR is performed.

TIP

You do not need to be lifeguard-certified to know how to perform CPR. As a matter of fact, there are many different level classes you can take to learn this lifesaving skill.

One of the more popular methods that anyone can perform is called *hands-only CPR*. Although lifeguards are trained to a higher standard as professional rescuers, we urge everyone to take the time to learn this simple skill. To perform hands-only CPR, all you have to do is:

1. **Call 911 if you see an adult or child collapse.**

2. **Using two interlocked hands, push hard and fast on the center of their chest.** See Figure 2-6.

   It is that easy! You can use the Internet to watch hands-only CPR tutorials. So, what are you waiting for?

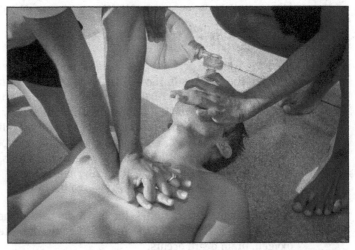

daviles / Adobe Stock

FIGURE 2-6: Lifeguards work together to administer chest compressions and deliver rescue breaths to the unconscious victim.

Controlling bleeding

Some days your job as a lifeguard will be as simple as applying a band aid. A day at the pool, park, or beach is always intended to be fun, but there are many ways this day can get quickly turned upside down! An important question to ask is whether your victim simply needs a band aid or should be taken in an ambulance to the local emergency room for some stitches and staples. Ascertaining the level of injury is no joke.

REMEMBER

There are many different ways to get hurt in the aquatic environment. One of the biggest problems around the pool deck is the ol' slip and fall. Running is the biggest rule violation on a slippery pool deck, in addition to the classic violations like jumping backward off the side of the pool and diving in shallow water. All of these things can and often do lead to injuries!

Knowing how to control bleeding is an important part of your job as a lifeguard, so become familiar with your facility's first aid kit sooner rather than later.

First and foremost, anytime you are dealing with blood, you need to take personal protective measures. Contact with someone else's blood and other types of fluids can put you at risk of contracting diseases. The best way to protect yourself from bloodborne pathogens is to glove up!

TIP

Our rule of thumb is simple: "If it's wet and not yours, don't touch it!" Protect yourself by wearing latex gloves or other PPE (personal protective equipment).

There are just a few simple steps you need to follow to control bleeding. The main idea behind controlling bleeding is to slow the bleeding process. You can do this by simply providing direct pressure over the wound using a clean, sterile dressing. One of the biggest mistakes people make is that they keep removing the dressing to peek if it is still bleeding, ultimately preventing the wound from clotting.

Resist the urge to look and apply pressure for several minutes. If there is excessive blood loss and blood is soaking through the bandages, continue to apply more pressure and add more dressings or bandages on top.

REMEMBER

Of course, *never* hesitate to call 911 or your professional emergency number if you think the situation warrants it.

Your last resort when it comes to bleeding control is to use a *tourniquet*. Using a tourniquet is pretty serious business, so if you plan on taking this route, you should first (quickly) assess if it is appropriate to do so. This is *not* your everyday bleeding control. The purpose of a tourniquet is to slow down or stop major bleeding.

Major bleeding like this typically comes from a number of injuries where arterial bleeding is present. It is not uncommon to see these types of injuries from explosive devices, shootings, stabbings, or major trauma (shark attack or boat propeller accident). A commercial tourniquet might be in your standard first aid kit. If one is not available, simply find something like a belt, T-shirt, or any other item that you can wrap around a limb and tie off.

Be sure to continue applying direct pressure over the wound.

Tourniquets should only be used on limbs — never around the neck or chest. Tie it off as tight as you can a few inches above the wound. Ideally, note the time the tourniquet was applied and write it on the victim's skin in bold, dark ink. Seek professional medical help immediately.

Tourniquets cut off all circulation to the limb in order to save the person's life. In some cases, the limb may need to be amputated. Although this sounds harsh, the alternative may be death.

It only takes a few minutes to lose the 2-4 liters of blood that causes an adult to die.

Handling heat-related injuries

Being out in the sun all day long has its consequences! As good as it might feel initially, overexposure to hot conditions can cause serious medical complications. Can you think of a time in your life when you were really hot and weren't dressed appropriately? How did you feel? What did you experience? Wearing the right clothes and fueling your body in the right way is the key to surviving a hot environment.

There are three types of heat-related emergencies — heat cramps, heat exhaustion, and heat stroke. As lifeguards, we often treat people suffering from them. We are also very much aware that lifeguards are not immune to heat injuries as well.

Heat cramps

It is important to be able to decipher the symptoms between the three, as they can become life threatening if they are not treated. Here, your muscles begin to cramp up in your legs and abdomen and you begin to experience muscle spasms. These are quite uncomfortable and painful. Often times, people suffering from heat cramps need IV fluids to help balance the water and sodium intake of the body. Cramping often accompanies the next tier of heat-related emergencies, heat exhaustion.

Make sure to drink plenty of water and other electrolytes to avoid dehydration.

Heat exhaustion

When heat cramps are not treated, it can develop into a more severe condition called heat exhaustion. With heat exhaustion, you typically feel overheated, tired, and faint. You might experience cool, pale, and clammy skin. In this case, your best bet is to seek shelter in a cool environment if possible. This usually occurs after strenuous physical activity in a hot environment.

Heat stroke

Lastly and most serious is heat stroke. This is when your body loses its ability to sweat. Here, unlike heat exhaustion and heat cramps, you become dry and red. Your body has physically lost its ability to cool itself, putting you at serious risk for sudden cardiac arrest and other medical complications. Think about how you would feel on a 100-degree day sitting in the car with no air conditioner. Your body's cooling systems are broken and you need to seek medical attention immediately!

Figure 2-7 breaks down the symptoms of heat stroke and heat exhaustion and includes methods for treating them.

Helping someone who is choking

As a lifeguard in a recreational environment, there is a chance that you will be approached or called for assistance in choking situations. Those mozzarella sticks from the concession stand can sometimes be no joke! These scenarios present themselves in one of two ways: either with a conscious victim or an unconscious victim.

When your victim is conscious

In the case of conscious victims, assuming that you have been given permission to assist them, you should encourage them to continue trying to dislodge the object by coughing.

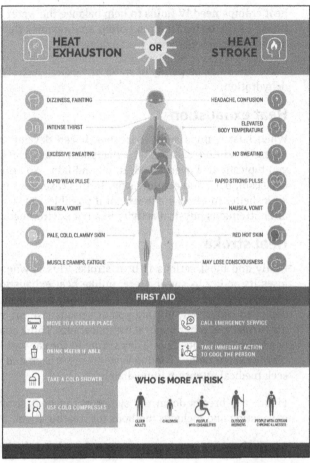

FIGURE 2-7: The differences between heat exhaustion and heat stroke, as well as the appropriate ways to respond to each; heat cramps, the least severe of the three, is typically experienced when suffering from heat exhaustion.

TIP

If they are coughing, consider this a good sign — their airway is not blocked, so they should keep coughing!

If their attempts at coughing are unsuccessful, you should begin by giving five back blows:

1. **Have them face away from you, bending over. Secure them with your nondominant hand and deliver five back blows between the shoulder blades.**

2. Locate the navel. Place the bottom of a fist against it and wrap it with your opposite hand. Thrust upward five times for abdominal thrusts.

3. Rotate between these back blows and abdominal thrusts until the object is dislodged or the choking victim becomes unconscious.

The process for infants is slightly different. Follow these steps to assist a choking infant:

1. Secure the infant's head and neck by resting their chin on your hand and turning them over with your forearm straight down the chest.

2. Face down and, at a 45 degree angle resting on your knee, deliver back blows with the heel of your hand. Aim between the shoulder blades.

3. Rotate them right over to your other leg to deliver five chest thrusts in the same manner as you would when delivering chest compressions, with two fingers.

When your victim is unconscious

If you find the victim unconscious or they become unconscious, you should commence CPR.

1. Begin with rescue breaths to determine whether their airway is blocked.

2. If it is blocked (their chest does not rise when you attempt to give breaths), deliver 30 chest compressions with the intention of dislodging the blockage.

3. Give their mouth a quick finger sweep if, and only if, you see something emerge from their airway.

4. Try for another two breaths to see if their airway has cleared. If not, repeat!

Treating a bad sunburn

When it comes to sunburn, some people just get it worse than others. We all have that one friend who somehow always returns home from the beach red as a tomato, and you can always tell which spots on their body they missed when applying sunscreen.

People with lighter skin are more likely to feel the effects of the sun's UV rays and get sunburned.

TECHNICAL STUFF

Melanin is found in all of our skin; it is the brown pigment that blocks out damaging UV rays and the reason that those with darker skin are less likely to burn.

WARNING

Do not be fooled. If the section about skin cancer did not reinforce this enough, *everyone* should be wearing an adequate amount of sunscreen, regardless of how naturally tan or dark you may be.

For starters, if you find yourself starting to burn even the slightest, get out of the sun! Cool down, loosen your clothes, and find some shade — it might even help to apply a cool compress to the affected areas.

TIP

Do not rush to the extreme and apply ice to a sunburn, because you don't want to shock the body, cause the vessels to narrow, and stop blood supply to the damaged skin. However, a cool shower may do the trick with larger affected areas.

Aloe vera works wonders on sunburn, as it carries anti-inflammatory agents to calm the skin and minimize swelling. It is recommended that you, your party, or lifeguard crew always have some handy!

TIP

Hydrate, hydrate, hydrate. Water makes up around 60 percent of our body, so it should come as no surprise that it is sometimes the cure for everything. Rehydrating and consuming beverages containing electrolytes will help the recovery process.

With more serious, second-degree burns, resist the urge to pop developing blisters. You'll learn your lessons soon that breaking a blister does you more harm than good. Opening a wound can lead to infection. Just clean the blister of any dirt and let your body take care of the rest.

TECHNICAL STUFF

The *UV index* is a weather metric that measures the projected risk of overexposure to the sun on a scale of 1 to 11+. You might have guessed that a UV index of 1 indicates the lowest level of risk of overexposure to the sun, while 11+ is the highest risk. This metric takes into account several factors to determine how much of the sun's dangerous UV rays will reach the ground, such as the amount of cloud coverage, altitude, solar elevation, pollutants, and a handful of others.

Managing injuries from encounters with marine life

When working in open water facilities, the idea of run-ins with marine life always lingers in the back of lifeguards' minds. For the most part, "encounters" with marine life are from a distance, as we observe them from the shore and admire their natural beauty many yards away.

For example, dolphins often pay a visit to our East Coast shores, and you can catch them grabbing waves if there's some active swell in the water. It's always a treat to see them come by in their groups, or *pods*. Dolphins almost never pose a threat to humans. In clear waters, you might witness a sea ray lurking along the ocean floor beneath you. And sometimes, you can catch the mist of a whale shooting out from its blowhole as it comes up for a breath — undeniably a majestic sight.

WARNING

There will be times, however, where run-ins with marine life are less-friendly encounters and the role of the lifeguard comes into play.

On the milder side of the spectrum, crabs roaming the shallow ocean floor may grab at swimmer's toes. Their sharp claws may give way to superficial cuts, where band aids are your best bet to shield that wound from the elements.

Some jelly fish sting, and these encounters can certainly be dangerous. These stings are their sensitive tentacles brushing against skin, and in most cases the victim will never see what stung them. They present as welts that resemble burns, and the sensation of pain may vary from prickly, to throbbing, to unbearable. A sting from a Portuguese man o' war, found in the Atlantic and Indian oceans, for example, requires immediate medical attention due to how venomous it is.

WARNING

Sting rays also pose a dangerous threat in that if you get "stung," it is extremely painful. These encounters occur frequently on the West Coast and Gulf shores. The best way to avoid being stung is to do the *sting ray shuffle*. Sting rays are not aggressive creatures and only respond with their tails when they are stepped on. The injury almost always goes to the lower part of the leg or foot. To prevent that from happening, swimmers should shuffle their feet as they enter the water. If they make contact with a sting ray, the ray will just swim away.

Treatment for a sting ray sting is to immerse the extremity in hot water — as hot as the victim can stand it. Relief is immediate! This has to be done continuously until the pain subsides, even when you remove the extremity from the hot water. Sometimes this can take up to an hour.

To treat all types of stings, remove the victim from the water first and foremost, and observe them for signs of shock. If any tentacles remain, delicately remove them with gloves. Wash the affected area with alcohol, as it will inactivate any intact *nemato-cysts*, or the stinging cells from the tentacle. Then, rinse it under cold, fresh water (or hot water for the sting ray sting). Finally, seek medical attention if necessary!

While it is rare, swimmers have been bitten by sharks and similar sea creatures. If this occurs, act fast. Retrieve the swimmer from the water (if you first deem the scene safe for you and your crew!) and assess the wound. If the victim is bleeding profusely, refer to the bleeding control instructions in the previous section. Call for professional medical providers and consider dialing the number of your local marine wildlife specialists.

REMEMBER

Remember that the ocean is their home, and we are the visitors. Respect sea life and always be cognizant of the oceanic environment. As a lifeguard, it is your responsibility to put the safety of your swimmers first, and if the ocean is deemed unsafe, keep the swimmers out.

Chapter **3**
The History of Lifeguarding

Everything has a story and behind that story often lies history. While you might not often think about what brought some of the world's greatest innovative inventions and or services to fruition, you might just find their history astonishing! Join us as we step into our time machine and see how the modern-day lifeguard was born.

Unearthing the Origins of Lifeguarding

Believe it or not, it was not until around the 19th century that people in the United States began to take to the ocean as a recreational activity. When the summer months began to blossom, people started to think of using the ocean to cool off during particularly hot days. The common consensus, however, was that these people were crazy! Most people did not know how to swim, and as people flocked to the seas, many wound up drowning.

As railroads in the United States were built, some wise business-men in Philadelphia decided to run them to the shore, which led to the first American seaside resort in Atlantic City, New Jersey in 1854. As expected, the drowning rate significantly increased as more average 19th century Americans tried swimming as a leisurely pastime without knowing how. The public quickly realized that the waters needed professional lifesavers, and the earliest signs of lifeguarding emerged.

Shipwrecked!

Let's backtrack a few years. Watchmen on the water were established to walk the shorelines at night, keeping an eye out for shipwrecks. They were not watching over and protecting recreational swimmers.

In the United States, it took the disastrous shipwreck of the steamer Huron along the coast of North Carolina for the creation of the first professional organization employed to save lives on the water. A full 98 people drowned during this incident, prompting Congress in 1878 to appropriate funds for the creation of the U.S. Life Saving Service (USLSS). This organized group upheld standards concerning professionalism and regulations. They emphasized competence, performance, schedules, and physical training. The USLSS expanded to 189 stations across the country, with crews sprouting up along the Atlantic Coast, around the Great Lakes, along the Pacific Coast, and even in Ohio.

In 1915, the USLSS absorbed the Revenue Cutter Service after saving a recorded 28,121 vessels and 178,741 swimmers, and the organization we now know as the United States Coast Guard was born. With steadily evolving technology and the development of motorized boats, the need for rescuing shipwrecked swimmers diminished as a role for the Coast Guard. The need for the professional lifeguard was born.

Recognizing the need for lifeguards

With seaside resorts on the rise, recreational swimming became more popular. Unfortunately, that meant more people succumbed to drowning. There was little knowledge of the ocean's mechanisms; few understood how rip currents, tides, and the surf worked.

On June 12, 1882, Atlantic City hired two men to be the first open water specialists, comprising what we now consider the first beach patrol. Very quickly, this organization grew. By the start of the 20th century, this group grew to 55 members. A decade later, there were 64. Around the country, similar groups began to pop up. The United States Volunteer Lifesaving Corps (USVLC) materialized near Venice Beach in 1892. Long Beach, California began hiring lifeguards in 1908, and the city of San Diego's lifeguard operation was led by their police department in 1914.

Around 1885, the Young Men's Christian Association (YMCA) spearheaded the construction of pools. They also initiated the first swim lessons. Seventeen pools were built that first year, normalizing the idea of recreation in bodies of water.

Come 1914, Commodore Wilbert E. Longfellow is attributed to the development of the Life Saving Corps of the American Red Cross, with the mission of teaching people how to swim and provide lifesaving services. The earliest Red Cross programs taught people about swimming, water safety, and lifesaving.

On the other side of the world in the early 1900s, other beach patrol services began to form. In some regions, national volunteer systems were established, leading to the birth of surf lifesaving in Australia, New Zealand, and the United Kingdom.

The U.S. government started to assume a larger role in recreational opportunities, acquiring park systems, programs, and departments that extended from national and local levels. Many public works projects were established during the Great Depression. Lifeguard services came right along with them. In 1960s, the present-day United States Lifesaving Association, then known as the Surf Life Saving Association of America, was born.

TIP

The 1956 Summer Olympics were hosted by Australia, and California lifeguards competed at the Australian Olympic International Surf Championships. Turn to Chapter 12 to learn more about the professional sport of surf lifesaving and its continual influence today.

Upon their return home to the United States, one of the biggest takeaways that the Americans garnered from the Australian lifeguards was their ever-present organization among their lifeguard groups. It was around this time that LA county lifeguard Bob Burnside was appointed president of the Surf Life Saving Association of America. His vision was to expand the organization to national status. Under his presidency in 1965, the organization's name changed to the National Surf Lifesaving Association. Over the next decade or so, the organization expanded to represent guards across the nation.

In May 1979, the organization decided that it should represent all open water lifeguards, whether at surf or non-surf beaches. At a board of directors meeting in Santa Cruz, California, they voted to change the name to the United States Lifesaving Association. The United States Lifesaving Association is still active today, an organization serving ocean, bay, lake, river, and open water lifeguards.

HISTORY OF THE JONES BEACH LIFEGUARD CORPS

On August 4th, 1929, the Jones Beach State Park in New York opened to the public. The official roots of the Jones Beach Lifeguard Corps, however, trace back to the year prior, in 1928, when the Long Island State Parks Commission made the decision to staff Jones Beach State Park. They brought in a German ex-sea captain named William Johns. Captain Johns was tasked with putting together a group of lifeguards to watch over the park, sourcing them from the beach patrol at Valley Stream State Park, another facility in the Long Island State Parks System. Among the dozen or so first Jones Beach lifeguards were a 1920 Olympian, a long-time Hawaiian surfer and Columbia University student, and a collegiate swimmer from NYU. That first year in 1928, the lifeguards were not watching over recreational swimmers from the suburbs; rather, the original swimmers at Jones Beach State Park were the construction workers who were developing the beach for the public to enjoy the following year in 1929. With the completion of the Wantagh Parkway and the opening of the East Bathhouse, the lifeguard staff in 1929 was composed of 18 guards; they operated for only about a month into September. The following year, the lifeguard patrol was made up of about 35 lifeguards, and by 1931, the beach consisted of about 66 guards: 15 petty officers, a captain, and about 40 fulltime and 10 weekend lifeguards.

The guards patrolled more than a mile of oceanfront and 1.5 miles of bay beach, with the usual crowd exceeding 25,000 on weekdays and 80,000 on Sundays. Watching over these large numbers of swimmers was no small feat, and the Long Island State Park Commission was well aware of it.

In those days, to be considered for a lifeguard position, you needed a Red Cross certificate and several years of experience in lifesaving. Candidates had to pass rigid tests before they were even considered.

Each applicant had to prove their knowledge of rapid lifesaving methods, first aid, swimming, handling surf boats, artificial respiration, and using an inhalator.

Perched on towers, the all-male guards were posted at regular intervals along the ocean and bay beaches. From this vantage point, they could command a clear and undisturbed view of that section of the bathing area designated to their patrol. On average, 30 rescues a day took place during the week with as many as 300 on Sundays. Records show that the Jones Beach Lifeguard Corps made more than 1,200 rescues during the 1931 season. The organization boasted non-fatality marks in 1929 and 1930.

Over the years, the lifeguard corps continued to grow as word got out about this incredible opportunity. The best athletes around Long Island and the metropolitan area fought for these coveted positions.

The Jones Beach Lifeguard Corps continued to grow through the years. It organized its first union in 1963, forming under Local 381 of the Building Service Employees International Union AFL-CIO. In 1966, the union stood in solidarity as state park officials tried to propose an age limit of 35 for all lifeguards.

The park continued to expand, with the East Bathhouse pool later opening in 1967. That year, the JBLC had an eight-day strike and settled it with a pay raise and retro check. The first female lifeguards in the corps were hired in 1968; these female guards didn't take an ocean test and only worked the pools and bay. It would not be for another decade (in 1977) that the women were required to take the same qualifying test as the men.

In 1971, state park officials wanted to cut down lifeguard staffing from 360 to 300 lifeguards. In addition, they wanted to eliminate their current pay scales and pay the lifeguards less. The lifeguard union attempted to discuss these concerns in good faith; however, on Memorial Day weekend of 1971, the lifeguards ultimately agreed to go on strike. This strike lasted for eight weeks, and unfortunately four people drowned in their waters. During that time, 150 replacement (scab) lifeguards were hired, but these under-qualified guards were not able to prevent the four deaths.

On July 27th, 1971 a deal was made and the lifeguards were given a pay raise, two safety directors, double-time pay on Labor Day, the ability to test out the replacement (scab) lifeguards, and $800 in lost

(continued)

(continued)

wages. It is said that the actions of the lifeguards in 1971 was the strongest showing of this union in its history. It is because of these actions that now, more than half a century later, the Jones Beach Lifeguard Corps stands strong and proud with the New York State Parks and the Long Island State Parks Commission.

Photograph by Jones Beach Lifeguard Corps Historical Archives

Jones Beach lifeguards stand together for a crew picture in 1966.

Modern-Day Lifesaving: Lifeguarding in the 21st Century

As recreational swimming became more common, pools began popping up everywhere. Public pools were often funded by local and state governments, and staff lifeguards became the norm. In the 1990s, with the rise of one particular television show that dramatized the job (*Baywatch*), lifeguarding got a reputation for being an action-packed, glamorous, real career.

The Baywatch effect

When the majority of the world's population hears the word "Baywatch," the first thing they think of is David Hasselhoff and Pamela Anderson running down the beach in slow motion. The iconic TV show took the world by storm in the 1990s, and *Baywatch* later became the most watched syndicated television show in the world! *Baywatch* was a worldwide name and it put California beaches and the lifeguard lifestyle/career on the map. It also made the red rescue can an iconic symbol.

Everything about it was glamorous, from the action, to the hot sandy, beach days in the California sun (especially for those watching in cold weather climates), to the lifeguards' physiques. For the first time ever, lifeguards were front and center for the entire world to see!

This came at a penalty, though. While we will always be thankful for what *Baywatch* did for lifeguarding in some respects, it also created an unwanted stereotype. All lifeguards must run in slow motion and have insanely built bodies, blonde hair, and bronzed skin. As they make rescues, they also solve murder mysteries, fight off marine life with their bare hands, and do all sorts of other ridiculous things. The reality is that a lot of this is amplified for entertainment purposes.

The kernel of truth was often there, but *Baywatch* was exaggerated to get that TV appeal (see Figure 3-1). Many (but certainly not all) of the episodes were based on real rescues and scenarios that did happen to LA county lifeguards over the years. These storylines were created by former lifeguards and *Baywatch* creators Gregory Bonann, Douglas Schwartz, and Michael Berk.

Baywatch pretty much defined pop culture in the '90s and there is no doubt it did more good for the lifeguarding community than harm. As a matter of fact, one of the main characters — Lt. Stephanie Holden (played by Alexandra Paul) — was a strong, independent, heroic woman saving lives equal to men. This is well before we saw many women in positions of power in this male dominated profession. Women and girls around the world automatically liked her character.

Young men and women around the world were inspired by the heroics of these TV lifeguards. As a matter of fact, it has been documented that people's lives have been saved based on the water rescue and CPR scenes from *Baywatch*! Mouth to mouth had never been so popular. Lifeguarding jobs became desirable, and lifeguarding was even seen as a career. The sunny, hot California coastline was depicted as this fairytale land of eternal sunshine, youth, and excitement. People from all over the world flocked there to vacation and many even relocated to the Golden State! To this day, if you work a tower in Venice, California, you are sure to get your photo taken by tourists from all over the world.

ZUMA Press, Inc. / Alamy Stock Photo

FIGURE 3-1: The cast of the hit television show Baywatch as seen in the late '90s.

TECHNICAL STUFF

Did you know Michael Newman, who played "Newmie," was the only real lifeguard on the show? A lifelong career LA county lifeguard, he was hired to ensure that the actors looked authentic when performing lifeguard-related duties. He did so much behind the scenes that the crew fell in love with him and he was written in as a regular main cast member!

THE REAL BAY WATCH:

A Quick Look at the Fleet of LA County's Lifeguard/ Paramedic Rescue Boats

by Joel Gitelson

I have intentionally titled this "bay watch" as two words because that is the way it was spelled back in August of 1947 when the first LA County Lifeguard rescue boat was christened, as pictured in the figure. It wasn't until Captain Bud Stevenson went to paint the name of the vessel on the transom that he combined the two words so it would fit evenly. The first lifeguard rescue boat dates to 1926 under the LA City Lifeguards and the Santa Monica City Lifeguard rescue boat in the 1930s. The name "Baywatch," as it is spelled today, was the result of a naming contest sponsored by the now defunct *Los Angeles Examiner*. A Mrs. Marsh of West Los Angeles was the winner and was present at the christening. Paramount Pictures starlet Carole Mathews broke the champagne bottle over the prow. Perhaps it was a sign of things to come — a Hollywood premonition send-off.

Photograph by Joel Gitelson

The first LA County Lifeguard boat is christened at Marina Del Rey.

(continued)

(continued)

The Los Angeles County Lifeguards currently operate seven, 32-foot rescue boats powered by twin Cummins diesel engines. They are equipped with full EMS gear as well as equipment to handle boat rescues, scuba search and rescue/recovery, and marine firefighting. A Volvo Penta engine pumps sea water and the boats carry foam as needed. The two paramedic rescue boats on Catalina Island — Baywatch Avalon and Baywatch Isthmus — also carry Advanced Life Support (ALS) equipment. When you dial 911 on Catalina Island you get Lifeguard paramedics on land and sea. Baywatch Santa Monica is put into service on an as-needed basis. Baywatch Malibu, stationed off the Malibu Pier, responds to the northern coast of Los Angeles County and backs up the beach lifeguards at Zuma Beach. The remaining three boats — Baywatch Cabrillo, Baywatch Redondo, and Baywatch Del Rey — are available 24/7. These vessels are responsible for 72 miles of coastline and waters 50 miles offshore, including Catalina Island. The mainland boats have the primary responsibility of backing up the beach lifeguards. I have had the honor and privilege to have worked as the deckhand on all the Baywatch rescue boats and with every Rescue Boat Captain during my tenure with the LA County Lifeguards, from 1981-2012.

Perhaps the most dramatic incidents ever performed by the Baywatch rescue boats involved two passenger jets that crashed into the Pacific Ocean in early 1969, six days apart! Baywatch was able to respond quickly to the first crash and saved 35 lives from the downed jetliner. Unfortunately, no one survived the second crash.

One might ask, "So how did the movie and television series *Baywatch* get named?". Greg Bonann, part-time LA County Lifeguard and the co-creator and producer of all 11 seasons of *Baywatch*, was my go-to person to answer that question. He told me that while he was sitting in the kitchen in his apartment in 1987, the phone rang. He couldn't get up fast enough to answer it, so his mother, who was visiting at the time, picked up the phone and answered it for him. She told him it was the lifeguards calling him for a 10-6 deckhand shift on Baywatch Del Rey the next day. He told her to tell them, "Yes," he would be there. When she hung up the phone, she said:" Son, that should be the name of your television show!" "Baywatch Del Rey?" Greg asked. "No!! Baywatch!!" she cried, and that's the truth.

The lifeguard shortage

At the time of writing this, we are nearly three years out from the peak of COVID-19, that strange stretch of months starting in March 2020 when the world essentially shut down. The United States is still feeling the effects of the pandemic in its pools, parks, and beaches. There was already a lifeguard shortage because it's a difficult job to begin with, and there are a number of physical restraints and qualifying procedures to hurdle in order to become one.

One of the larger contributions to the shortage was the lack of lifeguard training courses available during the pandemic. In the same way that schools closed to in-person attendance, lifeguard classes did as well. How could we hire more lifeguards if none were being trained? Our ability to backfill lifeguards who moved on eventually caught up to us, which is how a third of all pools in the United States found themselves affected by the shortage.

Other reasons for the lifeguard shortage were the suspension of visas when international travel was halted. Many pools in the country rely on foreigners with J1 visas to staff their facilities.

TECHNICAL STUFF

It is estimated that tens of thousands of lifeguards are sourced internationally to fill lifesaving positions around the United States.

There were many ways that the shortage was addressed, and several different avenues have eased the blow from the pandemic. From wage increases to sign-on incentives and end-of-season bonuses, lifeguard supervisors took unprecedented measures to hire new guards on their crews and avoid having to shut down their facilities.

We hope to help bridge the gap with this book and encourage all interested parties seeking an exciting and rewarding position to apply within. Find out if your local pool is holding a lifeguard course and sign up today!

LIFEGUARDING IN THE MIDST OF A PANDEMIC

When the entire world shut down in March 2020, there were very few places where people were free to go after being forced into lockdown for months and months on end. Indoor spaces, including indoor pools, were closed in fear of spreading the airborne disease. However, open water facilities, pools, and other outdoor bathing areas were faced with the question whether they could safely open. For the first time, lifeguards found themselves on the frontlines in a very unique way. While other first responders like police, fire, EMS, and all medical providers could wear personal protective equipment, lifeguards had very minimal options, especially when it came to going in the water. When making a rescue, which of course requires extremely close contact, there is zero protection and certainly no social distancing.

To add fuel to the fire, the beaches were the busiest they had ever been. Beachfronts saw record-breaking attendance. People had nowhere else to go. They were not going on vacations or flying to faraway lands — the world was home.

Lifeguards were forced to learn new ways of operating to protect themselves and adhere to local protocols. Trying to adapt to the unknown environment, they willingly put their selves at risk so that the public could experience the slightest sense of normalcy. Honored by their municipalities as essential workers, lifeguards rose to the occasion and continued to protect the public during those unprecedented times. These actions represent the spirit of what it means to be a lifesaver.

Looking at How Lifeguards Are Portrayed in Media

Even well before the world was introduced to *Baywatch*, lifeguards were portrayed by the media in a very distinctive way. Let's look at some of our favorite ways that lifeguards have popped up on the big screen and beyond:

>> **Sunscreen on their noses.** What a classic lifeguard move! Did you know your nose has a much higher chance of getting

sunburned? You would think every lifeguard would wear white zinc on their nose, but they don't. . .yet this became a staple stereotypical look.

>> **Iconic red bathing suits.** Everyone knows that a lifeguard's favorite color is red (or is it?!)! The red bathing suit became synonymous with the heroic acts of lifeguarding. Just an FYI — lifeguards can also often been seen in yellow and blue as well.

>> **The teenager look.** In every movie or TV show, why is it that the lifeguards are always so young and in peak physical condition? Although there are many young lifeguards, there are also plenty of senior guards (old ones) too! Even though the media might make you think so, lifeguarding is not just a teenager's job.

>> **Doing CPR on everyone!** The media loves to show off our CPR skills, but the reality is we are not doing CPR every shift. And, it almost never happens to your high school or college crush, especially while you're on duty!

We dove earlier into how *Baywatch* spurred a lot of the interest in the career, and in doing so created its own stereotype of how lifeguards are supposed to be portrayed. There are other sources on TV that showcase lifeguarding and have proved to be both accurate and inaccurate.

In Australia, everyone is familiar with the series *Bondi Rescue*, a reality TV show that portrays the ins and outs of the daily life of a Bondi Beach surf lifesaver. Viewing this from an American standpoint, there are many differences you will note right off the bat, from their rescue techniques to their dispatching system. Of course, as a prerecorded show, they are inclined to showcase the most extraordinary occurrences throughout the year. However, this production still provides factual insight about the day-to-day duties, the lives they save, and unfortunately, the ones who are lost.

While nothing nearly as successful has aired in the United States, some cable networks have produced similar documentary style productions over the years. Particular shows such as *Beach Patrol* on the True Crime Network and *Lifeguard!* highlight various lifeguard agencies across the country and some of their most momentous lifesaving situations.

2

Lifeguarding in the Different Facilities

Become familiar with qualifications of the lifeguard at your town's pool or waterpark.

Learn about lifeguards at a still water bay, lake, or open water facility and how they earned their role on the lifeguard stand.

Get to know the ocean lifeguard and what it takes to rescue victims in the most demanding of waterfronts.

Find out what types of options you have after deciding you want to pursue a career in lifeguarding.

Chapter **4**

The Pool and Waterpark Lifeguard

There is no denying how different the roles of a lifeguard are at a town pool compared to the duties of a lifeguard at a waterpark, but it seemed appropriate to group these two into a singular chapter. There is one thing for me, however, that these two types of facilities have in common. And that's nostalgia. The smell of chlorine infiltrates my nose, while the sound of other children laughing grows louder and louder as my brother and I make our way toward the gates that lead to the pool.

Was your local pool fancy enough to have everything included? A pool for splashing? Boards for diving? Perhaps slides for sliding? Maybe a food court? Few things tasted better than my local pool's chicken tenders from the concession stand. Just be sure to wait 30 minutes after eating before getting back in the water!

Knowing What It Takes to Be a Pool Lifeguard

You're going to need a little bit more than just a desire to be lifeguard if you want to be able to sit up on that chair.

There are a handful of boxes you have to check before you can become a lifeguard.

For starters, there is a minimum age to start employment as a lifeguard. This number varies from place to place as the minimum age for employment changes across borders, but it is likely around 15 or 16.

If you are under the legal age or are still ineligible to take the test, but you're interested in a job in lifeguarding, check out Chapter 13 to learn about junior lifeguarding programs and get a head start on your career!

There is, of course, a physical component, both on land and in the water, that you must pass to become a lifeguard. There's typically an educational portion to the qualifying process that includes a written exam. And before you can finally climb up on that chair, you cannot forget the list of certifications required to actually become a professional rescuer.

Passing the physical examination

You must be able to prove that you are physically fit to be a lifeguard, as your most important duty in this role requires you to act on the fly with both strength and speed.

For those of us who did not grow up swimming competitively on a swim team, it is very possible that the qualifying procedure will be a demanding test, which is why we highly encourage you to practice prior to the exam! Unless you are part fish, it should not be your first time in a while jumping in a pool for the qualifying procedure.

The physical portion of the lifeguard test for a pool and waterpark lifeguard will likely only take place in the water. This lifeguard test not only assesses how strong of a swimmer you are, but also how comfortable you are in the water.

Endurance test

The first part of the lifeguard exam tests your endurance. The swim ranges from around 200 to 300 yards. Demonstrate your ability to swim the freestyle or front crawl comfortably for an extended period of time. Don't let your stroke technique fall apart. Be sure to display your ability to breathe onto both sides, the left and the right. Make sure you stay on your stomach facing forward.

WARNING

Some exams may disqualify you for turning over onto your back, or rolling onto your side during your freestyle swim.

A few strokes of breaststroke may be permitted to catch your breath, but be sure to get back on your stomach and finish the swim in the allotted time period, which is typically about 4 minutes for 200 yards.

TIP

Wear tight fitting swimwear in the water to stay hydrodynamic and prevent drag! These types of swimwear I am referring to include jammers (pictured on the swimmer in Figure 4-1) or speedos. While they are not mandatory, they could help you be faster, more efficient in the water, and conservative with your energy.

FIGURE 4-1: The young swimmer prepares to take off from the block wearing a pair of form-fitting jammers.

This extended distance is designed to mimic the swim part of a rescue. It tests your ability to swim at an appropriate pace, as struggling swimmers require urgent help where every second is essential. It also examines your ability to swim for longer distances, because you may have to save someone at the opposite end of the pool. You must be able to make it there without taking a break!

Treading test

The next portion of the lifeguard exam tests your ability to tread water. Both experienced and unexperienced swimmers may find it difficult to complete this task, as it tests your endurance and lower body strength. Prospective lifeguards have to tread water for around two minutes with their hands either out of the water or tucked beneath their armpits; they cannot be used to assist you in floating.

TIP

It's best to employ a breaststroke or scissor type kick while treading, as opposed to a freestyle/flutter kick. Rather than try to get in as many kicks as you can, be efficient with your kicks and try to make every single one count so as to conserve as much energy as you can to last the entire duration of this component.

It's important that you are able to tread water for long periods if you want to be a lifeguard. When rescuing struggling victims, the only help you have in bringing the swimmer in is your legs. You may have one arm to help stroke you in, but the other arm will be holding your victim tight. In other instances, you find yourself in deeper water, communicating with other lifeguards and using your hands to take care of a victim. In the case of a head, neck, or back injury, you have to rely on your lower body to keep you afloat as you work with the victim and the backboard.

Brick test

Finally, you are faced with the brick test. This part of the pool lifeguard test is composed of retrieving a 10-pound brick submerged at the bottom of a pool. Sometimes, this simply means diving to the bottom of the pool and bringing it back to the surface. Then, you can drop it down for the next lifeguard to perform.

In other scenarios, there are additional components to this brick test. For example, you may have to begin at the opposite end of the pool, swim 20 yards or so to the brick, dive down to retrieve it some 10 or so feet below you, and bring it back up. Then, you must maintain the brick above the water and make your way back to the starting point. Which test you're faced with depends on where you are trying out.

REMEMBER

These three parts must be completed within an allotted time period as well.

Essentially, this part serves as a type of mock rescue.

Continuing your water training

After passing the lifeguard test, regardless of whether you found the physical portion of it to be difficult or not, you now have the pool at your disposal to improve upon your skills. Take it upon yourself to grow as a lifeguard and work on the test components so that they will be a breeze come the requalifying procedure. More importantly, these exercises allow you to become a more efficient rescuer in the water during real-life emergency situations.

TIP

Workouts for staying in shape throughout the season and for preparing for the lifeguard test can be found in Chapter 8!

Becoming certified

You are physically adept to become a lifeguard, great! But to finally call yourself a professional rescuer, you need certifications that are recognized by the national standard. In addition to the specific lifeguard certification required by your facility and granted after passing (among others) the physical exam requirements, you need certification and trainings that satisfy OSHA-mandated job requirements.

TECHNICAL STUFF

The Occupational Safety and Health Administration (OSHA) is an agency of the U.S. Department of Labor. The agency creates safe working conditions for employees by providing guidelines for training, education, and assistance.

The two certifications you definitely must have are Basic First Aid and CPR/AED for the Professional Rescuer. In the big picture, these certifications instruct students on how to approach and respond to respiratory emergencies, cardiac emergencies, physical injuries, and other medical situations. For these more serious types of encounters, the job of the lifeguard involves stabilizing the swimmer before higher-level rescuers arrive on scene and take over. These classes are designed to be interactive, including video components and hands-on exercises.

The Basic First Aid, CPR (cardiopulmonary resuscitation), and AED (automated external defibrillator) courses encompass all of the following:

>> Cardiac arrest
>> CPR – Adult

- » CPR – Child and infant
- » AED
- » Stroke
- » Choking
- » Vomiting
- » Neck injuries
- » Anaphylaxis (life-threatening allergic reaction that can lead to difficulty in breathing)
- » Breathing difficulties
- » Seizures
- » Bleeding
- » Wounds and abrasions
- » Burns
- » Musculoskeletal trauma
- » Environmental injuries
- » Poison
- » Shock
- » Psychiatric emergencies

Getting the classroom education

You can be the strongest swimmer in the group, but if you don't know the proper way to assist the different types of drowning victims, you can never be an effective lifeguard. In order to become certified as a lifeguard, a certain number of classroom hours are typically required.

Your classroom education covers everything from being in the water and going over backboard exercises, to cross-chesting a swimmer back to the wall, to the correct way to deliver chest compressions, to the proper course of action when dealing with a victim in shock.

In the classroom, you begin your earliest practice as a teammate on a lifeguard crew. This training does more than teach people lifesaving skills. You will also develop personal and professional skills. You learn about the most effective ways of communicating, as this skill is important to know in high-stress environments and in everyday situations. There are many exercises where you practice staying calm in emergencies and learn to collaborate with your crew members.

Another large part of the curriculum in a lifeguard class includes the instruction for escaping the grip of a struggling victim when things do not go as planned.

When someone is actively drowning, they will grab onto the first thing that they can in order to keep themselves afloat. That could be you if you don't use the proper techniques in approaching and securing them. As much as it is annoying that their first move might be to lurch onto you and pull you down underwater with them, we can't blame them for this survival instinct.

The generally accepted course of action in these scenarios is to take a big breath of air before pulling yourself underwater with them. For the most part, this should teach them a quick lesson and they will immediately let go before continuing to struggle at the surface. If they are particularly relentless and hold on tighter, tuck your head down, turn to one side, and simultaneously push up and away.

It helps as well that you aim for the underside of their arm above the elbow and grab the pressure point in their bicep.

The two commonly known escapes are the Front Head-Hold Escape and Rear Head-Hold Escape (if they manage to grab you from behind), which we discuss in detail in Chapter 10.

There are many different courses available out there. Verify what your facility requires in terms of certifications! If you have an option, look into the various lifeguarding organizations and what they have to offer. Among many others, these include the American Red Cross and YMCA. Some facilities do not require a third-party certification.

Working at the waterpark

Lifeguarding a waterpark undoubtedly includes all of the afore-mentioned topics, but it also incorporates lifesaving techniques that are exclusive to park attractions and unique to an average pool or diving well.

Entries into pools that have gradual slopes with a zero depth edge require the run-and-swim entry. Wave pools are good examples of these types of pools. Sometimes you need to employ a walking assist to help people get out of the water and/or up slippery staircases. A one or two-rescuer beach drag may also be used to pull victims who are struggling to find their footing.

Each waterpark (and facility) is different. It is important that you study and follow the EAP (Emergency Action Plan) of your designated facility. Depending on the attraction or ride, the way you go about tending to an emergency differs. Emergencies in the winding river attraction may require you to hit an emergency stop button to stop the current. Emergencies in the catch pool of a waterslide may mean pressing that emergency stop button to slow the rushing water, preventing further swimmers from going down and allowing for the best environment to provide help. In the tumultuous waters of a working wave pool, this stop button may be necessary to get to the victim and provide proper stabilization, or whatever intervention is needed.

REMEMBER

Once again, it is important that the park's EAP is followed so that all lifeguards are on the same page in these types of scenarios and the problem can be taken care of in the most efficient manner.

In all special situations, your best judgement may be the best tool and instruction that you employ.

Maintaining Your Facility

Depending on the way that your facility is run, you may find yourself in charge of a number of maintenance tasks in addition to your sits on the lifeguard stand. These roles are often split up among the crew, with the more senior guards delegating tasks and the younger guards, or "rookies," getting their hands dirty.

Monitoring chlorine and pH levels

Believe it or not, managing chlorine levels at a pool is part of keeping the facility safe and fun. Chlorine keeps the pool from becoming a gross, bacteria-filled hole of water in the ground. Unsanitized pools due to poorly managed levels of chlorine may lead to swimming-related illnesses like diarrhea, swimmer's ear, athlete's foot, MRSA, and many more.

Whether you are tending to your residential pool or preparing for a day at your workplace, it is important to verify that the levels of chlorine, the pool's first line of defense against germs, are up to standard.

TECHNICAL STUFF

According to the CDC, the concentration of chlorine (technically, free chlorine, or the active form of chlorine that kills germs) should be at a minimum of 1 ppm in pools.

Maintaining the pH levels in your pool also goes hand in hand with the chlorine. The sweet spot is between a pH of 7.2 and 7.8. Anything above 8.0 causes the germ-fighting ability of chlorine to deteriorate and is prone to causing skin rashes on swimmers. Anything below 7.0 increases the sanitizing ability of chlorine but causes the pipes in the pool to corrode and break down. It can also cause a painful stinging sensation in swimmers' eyes. Factors like heavy rain are culprits in fluctuating pool pH levels.

Training for chlorine and pH maintenance occurs in-house and the lifeguard hierarchy and work protocol varies from one facility to another. It may be your responsibility to check these levels either weekly, daily, or on a more frequent schedule. Testing will be more frequent if there are lots of patrons visiting, especially children. With outdoor pools, the weather plays a factor in how often a pool should be tested. After a storm, it should be checked multiple times that day.

WARNING

Depending on where you work and the staffing of your facility, you may be required to check or change chlorine gas tanks from time to time. It is important to be careful and be properly trained when performing maintenance checks on chlorine tanks, as chlorine leaks can cause serious health risks. The effects can be immediate and irreversible to your eyes, lungs, and other body parts.

TECHNICAL STUFF

There are three methods for checking the amount of chlorine in a pool: pool test strips, liquid test kits, and digital pool testing.

>> Pool strips are the most widely used method for checking the levels of chlorine in the pool; they are foolproof, inexpensive, and fairly accurate. Some strips will only test for either chlorine or pH, while others gauge the levels of more than one test in a single dip. After comparing with the labels on the little canister those strips come in, you'll have a much better idea of the pool's chemical balance and what needs (or doesn't need) to be added!

>> Liquid test kits are a little bit more money and a tad more complicated compared to pool strips, but they are more reliable and encompassing. Drops are gradually added one by one to the pool water you've collected. As you observe the color change, the water's composition is revealed through a series of complex chemical reactions.

>> Finally, digital pool testers capture the most accurate picture of a pool's chemical composition. They are also the quickest, easiest, and as you might have guessed, the priciest of these three methods. You can read the results of the pool's chlorine, pH, and many other chemicals with the electronic display right on the device.

TIP

Tips for measuring the chlorine levels at the pool:

>> Allow the pool pump to circulate the pool water for at least an hour before taking a sample. Results from water that has been sitting may yield inaccurate reads.

>> Retrieve your water sample at a depth of around 12-18 inches, or elbow deep.

>> Try not to take samples near pool returns or floating chemical dispensers, which may have the tendency to inaccurately swing the chlorine readings.

>> Keep an ongoing record of the chlorine and pH levels in the pool to get a good idea of the pool's pattern. (See Figure 4-2.)

If a pool's chlorine maintenance system is down for any reason, closing the pool is likely the best or only course of action. Your primary concern should always be to guarantee the health and safety of all recreational bathers.

REMEMBER

Safety is the number one priority as a lifeguard, and allowing swimming in an unsafe pool violates your oath as a lifeguard.

Checking for hazards in and around the pool

With safety being your number one priority, it is important that anything outside or around the pool that may cause bodily harm or produce an unsafe environment is either removed or swimming must be stopped.

Evgeniya Sheydt / Adobe Stock

FIGURE 4-2: A lifeguard uses a chlorine strip to check the levels in the pool.

Watch for these common hazards in and around the pool:

>> Loose drain covers

>> Shattered glass

>> Pooling water around clogged drains

>> Broken tiles, ladders, or stairs

>> Unsecured handicap lifts

>> Crowds past capacity

>> Scattered personal belongings

>> Blocked fire exits

>> Weathered diving boards

>> Any old or outdated safety equipment

Another safety factor that may come to mind is the weather. While not directly *in* the facility, the weather can be the most obvious sign that swimming is no longer safe. Any sort of lightning or electrical storm in an outdoor pool should prohibit swimming in all capacities. Because water is a conductor of electricity, lightning striking water causes a lethal current to pass throughout the entire pool.

Poor lighting in a swimming pool facility can pose a dangerous situation, as swimmers and visitors must be able to clearly see where they are going. Sometimes something as simple as seeing a puddle before stepping in it could prevent a nasty fall. Slippery signs should be readily available at your facility, especially in waterparks, where children running with excitement have little regard for their environment. In poor lighting, the lifeguard's vision is also hindered. You should be able to see the facial expressions on your swimmers, and a poorly lit facility might prevent you from being able to do so.

Using an equipment checklist

It's always important to keep a mental note in your head of your essentials. The same way that you sound out "phone, keys, wallet. . ." in your head before walking out your front door (or is it just me that does that?), it's important that you check off the different items on your pool/waterpark checklist prior to making your way to the lifeguard chair or stand.

Do you have your rescue tube? Without this flotation device, you are already at a deficit when it comes to pulling a struggling swimmer out of the water and being able to fulfill your duties as a lifeguard.

REMEMBER

Swimming your victim to safety on a Styrofoam tube is a whole lot easier than swimming your victim in when the only thing supporting them is you.

Don't forget that stylish fanny pack! I can't be the only one who thinks that the fanny pack and visor is an incredibly flattering look. That fanny pack should have many essential items in the case of all types of emergencies. It should have both an adult and pediatric CPR breathing mask for delivering rescue breaths. A pair of gloves comes in handy (pun intended) for protecting yourself and others. Some sterile pads in there are essential in instances of uncontrolled bleeding. Triangular bandages in the fanny pack would be great for wrapping a wound or a quick sling. And you most certainly cannot forget handful of small band-aids, as adults and children alike will be asking for these on a whim.

Since the COVID-19 pandemic, an N-95 mask and a surgical mask or two tucked into your lifeguard fanny pack have become standards. Don't forget that your safety and the prevention of disease comes before all else.

Finally, make sure you have your whistle on you! Whether it's clutched to your bicep, around your neck, or looped into the strap of your hat, your whistle should not be left behind. Moreover, it should be easily accessible in case that you need to speedily get the attention of a particular swimmer or another lifeguard.

The Biggest Danger: Head, Neck Back/Spinal Injuries

Can you think back to a time when it was a hot, sweaty day at your local pool and the only thing you could think about is jumping into that refreshing oasis? Sometimes in these scenarios, the excitement can cause people to become careless.

It is very important that signs prohibiting diving are very clear to the public.

As a lifeguard, it is simply impossible for you to remind every single person on the pool deck that they cannot dive headfirst into the pool. However, it should be you and your crew's duty to make sure that the sign prohibiting diving in the shallow water is not only visible, but inconveniently obvious. The depth at the ends of the pool deck should also be clearly painted or indicated. Too many times I have seen the depth of a pool fading away or missing entirely, creating a very unsafe environment. It can be very difficult to gauge how deep a pool really is from the deck.

Between 3 to 5 percent of spinal cord injuries are attributed to swimming or diving accidents. When swimmers dive headfirst into a pool and meet the bottom with their head or necks, they are at high risk of breaking or damaging their spinal cord. These types of accidents may cause a swimmer to become paralyzed. The two types of paralysis are *quadriplegia* (paralysis of all four limbs) and *paraplegia* (paralysis of the legs and lower body).

When lifeguards witness a swimmer with a suspected spinal cord injury, they must first activate their facility's EAP, calling for a backboard to arrive at the scene. The first lifeguard is responsible for keeping the victim's head in stabilization. Head stabilization is the process of maintaining the head, neck, and spine in a neutral position to prevent further injury to their central nervous system. Once the backboard arrives on the scene, the victim should be safely, securely, and efficiently strapped to the board. See Figure 4-3.

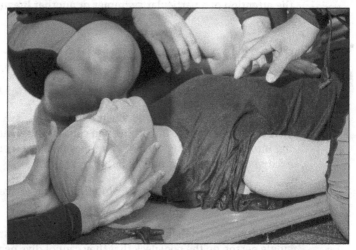

hooyah808 / Adobe Stock

FIGURE 4-3: The lifeguard at the head of the victim holds their head in stabilization, preventing motion and further injury of their head, neck, and back.

The lifeguard who was the first to respond to the victim must never let go of the patient and lose stabilization of their head until the victim is transferred to a higher standard of care.

This lifeguard who is holding the head in inline stabilization is also the leader in charge and delegating tasks. It is important that higher-level rescuers such as EMTs be notified as soon as possible. Care is passed along to them before the victim is transported to a hospital or medical facility with more advanced resources.

Blowing the Whistle on Bad Behavior

The sound of the lifeguard whistle is familiar to people of all ages. On the pool deck and at the waterpark, you might constantly hear the sound of a whistle being blown . . . the big question people might ask themselves as they look up toward the lifeguard stand is "are they talking to me?"

While some people look at the lifeguards as the "water police," it is our job to make sure people have a great time in a safe manner! While they might think we are purposely out to ruin their day of fun, it is actually the exact opposite! Lifeguards really just want to make sure no one loses sight of certain safety measures that can result in serious injury or death.

Blowing the whistle on bad behavior is one of the most important jobs of the lifeguard and even though you might feel bad about it, you must remember that once an accident has occurred, there is no going back. Keep the rules tight and apply them equally to everyone. No one gets a hall pass!

Using clear, basic hand signals and pointing directly at the person in question should help you get the job done (see Figure 4-4). Enforcing the rules cuts down on bad behavior and ultimately reduces the number of emergencies at your pool or waterpark!

"No running on the pool deck!"

Hands down, one of the biggest violations on the pool deck or waterpark is running! While most of us, adults included, may not be able to contain our excitement for the day's activities, running on the pool deck is one of the more dangerous things swimmers can do. Pool decks often are constructed with concrete or various types of tile. Concrete pool decks typically give you more grip even when they are wet; however, tile pool decks tend to be more slippery and a hazard even when walking.

Michael O'Neill / Adobe Stock

FIGURE 4-4: This lifeguard enforces pool rules and attracts the attention of his swimmers by blowing his whistle.

The idea behind the "no running" rule is to prevent basic slip and falls. More serious slip and falls can result in injuries to the head, neck, and back, on top of any potential trauma (such as bleeding or other injuries).

Additionally, running on the pool deck could result in someone being knocked unconscious or even landing in the pool. This poses a very serious situation for children and adults, as it only takes a small amount of water inhaled into your lungs to drown. Even with lifeguards on duty, this is a much more serious and complicated rescue.

All aquatic facilities have signs like "No Running," "No Diving," "No Jumping," and so on. These are all safety reminders, for all the bathers who visit the facility. As a lifeguard, you should know where these signs are located and point them out to visitors and patrons. If you find that any of these signs are not in plain sight, make an effort to bring this up to upper management. Make sure these signs are clearly visible to help make your facility a safer place!

Walking on the pool deck is a simple rule, but hands down one of the most difficult to enforce as a lifeguard. For many people, they simply just let their excitement get the best of them!

90 PART 2 **Lifeguarding in the Different Facilities**

"Cut out the horseplay!"

Nothing is more fun than a day at the pool or waterpark with friends or family. Chicken fights, rough housing, playing near the drain, or anything that puts or forces anyone underwater can quickly go from a good time to tragedy in a matter of minutes. Because your swimmers may not know any better, it's important that you put an end to the horseplay. The reality is, what starts off as just plain good old fun can quickly turn into a real emergency. Consider just a few of these dangers:

>> Chicken fights usually call for four players. One player sits on top of the other players shoulders and the two pairs face off at each other. The purpose or intention is for one team to knock off the player who is sitting on their opponent's shoulders. This game often gets extremely physical and often times leads to injuries. We have seen people get punched, kicked, and even break their noses. It is not uncommon for players to fall backward and smash their heads on the concrete deck! While this is certainly not supposed to happen, that is why it is called an accident!

>> Another very dangerous thing that most people simply just aren't educated about is the danger of the pool drain. Most pool drains do not create a powerful suction; however, it has been documented in several cases that swimmers with long hair or jewelry can get caught in the drain and drown.

   Many children love to fetch dive sticks and other toys that sink to the bottom of the pool. Being able to touch the bottom and swim up to the surface is a rite of passage of all children. Both activities may seem innocuous but can lead children too close to the treacherous pool drain.

TIP

Know where the pool drain is located and keep an extra special eye on that area. Educate children and parents who visit your pool or waterpark. If you see them diving with jewelry on, recommend that they take it off and explain why! No one should ever be playing by the drain, ever. Safety should always be the number one priority when watching your swimmers.

THE VIRGINIA GRAEME BAKER POOL AND SPA SAFETY ACT (VGBA)

This U.S. law is named after Virginia Graeme Baker, who succumbed to a pool suction-drain injury in June, 2002. A spa drain held her underwater, causing her to drown.

As a result of this incident, on December 19, 2008, the VGBA was written into law to make private pools and spas safer. The law brought more overall awareness about the dangers of underwater drainage systems and the importance of keeping a constant eye on children in and around the water.

"Quit the diving board shenanigans!"

Hands down one of the biggest attractions at any pool is the diving board. There is something powerful that just draws people to want to climb up that ladder and walk the plank! While the diving board is hands down one of the most fun parts of spending the day at the pool, it can also be one of the most dangerous. A typical diving board is approximately 8 to 10 feet long and several feet off the water. For safety reasons, diving boards shouldn't be installed in water that is less than 8 feet deep.

Of course, if we are talking about larger diving boards, pools are typically 10, 12, or even 15 feet deep. Spring diving boards are the ones that you are probably most familiar with. They typically have some flexibility in them and some even have a fulcrum that allows divers to adjust the spring of the diving board. Platform diving boards are hard flat surfaces and the divers dive from either 5, 7.5, or 10 meters.

All diving boards have serious potential for injury, which is why when it comes to diving board safety, there is no room for shenanigans! You should never let more than one person jump off a diving board at the same time. It is imperative that the lifeguard who oversees the diving board area of any pool must be in full control of what is going on. Two people on the diving board at once can create a hazard, since it is very easy for one or both people to lose their balance and fall off, either into the water or worse, onto the deck.

The most common diving board hazard is the possibly of hitting your head on the diving board. This is why most facilities do not allow you to do somersaults and or other fancy dives other than jump straight in or do a cannonball. Even trained professional divers have been known to occasionally bump the board at times.

Back in the 1988 Olympics in Seoul, Korea, U.S. diver Greg Louganis smashed his head on the diving board during the preliminary rounds. He got five stitches and was back diving for finals. He managed to finish in third place.

Another dangerous aspect of diving boards is the possibility of getting jumped on in the water. The lifeguard needs to control how quickly swimmers are allowed to enter the diving board platform. This plays a big role in the safety of the swimmers on the board and in the water.

If a patron jumps off the diving board and hasn't yet reached the side of the pool and then another person jumps off the board, both people are now at serious risk for traumatic injury, including potential head, neck, and back injuries. The lifeguard must communicate clear stop and go commands. Establish stop and go commands early and never let your guard down. A fun day on the diving board can quickly become tragic if you aren't on top of it all of the time!

Having Eyes in the Back of Your Head

Lifeguards are professional people watchers and a good lifeguard is said to have Spidey-like senses! We can't even begin to express to you how important it is not just to look, but to process what you are looking at while on the lifeguard stand. As a lifeguard, you will eventually become an expert at understanding and reading body language and facial expressions and even be able to make assumptions about who will need help before they are in trouble.

Scanning the area

Scanning is a very important skill that every lifeguard must eventually master! Scan your area and look for hazards or clues that help you recognize that a person is in trouble or needs your assistance! When you're scanning, you should not just be looking. You should be looking and processing what you are seeing.

There are many different types of scanning techniques. One isn't necessarily better than the other, but it is important to use a variety of scanning techniques to make sure you keep your mind and body engaged. When scanning any body of water, you have overlapping areas or zones of coverage (unless you are a single guard facility!). There are five components of effective scanning:

>> Eye movement

>> Head movement

>> Body position

>> Alertness

>> Engagement

Anyone can be a body in a lifeguard stand. To be a good lifeguard, you need to be 100 percent fully attentive at all times when on duty, and that means scanning your area of responsibility for clues and or problems. While some things might be obvious to the naked eye, others may not. Do it long enough and you will eventually be able to pick out the needle in the haystack! Depending on your facility, the amount of time you sit in one particular lifeguard stand can vary anywhere from 15 minutes to an hour. This is designed to prevent lifeguards from becoming complacent, sleepy, or bored and ultimately miss something important in front of their eyes.

To be at your best, make sure you are also taking care of yourself. That means to eat, drink, wear sunscreen, and spend some time out of the sun by using an umbrella, wearing a hat, and spending your breaks in the shade. The last thing you want to do is compromise your own health and safety. Lifeguarding out in the elements can take a toll on you and ultimately affect your ability to scan properly!

Some things you might want to look for while scanning:

>> Fully clothed swimmers

>> Water wings or other flotation devices

>> Young children and the elderly

- >> Excessive splashing (that could be drowning)
- >> Fearful or pensive body language
- >> Patron entering the water who has no tan in the middle of the summer

Paying attention to your blind spots

You can't make a rescue if you can't see it happening. There are certain special areas of the pool that you should never forget about. For example, one of the most common places that can often be neglected is directly underneath the lifeguard stand! When you're sitting upright in the lifeguard chair, you tend to want to look out and not down. Not to mention, if you really want to see what's going on underneath your stand, you might actually need to lean forward and then look down. As a matter of fact, if you see someone hanging underneath the lifeguard chair, you should kindly ask them to move and don't forget to explain why.

The lifeguard sitting across from you or on your side should keep an eye on your blind spot under your chair and you should do the same for them. Lifeguarding is about teamwork and communication. If you see something, even if it's not in your zone, don't be afraid to say something! Or do something! Never assume.

Blind spots can also be created various other ways. Sometimes the glare of the sun on the water can create a section that you can't really see. This is why wearing a solid pair of polarized sunglasses is important, as well as a hat or visor to keep the sun directly out of your eyes.

Blind spots can also be created by the presence of large, blow-up floats. While each facility operates on its own rules, it is not uncommon for this exact reason and many more that these large, blow-up toys are not permitted in many public pools around the country.

Chapter **5**

The Stillwater Lifeguard

Many of you are familiar with pools, waterparks, and oceans, but you might be asking yourself what we mean by *stillwater*. A stillwater facility is made up of an open body of water that simply has no current. This can include campgrounds, public parks, resorts, summer camps, and so on. While some still bodies of water can experience water movement due to tidal changes like low and high tide, there is no current or sweep. A current typically carries objects in a certain direction. Currents often change in bodies of water like a river or an ocean. In an ocean, you'll commonly hear the sweep moving parallel to the shore (east to west, west to east, north to south, or south to north). Rivers usually flow downstream, although there are exceptions.

The biggest problem with stillwater bathing areas is that they often look appealing and appear to be less dangerous. This is the perfect example of a wolf dressed in sheep's clothing. Swimmers often incorrectly judge these books by their covers. Stillwater facilities can be very dangerous even though they don't look it.

Knowing What It Takes to Be a Stillwater Lifeguard

A natural progression for some may be to graduate from working as a pool lifeguard to working as a stillwater lifeguard. There are many different types of stillwater facilities. These recreational bathing areas are typically made of up of bays, lakes, reservoirs, and estuaries. Being a stillwater lifeguard requires additional training compared to pool lifeguarding. Figure 5-1 shows one ever-watchful guard on the job.

Andrew / Adobe Stock

FIGURE 5-1: A guard sits on their stand at Pear Tree Point Beach in Fairfield, Connecticut scanning the water.

Physical training

Working as a stillwater lifeguard requires you to be physically fit. The demands of the job tend to be greater than the demands of pool lifeguards. Not everyone is cut out to work on the open water. To even be eligible to become certified as a stillwater lifeguard, you usually have to pass the swim pretest given by the American Red Cross or another nationally recognized aquatic training program.

REMEMBER

The American Red Cross is one of the largest national organization that provides lifeguard and aquatics training. While many jobs require their courses, some may not. Check with your local facilities to determine what training is required!

The following skill prerequisites are based on the American Red Cross' Waterfront Skills module. Candidates must:

» Be 15 years old on or before the final scheduled session of the lifeguard class.

» Swim 550 yards, continuously demonstrating breath control and rhythmic breathing. Candidates may swim using the front crawl, breaststroke, or a combination of both, but swimming on the back or side is not allowed. Swim goggles can be used.

» Swim five yards, submerge and retrieve three dive rings placed five yards apart in four to seven feet of water, resurface and continue to swim with the dive rings another five yards to complete the skill sequence.

» Tread water for two minutes, using only your legs. Candidates must place their hands under the armpits.

» Complete a timed event within one minute and 40 seconds:

   ● Starting in the water, swim 20 yards. Your face may be in or out of the water. Swim goggles are not allowed.

   ● Surface dive, feet-first or head-first, to a depth of seven to ten feet to retrieve a ten-pound object.

   ● Return to the surface and swim 20 yards on your back to return to the starting point. Both hands must hold the object and you must keep your face at or near the surface so you can get a breath.

Classroom education and water training

The classroom component of your education to become a stillwater lifeguard builds on your knowledge from the pool curriculum. There are several rescue techniques and skillsets that are unique to the stillwater lifeguard environment.

Table 5-1 lists the skills taught to stillwater lifeguards.

TABLE 5-1 Skills Taught to Stillwater Lifeguards

Skill	Purpose
Walking Assist	To help walk out an injured or ill victim from the water
Beach Drag	To remove an unresponsive victim from the water to the shoreline
Head-Splint–Face-Down in Extremely Shallow Water	To stabilize a spinal injury in extremely shallow water
Searching Shallow-Water Areas	To aid a search effort for a missing swimmer
Feet-First Surface Dive	To submerge yourself feet-first in areas with possibly dangerous bottoms
Head-First Surface Dive	To dive down head and hands first for a quick and efficient sweep
Searching Deep-Water Areas	To aid a search effort for a missing swimmer
Approaching a Victim on a Rescue Board	To approach a struggling victim on a rescue board
Rescuing an Active Victim with a Rescue Board	To assist an actively drowning swimmer on a watercraft
Rescuing a Passive Victim with a Rescue Board	To assist a passive swimmer on a watercraft

Required certification

When considering a job as a stillwater lifeguard, you should look into the specific certifications required for your desired facility. There are many jobs in different municipalities that could require different certifications and/or licensure.

TIP

You can never go wrong taking one of the nationally recognized certification programs; however, it's a good idea to find out exactly what is required where you live or want to work, so you don't waste your time and money before you start a particular training program.

Understanding the Silent but Deadly Nature of Water

Many swimmers have a false sense of security when it comes to stillwater bathing facilities. This can be a special concern for people who aren't strong swimmers and for those who have young children. The problem typically lies in the lack of education when it comes to understanding water safety and the challenges of different bodies of water. While still bodies of water might look less dangerous, they have their own set of unique dangers that sometimes rival the ocean!

Before swimmers get in the water, they should look for any signs that might give them clues to certain dangers specifically related to that facility, as shown in Figure 5-2. In fact, the best thing to do is to talk to the lifeguards on duty before swimming.

Claudio Divizia / Adobe Stock

FIGURE 5-2: Posted warning signs remind visitors of hazards such as strong currents and deep water. No swimming advised!

WARNING

As a general rule of thumb, if there are no lifeguards, no one should be going in the water. Swimming without a lifeguard on duty is the number cause of drownings across the world. The likelihood of an on-duty drowning is possible but highly unlikely. Taking this simple piece of advice can literally save someone's life. While it might be tempting go for a quick dip, the question is, is it really worth it?

Unique dangers in stillwater

Depending on the body of water, you likely can't see the bottom from the surface of the water. Unlike a pool where you can see all your swimmers, the bottom of a lake or bay and similar landscapes are clouded. This makes any lifeguard's job that much harder, for the obvious reason that you can't see those swimmers who are submerged. Are they just having fun diving down deep, or are they in real distress and needing assistance?

Nature's hazards

Soft silt or muddy bottoms can cause a swimmer to slip under. They resemble the effects of quicksand. Submerged objects such as rocks, trees, stumps, and underwater plants can force swimmers to lose their footing and cause poor swimmers to fall into the water, leading to a struggle. Even those with strong swimming abilities can trip on something underneath, get caught off guard, topple over, and hit their head. They might even become unconscious, with a possible concussion or other head injury. Shells, barnacles, and other marine-like creatures dwelling beneath the surface are all hazards that require lifeguards to spring into action.

Uneven and rocky bottoms

The bottoms of these stillwater sites are also likely to be uneven and less forgiving than the sandy ocean floor. The slope of the water's floor is also subject to change at a moment's notice. It happens all too often, where a parent takes their eyes of their child for a second, and as they walk farther out from shore, just one sudden step takes them into deep territory. In these moments, it could be a race to get to the victim.

Less buoyant than salt water

This has been mentioned earlier in this book, but it warrants repeating. Most still bodies of water are made of freshwater, not salt water. Recall that saltier water is more buoyant, and swimmers are more susceptible to slipping underwater and drowning when the salinity decreases.

Marine life hazards

Our world's waterways are filled with many diverse living things. As a stillwater lifeguard, you should be aware of the various types of marine life that may end up being hazards to your guests. From sharks and leeches, to jellyfish and crabs, to gators and crocs, to dolphins and snapping turtles, to manatees and seals, there is no shortage of life out on the water! Make sure you are trained on the proper first aid, protocols, and emergency procedures in your area.

No rip currents, no problem!

While treacherous rip currents (covered in Chapter 6) may not typically be found in stillwater environments, there are many other hidden dangers that you should be aware of. In saltwater bays, tides can create inflow and outflow currents, which can sometimes be even stronger than rip currents! The biggest problem when it comes to stillwater bathing areas is that they don't seem dangerous to the uninitiated swimmer. That couldn't be further from the truth.

TIP

When visiting a new body of water, make sure to look for signs that might point out hazards specific to that area. Many people do not take the time to read posted signage.

The following list briefly discuss some of the dangers you'll find at your favorite stillwater swimming holes:

>> A *seiche* (pronounced *saysh*) is a rare condition that occurs in a landlocked body of water. This can occur when strong winds combined with variations of atmospheric pressure push water on the surface to one side and then subsides. When rapidly rising and falling lake levels occur during a seiche, they can sweep people off piers and breakwaters and pull swimmers far away from shore. Although they are not common, it's important to know when a seiche can occur. In most cases, it's during a weather-related event with strong winds or even an earthquake.

>> The *currents* in rivers are often times underestimated. River currents can rival or be even stronger than ocean rip

currents. There are many factors that shape the strength of a river current, including channel width, depth, and water volume. As a lifeguard, you should always know what the currents are doing in your area.

>> A *low head dam* is a barrier across the width of a river that alters the characteristic flow of water and usually results in a change in the height of the river level. The purpose of a low head dam is to raise the water level upstream on a river; however, sometimes they occur naturally from logs or trees that have fallen in the river and become lodged. They can help boats navigate a channel, create a drop for generating hydropower, and make water available at intakes for water supply and irrigation. These very powerful currents can create reverse currents just below them, which essentially traps large debris (and sometimes people). Most swimmers cannot escape these areas if they get stuck in them. Debris that's caught in these areas may cause something called *strainers*. These strainers allow water to move through, but catch and trap larger objects, such as human bodies. Drowning victims are often found by divers in these areas, their bodies pinned underneath low head dams.

TIP

>> If you are ever caught in a river current, your best bet is to *not* swim against it. Try to swim downstream with the river at a 45-degree diagonal angle. The river will flow the strongest in the middle. Getting to the side gives you the best chance of survival. If you get tired, float down on your back with your feet pointed downstream and your head upstream.

>> *Heavy rainfall* makes a lake or river rise. Potential hazards, like tree logs, branches, or boulders can be covered up, which creates a serious hazard for bathers, especially those jumping and diving in the river.

>> A *long dry period* can even make waters shallower for diving, risking spinal injuries. Spinal injuries are one of the leading causes of injury in and around the aquatic environment. Accidents such as diving into the bottom and striking the sea floor or an any other object often lead to serious injuries to the head, neck, and back.

>> Most open water facilities also experience *high and low tides* throughout the day, which can be exacerbated by the moon at different times of the month. The difference in the tides at stillwater bays, for example, are far more prominent than differences in the tide at the ocean.

>> *Manmade holes!* Lifeguards have to be careful with the floor of the water as the tides change. In many instances, patrons dig holes in the sand, which become hidden when the tides come back up. Driving a lifeguard vehicle in these manmade holes, when undetected, can cause your vehicle to get stuck, or at the very least, rattle your teeth. They also create a dangerous situation when people are walking slowly out in shallow water and suddenly fall into a hole, which could lead to injury as minor as a sprained ankle or cause the swimmer such as a child to straight up disappear!

When swimmers step in an unexpected hole, they typically do not struggle. They will just quickly slip underwater and be gone. Comparing this to working on an ocean, where most rescues are because of rip currents, you typically can see them forming, giving you a heads up that swimmers could end up in trouble. These manmade holes give you no warning signs whatsoever. This is why these facilities can be dangerous.

>> *Sandbars* move and shift from season to season or from one storm to another. Storms that produce heavy rain or currents are certainly responsible for shifting sandbars. These changes in the waterfront floor can create unexpected drops and dangerous hazards. A bather could be walking in the water and suddenly drop from knee to waist deep in a split second. In some cases, the water may even be over their heads!

REMEMBER

The Great Lakes are the five largest lakes in the United States and include Lake Superior, Lake Huron, Lake Michigan, Lake Erie, and Lake Ontario (if you care to remember, the mnemonic HOMES works). They are located in the northern Midwest along the border between the United States and Canada. While these might technically fall in the stillwater category, that can be misleading because of their ability to generate waves, primarily due to wind swell and storm surges. What can make these waves even more dangerous than the ocean is how short their periods are. Waves can crash every three to five seconds, giving weaker swimmers a shorter time to recover in these rough waters when they are toppled over. In addition to wave generation, structural currents created by manmade jetties or piers can pull swimmers off the shore and out toward deeper waters.

A *breakwall* is a manmade structure that runs parallel to the shore. Its purpose is to prevent the coastal area from tides, currents, waves, and storm surges. Waves crash with extra force at breakwalls, creating a potentially dangerous situation if a swimmer gets caught in one. A *jetty*, on the other hand, runs perpendicular to the shore.

While there are certainly lifeguards along the shores of the Great Lakes (you'll learn later that the first Junior Lifeguards began in Chicago on the shores of Lake Michigan), there are many coastal parts of the lakes that lack lifeguards. This creates unsafe circumstances, as swimmers are forced to swim at their own risk when they want to cool off.

Maintaining Your Facility

Every open water facility must be maintained at a level of safety. When you're considering the challenges of lifeguarding at a waterfront, think about these unique tasks you need to do in order to safely operate and keep the public safe.

>> *Is the bottom free of hazards?* Is the shoreline free of sharp objects, broken glass, and litter?

>> *Is the sand in front of and around the lifeguard stands clear of objects?* Are docks and piers stable, lacking any protruding nails, rotting wood, or weak/frayed anchor lines?

>> *Are rescue craft such as rescue boards, rowboats, and kayaks in proper operating condition and do they contain the appropriate rescue equipment? Are they located where lifeguards expect them to be found?*

>> *Are communication devices, such as phones, two-way radios, air horns, whistles, and megaphones in good, working order?*

These are just some of the questions you should be asking yourself as the opening lifeguard and as a member of your crew throughout the day.

Watercraft

Similar to working on the ocean, having additional "tools in the toolbox" is key when it comes to performing any type of open water rescue. There are various types of watercraft you might find at any one of these stillwater facilities. Kayaks and rescue boards tend to be the most popular, mainly because they are easy to use, have many purposes, and are affordable. Small, motorized boats, rowboats, or even jet skis are common at these facilities, depending on the size and operating budget (see Figure 5-3). Make sure you know how to safely operate all watercraft before using them. See Chapter 10 to learn more about specialized equipment.

Libby / Adobe Stock

FIGURE 5-3: A lifeguard patrols on a kayak in stillwater.

Environmental concerns (sewage runoff after rain)

Stillwater is particularly susceptible to the effects of the weather and to precipitation because it does not move. Constantly moving bodies of water, such as rivers or oceans, and their generation of kinetic energy, ward off bacteria. That is why pools, which are technically stillwater, have to be chlorinated to make them safe to swim. Lifeguards cannot simply chlorinate freshwater, and if the composition of the water becomes unsafe for swimming, the facility may be forced to close. Thorough testing is therefore critical.

After large rainfall events or storms, stillwater facilities are sometimes forced to close due to high levels of bacteria. The storm water runoff goes into the lakes, contaminated with fecal bacteria, oil from the street, and pesticides from lawns, which can lead to gastrointestinal illness. The water quality standard set by the Environmental Protection Agency dictates what water is safe for swimming and recreation based on the levels of a bacteria called *enterococcus*. See Figure 5-4.

FIGURE 5-4: A sign warns of unsafe swimming due to high levels of bacteria.

When environmental hazards render your facility unsafe for swimming, your job that day could simply be to keep people out of the water. Keeping the public safe takes many forms.

» **Learning how to escape the strength of a rip current**

» **Knowing the day to day routine of these types of surf lifesavers**

Chapter **6**
The Ocean Rescue Lifeguard

While all lifeguard positions at their essence perform the same duties and are well regarded, there is no doubt that the ocean lifeguard is the most arduous and well respected position in the community of lifesavers. To work at a beach requires a more demanding level of physical fitness, as well as the ability to make decisions and absorb information in a large and ever-changing environment.

The process of becoming an oceanfront lifeguard differs from the pool and waterpark process. The training, classroom education, and day-to-day experiences are drastically different as well. Looking out toward the horizon, you will immediately recognize that the dangers in this oceanic environment outnumber those in stillwater facilities.

Knowing What It Takes to Be an Ocean Rescue Lifeguard

Do you have what it takes to be an ocean lifeguard? That's a question that may not have crossed your mind when you picked up this book.

Perhaps you have seen lifeguards at the beach perched on chairs or staring out from the lifeguard tower and thought to yourself, "What a cushy, easy summer gig!" The physical and mental conditioning needed to get to that lifeguard stand is considerable. We start by sharing with you this one, simple fact: This is not a job for everyone, and typically only the strongest and most well-rounded candidates are successful.

This chapter sheds some light on the major components of what it takes to become an ocean lifeguard.

Physical training

There are three phases to the physical training that goes into being an ocean lifeguard. It all begins with the practice you should do on your own to prepare for the qualifying procedure so you can come out on top and land the role you want.

TIP

Dive into Chapter 8 for our best tips on how to be prepared for the certification test and show up as the best athletic version of yourself.

Next, you must handle the physical training required of you as you go through the standard training, academy, or program. If the qualifying procedure did not do its job of letting in only the most competent candidates, the demands of these "rookie training" periods are meant to weed out those who are unfit to be an ocean lifeguard. There's no beating around the bush that days on days of swimming, running, mock rescues, and calisthenics in all types of weather conditions can certainly take a toll on your physical and mental wellbeing.

WARNING

Going through ocean rookie training is not for the meek or weak! It is truly a grueling process.

Being able to endure this training period proves your ability to be successful in the field when the time comes. If you're picturing this to be like some sort of military boot camp, you have the right picture in mind.

Finally, we must not forget the physical training required day in and day out to be able to keep up with the demanding duties. You must maintain the strength and endurance to run on sand, swim in unpredictable conditions, and pull struggling victims out of rough water — not just once, but over and over and over again on particularly treacherous days.

TIP

Turn to Chapter 10 to read a bit more about working on various in-service trainings and drills. It explains some of the best ways to sharpen your skills after you've landed this dream job. It also dives into the various in-service trainings and drills that focus on open water rescue techniques.

Classroom education

Before you can be successful as an ocean lifeguard, you must learn the various technical aspects of the job. In every lifeguard program across the country, there is some sort of formalized classroom lifeguard training. This is where you learn about the various topics of professional ocean lifeguarding.

The classroom component is designed to provide you with the knowledge and base level skills that will eventually be combined and incorporated into drills and training scenarios out on the field.

WARNING

The classroom component includes periodic checks of understanding in the form of unit/chapter quizzes and a final exam. It is not uncommon to require minimum passing grades of 80 percent in order to continue. However, every academy has its own set of academic guidelines and rules that you must follow in order to be successful. In many circumstances, if you don't meet these academic standards, you will be dismissed from the lifeguard training program.

REMEMBER

Take the classroom training seriously. Although it might not be as exciting as the hands-on work, it helps you become a better and more prepared ocean lifeguard!

You might be asking yourself what will be covered in the classroom. Here is a list of some (but not all) of the topics you will learn in the classroom training as an ocean lifeguard:

>> Responsibilities of a lifeguard
>> Rip currents
>> Oceanography
>> Rescues
>> Effective scanning
>> Characteristics of drowning victims
>> CPR/AED/first aid
>> Special weather conditions
>> Dangerous marine life
>> Beach and facility maintenance
>> Specific agency regulations, policies, and procedures

Water training

It should be no surprise that a very large part of an ocean lifeguard's training regimen happens in the water. As an ocean lifeguard, you should expect to be getting wet and wild every day! You should always be in the water and you should always be training.

Rookie ocean lifeguards should expect to spend an extensive amount of time in the water, as this is where you begin sharpening your skillset. From equipment handling to mock rescues, you will find that as the conditions of the water change, so will your ability to perform swiftly and efficiently.

At the end of the day, every person who goes in must come out, and you must be equipped with the appropriate skills to pull out any type of victim in any situation.

Sometimes training is just learning how to adapt to the ever-changing environment. You'll go through various scenarios with the hope that when it is your time to shine, you'll know how to properly tackle the task head on. Here are just some of those scenarios:

>> A large focus of water training involves handling spinal injuries in the surf zone and beyond.

>> Rescuing active drowning victims with a rescue can or tube is a simple classic mock rescue that you'll practice in various conditions.

>> Entries and exits in and out of the water play a key part of any rescue and can be performed daily.

>> Specialized equipment such as the rescue boards, dory boats, kayaks, and jet skis require a larger skillset to avoid injuring yourself or members of the public. You have to be competent enough to execute the rescue while operating this equipment.

Required certifications

Just like the other types of facilities, you need the credentials or certifications to back you up as a first responder and professional surf lifesaver. For starters, every lifeguard must be certified to perform basic life support measures with CPR/AED for the Professional Rescuer and Healthcare Provider and First Aid (or equivalent) through a nationally recognized organization.

TECHNICAL STUFF

The two most well-known organizations that can certify you to perform CPR are the American Red Cross and the American Heart Association.

TIP

Note that ocean lifeguard certification requirements, while very similar in comparison, can vary from agency to agency. Do your research and look into the different beach lifeguard jobs available in your area. Inquire about the minimum requirements and qualifying procedures. The biggest thing you want to find out is if you must hold an American Red Cross Lifeguard Training certificate or equivalent. Many agencies require one, while others provide their own in-house training programs. As examples, the following sidebars list the requirements to be an ocean lifeguard in New York at Jones Beach and Los Angeles county, California.

JONES BEACH LIFEGUARD CORPS.: LIFEGUARD QUALIFICATION EXAM

The Lifeguard Qualification Exam for New York State Parks, Long Island Region, where both authors work, is as follows:

- *100-yard timed swim.* Applicant must finish swim in 75 seconds or less to continue.
- *50 yard cross-chest carry: 25 yard swim; 25 yard carry.* Applicant carries manikin in cross-chest position in 70 seconds or less to continue.
- *¾ mile (1,320 yards) timed endurance run.* Applicant must complete the ¾ mile (1,320 yards) run in six minutes or less to continue. (Sneakers recommended.)
- *Timed ocean swim.* Applicant must complete the approximately 350-400 yard swim on prescribed open water, run-swim-run course to continue. Stopping will result in disqualification. The faster you go, the more points you get. The more points you get, the higher you will finish!
- Successful completion of 40 hours of rookie training with minimal passing final exam grade of 85 percent.

THE LOS ANGELES COUNTY FIRE DEPARTMENT LIFEGUARD DIVISION QUALIFICATIONS

Los Angeles county has its own qualification requirements, as follows.

- 1000 meter swim, followed by a run-swim-run
- Multiple choice test
- Evaluation of training and experience
- Background check
- Physical exam with stress test
- Successful completion of 100-hour lifeguard academy, which includes classroom instruction, physical training, and learning rescues/other lifeguard skill sets

Avoiding the Biggest Danger: Rip Currents

On shores and beaches around the world, the vast majority of rescues are directly attributed to the merciless pull of rip currents. Most beachgoers and recreational swimmers have heard of rip currents but are unable to tell you what they are, and more importantly, what they look like.

As an ocean lifeguard, you must have a good grasp of its mechanisms and know how to properly escape one. Even for a professional lifeguard, understanding all the components of a rip current is critical in order for your rescues to be successful and efficient. No one rip current is the same. Learning to read the water and make important decisions about how, where, and when to enter one all play key roles. As a professional ocean lifeguard, you are expected to be the expert. You should be able to explain to your everyday recreational swimmer how to recognize a rip current and what to do if they get caught in one.

TIP

Tell your swimmers to swim near a lifeguard! This is hands down the most important rule everyone should follow when visiting any oceanfront beach. That way, if swimmers get caught in a rip current, there will be a professional there to save them! Tell them to face the beach and if they are able, wave their hands over their head for help.

Understanding the mechanisms of a rip current

The reason that rip currents are exclusive to oceans is because they need breaking waves to develop.

REMEMBER

The Great Lakes are so massive that they can generate their own swell and waves, and it is possible for rip currents to form in these bodies of water.

When the waves break and move toward the shore, all that extra water needs a way to get back into the ocean. It does not just stay on the shore and accumulate there. The water feeds into the deepest part of the ocean, almost like a hole on the ocean floor. In many cases, this happens when sandbars close to the shore collapse, creating a section of rushing water (see Figure 6-1).

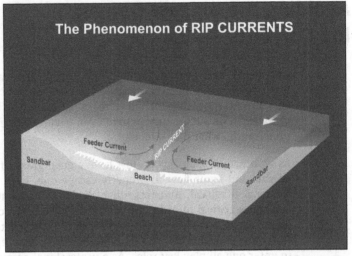

The Phenomenon of RIP CURRENTS

PATTARAWIT / Adobe Stock

FIGURE 6-1: How rip currents work.

Waves do not need to be huge for rip currents to form! This is a big misconception! All that is required for a rip current to form is the breaking of waves toward the shore that need to find their way back into the ocean.

The first part of the rip current is known as the feeder rip, and it can move at various angles. As the name suggests, it feeds into the neck of the rip current. This neck of the rip current almost resembles a runway that goes out to sea, leaving you in the head of the rip current. A picture-perfect rip current head often looks like a mushroom top. Depending on the depth and contours of the ocean floor, a rip current can stretch over hundreds of yards. However, the width of a rip current will not exceed more than several yards. When swimmers get caught in the neck of a rip current, the current can gain speeds of up to five feet per second, essentially shooting the swimmers out to sea.

TECHNICAL STUFF

It is important to know that rip currents do *not* pull swimmers down under the water. They simply pull swimmers out to sea. It is primarily body mechanics combined with fatigue and panic that cause swimmers to go under!

The ocean is very dynamic; it constantly changes throughout the day. The tide comes up and goes back down. Swells increase and decrease. In the same way, rip currents come and go but are bound to reappear in the same spot. The best lifeguards take note of changes in their environment and remember where the deep parts of the ocean are, and consequently, where the rip current will open up and absorb its next group of victims.

TECHNICAL STUFF

When going in to rescue someone from a rip current, it is crucial for you to know and understand which way the ocean is moving. Whether you refer to this as the current or the sweep, this is the way the ocean water is moving parallel to the shoreline as a result of wind, tide, and water densities. Mastering this motion is key to reaching your victim head-on during rescues.

If you enter the water to make the rescue in the wrong place, you can end up downsweep of your victim, which will force you to swim the opposite direction against the flow. On a heavy day, this can be like swimming on a treadmill, and you may not even make it to your victim! It is always best to enter the water upsweep of your victim and swim down toward them with the flow of water. This is called "playing the sweep."

Recognizing a rip current in the water

So now that you have a better understanding of what a rip current is and how they are formed, the big question is how do you identify one? There are several ways lifeguards and beachgoers can identify a rip current. You might not know this, but it is a lot easier to recognize the characteristics of a rip current from up high than when standing on the beach. This is one of the main reasons that lifeguard stands and towers are elevated. This vantage point allows lifeguards to spot rip currents more easily and see the bathing area as a whole. Being able to compare sections of the water from an elevated height makes spotting rip currents easier.

It is important to understand that when you're trying to identify rip currents, not all rip currents look the same. Some rip currents share similar characteristics, but it is important to recognize that there is no cookie cutter representation; they are all different. Some of the most common characteristics of rip currents are covered in the following sections.

Water discoloration

One of the most common characteristics of rip currents is discoloration of the water. When water rushes back out to the ocean and funnels into its deepest channel, it often kicks up the sand on the bottom of the ocean floor. When this happens, it creates a lighter, sandy color in the water. The distinctive change in the water's color makes it easier for lifeguards to recognize that a rip current is present. From here, you will see the water channeling up though the neck and into the head. Looking at this discoloration of the water from the perch of your lifeguard stand or tower, you should start to see a very clear picture of what is going on. Oftentimes, the neck and head of the rip looks like a giant mushroom head.

TIP

Polarized sunglasses allow you to spot these rip currents more easily. By removing the glare of the sun from the surface of the water, they give you a clearer and more comprehensive perspective of the water.

Wave recognition

As explained, the excess water brought on shore by breaking waves must be returned back out to sea. Rip currents, therefore, have no waves, as they are moving in the direction opposite of the surf. Due to the lack of waves in this channel, the water in rip currents has a tendency to look darker, without any of the whitewater present. Although this may sound contradictory to the sandy, light color of rip currents, the most important takeaway here is there are no breaking waves. Lastly, looking for a break in the incoming wave pattern could be a hint that a rip current is pulling!

Surface water recognition

Water at the surface of the ocean rip current can look different when compared to the surrounding water. Often, surface water of rip currents appears as if it is churning or choppy. Other times, it might display as constant ripples at the top of the water. Debris, foam, or seaweed at the surface that is moving out to sea or in a circular motion — in toward the beach and back out again — can be a telltale sign that a rip current is present.

TIP

There are some great videos on YouTube that show you how to spot real rip currents. Check them out:

>> National Oceanic Atmospheric Administration: Rip Current Science: www.youtube.com/watch?v=RJ4hcaJ91TY&t=10s

>> How to Spot a Rip Current: Surf Life Saving Australia: www.youtube.com/watch?v=PuA1DTC_gIQ

Breaking the grip of a rip

If you ever find yourself in a situation where you might be caught in a rip current, the first and most important thing to remember is not to panic! The National Oceanic Atmospheric Administration (NOAA) and the United States Lifesaving Association have teamed up to help educate the public about how to break the grip of a rip! Of course, as a lifeguard, you will be diving headfirst into rip currents to get to your victims out quickly, so it is important to be able to pull both yourself and the victim back to the shore.

You might already be telling yourself that you know the answer to this: Swim parallel to the shore. While this is the best course of action when finding yourself in a rip current, this is not the be-all and end-all solution. Different rip currents take on various shapes and routes, and sometimes swimming parallel to the shore may take you right back into the feeder rip, right up the neck of the rip, and back in the head. In most cases and especially for poor swimmers, these situations will end with a lifeguard coming to the rescue. Only very strong swimmers will find themselves being able to swim out of the rip current; even lifeguards sometimes struggle to escape the pull of a rip current.

REMEMBER

As long as you are able to stay afloat, you will be okay. Swimming toward the shore in the opposite direction of a rip current will only force you to expend energy. This is the equivalent of swimming on a treadmill! In most cases, swimmers are facing the beach (the direction they want to go) and are either stuck in the same spot despite their efforts or moving backward. For more confident, stronger swimmers, this can be less of a problem.

TIP

Weaker swimmers who cannot sustain the effort for a longer period of time are better off letting the current carry them away from the beach and waiting until it subsides before attempting to swim to safety by swimming parallel to shore. Rip currents are not going to carry swimmers out to the horizon line! They can at times pull swimmers up to hundreds of yards off the beach, but that is it. Eventually, they will find themselves in water that is not pulling, and this is when they want to make their move. Break the grip of the rip! Swim parallel to the shore, with the prevailing current, as shown in Figure 6-2.

Courtesy of US Department of Commerce National Oceanic and Atmospheric Administration

FIGURE 6-2: This flyer by the NOAA (National Oceanic and Atmospheric Administration) and USLA is often posted at beaches around the country and explains how to make your way out of a rip current.

TECHNICAL STUFF

The ocean drowning process begins as soon as swimmers panic. Less effective breathing decreases buoyancy, and when people psychologically enter panic mode, stroke technique and efficiency is quickly thrown out the window, causing them to sink.

So although this section is titled "Breaking the grip of the rip," in most situations it ends with you, the lifeguard, needing to make the rescue. The victim, unless they are a great swimmer, won't break the grip of the rip. Lifeguards, who are better at reading the ocean than the average swimmer, have a primary objective of getting and keeping the victim above water. Once they are floating, they can begin to make forward progress back to shore. If the pull is too strong, they can wait it out for the rip current to pause, otherwise known as a *lull* in the ocean. In other cases, some beach patrols will deploy secondary rescue methods. These methods vary from agency to agency and depend on the equipment they have. In most cases, this could call for a rescue line or watercraft such as a rescue board, jet ski, or boat.

TECHNICAL STUFF

Watercraft are explained further in the specialized equipment section of Chapter 10. A rescue line is yet another tool in the lifeguard toolbox. It requires a second lifeguard, also known as the line swimmer, to swim out to the victim on a buoy with the first lifeguard. As you probably guessed, the purpose behind this type of rescue is to pull the lifeguard and victim in the water back to shore. The lifeguard(s) on shore help feed the line out for the line swimmer before tugging the group back onto dry sand.

Maintaining Your Facility

It's especially important to keep your facilities in good working order so they are safe and clean. While the lifeguard's "office" is composed of the beaches around the world and is certainly less traditional than most, lifeguards are held to the highest standard of professionalism and care when it comes to operating and maintaining the facilities and equipment. Not to mention, a lot of these items around the workplace are not cheap! These items must be in working order to save lives and are crucial to the title of first responder.

Without proper maintenance, lives would be at risk and lifeguards would be operating in a dangerous work environment, which is contradictory to their mission.

Lifeguarding equipment

Without your equipment, your job as a lifeguard becomes more dangerous, more difficult, and less effective. There are many tools in the "lifeguard toolbox" and it is up to you to make sure that everything is where it should be and in working order. Not taking care of your lifesaving equipment puts you and the victims in harm's way!

At the start of every day, the opening crew should take a moment to investigate each piece of lifeguard equipment. Many patrols require that you call in a morning report at the start of the day, communicating up the chain of command and detailing what works and what might need to be replaced or repaired. The last thing you want is for a piece of equipment to malfunction or be broken when you need it.

Lifeguard stands/towers

Having fully functional lifeguard stands or towers plays a very important role in effectively performing your daily responsibilities. These integral lifeguard structures provide lifeguards with a bird's eye view of the entire beachfront, providing an unmatched perspective to catch a rescue, recognize a rip current, and help struggling swimmers.

There are many things that can make these structures unsafe or unstable. Most lifeguard stands and towers are constructed of wood. Something as simple as exposed nails or broken slats can create a safety hazard. Some lifeguard towers have windows that could shatter and doors that could come off hinges. Each morning, at the start of your shift, you should inspect your lifeguard stand or tower to make sure it is fully operational. You should report any problems or concerns regarding repairs to the appropriate personnel, based on your chain of command.

Rescue equipment

There are many choices a lifeguard needs to make when they decide it is time to make a rescue. One of the first things they need to think about is what piece of equipment they plan to use in order to execute the save. From rescue boards, to rescue buoys and rescue lines, there are many options available to most beach lifeguards.

The biggest difference you see between beach lifeguards and still-water lifeguards are the buoys they choose to use. While you might still see some agencies around the United States that are known for big surf using soft rescue tubes on the beach, the majority of beach patrols in the United States and around the world use a hard plastic rescue can called a Burnside buoy, as shown in Figure 6-3.

FIGURE 6-3: A Burnside buoy (and a pair of fins) are set up in the sand in front of a lifeguard stand, ready for use at a moment's notice.

The rescue line also plays a big role in long distance rescues. While not utilized in every beach patrol or rescue organization around the world, the rescue line has become a great way to assist lifeguards in conditions where it is difficult for the rescuer to get to shore. For even farther rescues, proper deployment of a boat, jet ski, or rescue board may be more appropriate.

TECHNICAL STUFF

The landline rescue race is always a showstopper at the National Lifeguard Championships (it's discussed in Chapter 12).

All equipment is subject to wear and tear, and lifeguard equipment is no different. Whenever anything starts to break down and become ineffective for lifesaving, it is time to throw it out. Water, particularly salt water, is destructive and a common culprit of this wear and tear.

>> Heavily used buoys, regardless of what they are made of, can become waterlogged, which adds significant weight to them.

>> The lines attaching the buoys to the strap that go across the rescuer's chest also break down after several seasons and need to be checked and replaced as needed.

>> Rescue lines have also been known to tangle themselves if not packed back in correctly or often stretched. It is up to the lifeguards to identify when a piece of lifeguard equipment needs to go out of service and/or be replaced.

First aid

As a lifeguard you will handle plenty of first aid related emergencies. In order to provide the best patient care, you must have all your equipment ready to go and in working order! All lifeguards will be trained, at a minimum, in CPR/AED and first aid skills. Some hold more advanced certifications, such as Certified First Responder (CFR) Emergency Medical Technician (EMT), and Paramedic. Regardless of your rank, your goal as a surf lifesaver remains the same, and that comes with the responsibility of checking on and knowing your supplies. This means knowing how to use the various items in your first aid bag and being familiar with where each item can be found. Some items have expiration dates, so be ready to replace them as needed.

WARNING

You don't want to be caught fumbling with the first aid bag when an emergency is at hand! This is a very unprofessional look and can put someone's life in danger!

One of the biggest problems that lifeguards and other first responders run into is not replacing equipment after it has been used. This is one of the main reasons that you must do equipment checks every day! Assuming that something will be where it was when you saw it last is not professional. Know your beach patrol system when it comes to checking and replacing all first aid equipment.

An oxygen tank will come in handy many more times than you might expect. On many occasions, a victim you pulled from the ocean can benefit from a good ol' non-rebreather mask and 10-15 liters per minute of oxygen. Remember that after using oxygen, you should check the PSI (pounds per square inch) to see how much is left in the tank!

TECHNICAL STUFF

Any oxygen tank lower than 500 PSI needs to be replaced.

Phones and radios

Communication is key! You have probably heard that phrase a thousand times, but it is true, especially when it comes to dealing with emergencies. There are many ways that lifeguards communicate on the beach for non-emergent and emergency reasons. Communication is especially crucial when the beach patrol covers miles of beach.

Two of the most effective ways that lifeguards talk to each other in 21st Century lifeguarding is by phone (no . . . not cell phones) and radio!

Each beach patrol/lifeguard service has different protocols and operating procedures for communications. Most organizations equip individual lifeguards stands or towers with walkie talkie radio communication. In addition, ocean lifeguard supervisors (in many cases, this could be the lifeguard officers) will communicate with a main dispatch office or communications center.

Just like the 911 system, the communications center acts as the main hub or command to help organize the additional resources that lifeguards request (such as additional lifeguards, police, fire, EMS, or Coast Guard). Mobile lifeguards on trucks or quads should always be equipped with a walkie talkie of their own so that they can be notified when and where a situation is going down.

TIP

Just like anything and everything else at the beach, radios can break and malfunction. It is important to test your radios each morning to make sure they are working. This means they transmit and receive messages. Having a fully charged battery (and a back-up battery) is essential to making it through a busy beach day! If you run into radio-related problems, you must notify the appropriate personnel and get it replaced ASAP. This type of communication is essential to running a safe and effective operation.

Sometimes the information you need to relay requires more than just a few words or lifeguard codes. Or perhaps you don't want to take up the radio space for more than a typical walkie talkie message. This is where using the landline phone comes into play, allowing for more normal conversations to get your thoughts, emergency or non-emergency, across.

In some municipalities, you'll find that lifeguard stands have an actual wire running from the chair, dug beneath the sand, all the way to a distant telephone pole. In Los Angeles county, this has been replaced by cell phones strictly for work-related functions. Other large agencies have lifeguards who work exclusively in a lifeguards dispatch office and serve a crucial role in receiving information and delegating tasks.

Setting up the beach

Setting up the beach each morning looks a bit different at every agency. While the goals and mission of the day that lie ahead are the same, over the years, each beach patrol has adopted its own operational methods. However, the process more or less follows these steps:

1. You first need to inspect all rescue equipment followed by the designating the swimming area by opening up the lifeguard stand or tower.

2. Next, you set up the appropriate flags for that day's swimming conditions. In most lifeguard operations, lifeguards use a flag system to designate a variety of hazards, typically ranging from rip current warnings and swim/surf areas to marine life sightings such as jellyfish, man-o-war, and sharks!

   Whether you are raising the flags on the tower's flagpole or planting them in the sand on the beach, it is important to set up each morning with pride, as it is your responsibility to inform the public of the day's dangers and hazards. While I wish we could say there was a national flag system in place, the reality is that one flag at one beach could mean something completely different at another beach.

TIP

Most beach patrols use the traffic light system to warn swimmers of hazards or problems. Green typically mean safe and it's okay to swim, while yellow usually indicates caution. Red signifies danger, no swimming, or high rip current warning.

Since flag colors and symbols are different at every beach, it is best to educate your swimmers about what the flag colors mean. Education is a very important part of a lifeguard's job. Likewise, when you're visiting another beach, ask the lifeguards there about their flags. Their system may be different!

You need to know the specific rules and regulations of your home beach very well. Believe it or not, this will help you when visiting beaches on vacation or even locally around your area. Some beaches have rules that others don't, so be sure to pay attention to signs and keep an eye out for flags, signs, or other markings designed to inform the public. As a lifeguard, you can set a good example and be a good visitor to other beaches. Practice what you preach!

JONES BEACH EXAMPLE: A STANDARD OPERATING PROCEDURE

A perfect example of a unique standard operating procedure practiced by the Jones Beach Lifeguard Corps, a part of the New York State Parks system is something called "umbrella lines!" Umbrella lines are giant popsicle-stick-like signs that look like life-size lollipops and have the words "umbrella line" on them. These eight-foot sticks are placed in the sand in sets of three or four in a row at a specific angle. They prevent beach-goers from setting up their umbrellas and obstructing the view of the water's edge from the main lifeguard stand. We spend a large portion of our day educating those who are unaware that you must place your umbrellas behind the umbrella lines with a megaphone! Now, if you hear our lifeguards saying "UMBRELLA, UMBRELLA, UMBRELLA," you know why!

Cameron DeGuzman (Author)

The umbrella lines at Jones Beach State Park are pictured in action, keeping the water's edge clear for lifeguards to see bathers.

Maintaining your vehicles

Swift, motorized vehicles have grown to be more and more important in the evolving lifeguard environment. Lifeguard trucks, beach 4x4s from companies like Kubuta, John Deere, or Polaris, and jet skis have revolutionized the lifeguarding landscape. They allow lifeguards to get from point A to B much quicker, and in times of emergency when a lifeguard could benefit from additional manpower, these vehicles can expedite the response and get people the help they need in a shorter amount of time.

In many agencies, those driving the trucks must be certified EMTs on top of their lifeguard certifications, and their vehicles are stocked with more specialized equipment (see Figure 6-4). One of the most integral roles of these vehicles is their ability to bring patients from the shore, up the sand, and onto the street where an ambulance awaits.

TIP

Salt water is incredibly corrosive, causing metal to rust and break down. A good rinse with a hose at the end of the day can go a long way in preventing damage to these vehicles and prolonging their lifetime. Plus, who doesn't love a good car wash?

Cary Epstein (Author)

FIGURE 6-4: The Los Angeles county lifeguard vehicle with mounted rescue cans, a rescue board, and all first aid equipment patrols the beach, prepared for any emergency.

Headquarters

Lifeguard headquarters are unique to each beach patrol. Typically, headquarters are staffed or operated by your most senior ranking lifeguard officers. This is often where lifeguard offices, training classrooms, or even locker rooms are. It is typically the place where larger-sized equipment — such as jet skis, trucks, ATVs, and other more expensive equipment — is stored. It is important to understand that the role of lifeguard headquarters vary from one beach to another.

For example, at Jones Beach State Park, instead of having one large, headquartered building for our entire beach patrol, each individual field (which is approximately ½ mile-1 mile long) has its own lifeguard shack. Each of these individual lifeguard shacks (although smaller than what you might picture when you think of headquarters) is exactly that — headquarters for that area of the beach. This is where equipment is stored and where officers and crew members seek shelter, complete lifeguard paperwork and reports, monitor the weather, work out, and handle weekly scheduling duties.

While they are only a few miles away along the coast, a few of our neighboring lifeguard agencies have completely different systems. At the end of the day, what every lifeguard "headquarters" has in common is that they support all lifeguard operations and are the source of all administrative orders. See Figure 6-5.

lazyllama / Adobe Stock

FIGURE 6-5: Beach Patrol Headquarters in South Beach, Miami, Florida.

Enjoying Recreational Activities

Working on the ocean, your office is also your playground. As a lifeguard, your number one priority is to keep the public safe by watching the water. At any given moment, whether you are on the stand or taking your lunch break, anything can go down. Swimmers rely on your team of lifeguards to settle the situation.

You might find that on your breaks or on particularly slow days, you wind up with a little extra time on your hands while on the clock to do other things. Sure, you might decide to get a quick iron pump and lift some weights. But if the ocean is pumping and Mother Nature is unleashing her wrath, most lifeguards cannot help but to jump in and splash around. There might just be no better time to get salty.

TIP

One of the best ways to stay in shape and sharpen your water skills is by getting in the water. As a lifeguard, you have plenty of opportunities to surf, boogie board, and body surf. As a matter of fact, we *want* lifeguards to be active and in the water. These are the best training days.

Surfing, boogie boarding, and body surfing are some of the most common aquatic activities you will find lifeguards participating in when working at the beach. In addition to the adrenaline rush, these activities translate into sharp lifeguard skills. Simply being in the water sharpens your body language in the ocean. These water sports force you to learn how to read the ocean and its patterns or waves. You quickly pick up on proper positioning and timing of a wave, which translates into making good decisions during tense rescue situations.

REMEMBER

The most memorable days on the beach hands down are the big rescue days, when you are charging the shore non-stop and pulling distressed swimmers back to safety. But the second-best days are those spent in the water with your crew, catching waves and making memories.

We all share a love of the ocean. At the end of the day, any time in the water translates into being a stronger and well-versed lifeguard. Because the ocean is not static, no two days are the same. You are constantly learning to adapt, and therefore your training never ends.

Chapter **7**

Lifeguarding as a Career

S o what do you want to want to do when you grow up? How many times have you been asked that? Many of us, even in our adult lives, are still trying to figure out the answer to that question!

When children are asked this question, we often hear answers such as fireman, police officer, doctor, singer, or actor. When my parents asked me (Cary) what I wanted to be when I grew up, my answer was a little bit different. "A red crayon in the shape of a lifeguard!" Yup. You read that correctly. Well my favorite color was red and I guess from an early age I knew I loved the water and yearned for a career in lifeguarding!

Most children, teens, or even adults don't know they can have a career in lifeguarding. A very rewarding career, might I add, although I'm still working on the red crayon part!

This chapter reveals what you need to know about working as a lifeguard, as a full-time career, a part-time career, or side gig. It also tells you about different work opportunities around the United States and the world.

Seeing What Opportunities Are Available

Being a lifeguard can be a full-time career in many places around the world. It is also a unique job where many lifeguards around the world can work part time or seasonally (depending on geographic location). Who said you can't have your cake and eat it too?

Lifeguards, like many other first responders, share a multitude of responsibilities. The primary responsibilities of a lifeguard are to provide surveillance to swimmers and visitors of aquatic environments, prevent accidents from occurring, and respond to various types of emergencies in and around the water and surrounding landscapes.

While many people automatically think that all lifeguards work outdoors, let's not forget that there are plenty of indoor pools, waterparks, and other facilities that are open year round that require lifeguards. The following sections give you an idea of the full- and part-time opportunities available to you as a lifeguard.

Making a living as a lifeguard

Full-time lifeguards typically work 40 hours a week, and like many first responders, may accrue additional opportunities for overtime. Many full-time lifeguards are often employed by government entities such as city fire departments. In other cases they work for the state park systems or local government entities such as counties and independently run townships.

Wages and salaries

Lifeguard wages vary, but for some tidbits about wages and other remuneration factors, consider this helpful information that you can toot your whistle at:

>> Open water lifeguards tend to get paid more than pool or stillwater guards.

>> Some agencies and organizations take into consideration years of experience and additional certifications such as Certified First Responder, Emergency Medical Technician, and Paramedic.

» On average, a starting first year pool lifeguard makes approximately $13-$17 an hour, while beach lifeguards typically start at $18-$29 an hour.

» Full-time lifeguard salaries, not including overtime, make approximately $50,000 a year. Many lifeguards have been known to work full time for one agency and part time for another. By doing this, they may be able to supplement their income by an additional $10,000-$15,000.

» There is room to make more money based on title promotions, specialty bonuses such as rescue diver, being bilingual, the longevity of your position, and the amount of overtime you work.

Opportunity for advancement

In most cases, when they meet certain criteria, full-time career guards can move up in title/rank. Similar to any para-military organization, common titles in lifeguard rank include, but are not limited to, chief, captain, lieutenant, sergeant, and boatswain. These are supervisory positions that require promotion from within the regular ranks of lifeguard and are typically only filled by full-time career lifeguards. Promotions may be based on various factors, such as seniority and in some cases civil service or internal department exam scores.

Moving up in rank typically increases your salary and offers you additional supervisory and administrative duties. The roles and responsibilities affiliated with each title are similar but vary from facility to facility.

TIP

While the majority of full-time lifeguarding careers are in places with warmer year round weather, such as California, Florida, and Hawaii to name a few, opportunities do exist in many states and places around the world. We guarantee that if it is your life's mission to become a full-time career lifeguard, there is a career out there waiting for you. At the time this book was published, there was a lifeguard shortage throughout the United States.

Public sector benefits

There are many benefits for someone who works as a full-time lifeguard in the public sector. A large portion of career lifeguards jobs are pensionable. Bonuses are pensionable as well but not overtime. A pension is a fixed monthly payment in retirement that is guaranteed for life. It is based on the final average salary, which is an average of the last five years of employment or the three to five highest years of salary. Every state determines this slightly differently.

For example, lifeguards who work for a state park system or the county fire department can retire after a certain number of years on the job. When calculating a pension, a typical multiplier is 2 percent (although this can vary). For example, if you worked 30 years as a lifeguard and your final average salary was $75,000, your pension would be 30 x 2 percent x $75,000= $45,000 a year. That $45,000 becomes your guaranteed lifetime income. Any job that allows you to collect a pension is a huge benefit. In many (but not all) places, you can add lifeguard to that list of jobs!

Exploring part-time lifeguarding options

Part-time lifeguard jobs abound throughout the United States. When you work part time as a lifeguard, that can be seasonally or year round.

The seasonal lifeguard

A lifeguard who works seasonally is usually employed from Memorial Day to Labor Day. This is peak summer season for most areas of the United States. These facilities close when the weather cools. These lifeguards take on the responsibility of keeping swimmers safe for a few months out of the year. Since they are not year round lifeguards, they are known as seasonal guards or part-time career lifeguards!

Many people think that the seasonal lifeguard is always a high school or college aged teenager. They would be very surprised to know that there is a very strong lifeguard culture here in the United States of adult seasonal career lifeguards. These are the men and women who, year after year, return to protect the waters of their beaches, pools, parks and other facilities.

GETTING PAID TO DO WHAT YOU LOVE

Adulting isn't always easy. At a certain point in everyone's life, you get your first job. At first, working is way to put a few extra dollars in your pocket or your piggy bank. Later on it turns more into understanding the importance of responsibility and maturity. Some of us start career oriented jobs right out of high school, while 37.9 percent of Americans go on to pursue a Bachelor's degree.

Lifeguarding can enable you to work throughout your other career. Teachers have a unique schedule that allows them to be available during the summer months. Taking vacation time off to work as a lifeguard might not always fit into your family's summer schedule, but many agencies require a minimum number of work days to remain eligible. In Los Angeles county, for example, you need only work ten days a year between September 1st and August 31st to remain on the hiring list. It's possible to pick up shifts from time to time outside the normal summer schedules.

There are endless roads you can take when it comes to answering the good old question, "What do you want to do when you grow up," but the best piece of advice is to do what you love!

It's that simple. Think about it. What gets you excited? What makes you tick? What can you talk about or do all day and never get tired of? The beauty of the world is that we all have different likes and interests. That's a wonderful thing, because I (Cary) would make a horrible accountant or handyman! Whatever you decide you want to do, if you love it, every day you will be genuinely excited to go and do it! Some people are driven by excitement and adrenaline, while others are happy sitting behind a desk all day and some of us can't sit still for ten seconds! What is exciting to you might not be exciting to someone else and that's the best part . . . you get to do you!

For me personally (Cary), I fell in love with swimming, which lead me to lifeguarding. Once I had my feet in the sand and felt that warm sunshine on my face during the summer of 1998, I instantly fell in love and knew I was never leaving. After my first real rescue and rookie summer came to a close, I walked off the beach and headed to college literally counting down the days to summer. I truly felt the love

(continued)

(continued)

> for this job. Each season, I walk off the beach and the countdown begins.
>
> Many people think that money equates to happiness. The more money you have, the happier you will be. While we do think that money can certainly buy you materialistic things that might make you happy in the moment, money can't actually buy happiness. Happiness comes from being self-fulfilled and living with a purpose. *Your* purpose. Waking up every day and doing what you *love* . . . that equals happiness! I am personally in my happiest place when I am at the beach, whistle in hand, and perched up on my lifeguard stand.

Most of them have other full-time jobs that allow them to have time off over the summer to lifeguard. Some may only work as part-time seasonal guards (meaning weekends or other days of the week). It is not uncommon to have seasonal lifeguards with 20+, 30+, or 40+ years of dedicated service! Seasonal lifeguarding for many of these "lifers" becomes not just a part of their careers, but a huge part of their lives. On average, a full-time seasonal lifeguard can bring in anywhere from $8,000-$15,000 a season! Of course, there are many variables that determine the high and low end of the pay scale.

As of July 1, 2022, the LA county starting salary for new seasonal lifeguards was $30.65/hour. Add 5 percent to that if you already have an EMT certification. Health benefits are available but require working some minimum hours during the winter, which can be challenging for a new lifeguard with little seniority. LA county also provides seasonal lifeguards with sick and vacation time, accrued with time worked.

In some cases, you might even be provided with employers who offer lucrative benefits to attract employees. Check with your local agencies and municipalities to see where their pay scale falls and what else they offer their full-time seasonal employees!

TIP

What kind of job are these seasonal lifeguards doing when they aren't lifeguarding? These and many more:

>> Teachers (off all summer)

>> School administrators

>> College professors

>> Public servants (fire, police, and EMS)

>> Private business owners/entrepreneurs

>> Anything if you can make the schedule work!

Year round part-time lifeguards

Folks who work year round as part-time lifeguards typically come from all walks of life, but choose to take on a part-time role in places where lifeguard operations are ongoing 365 days a year.

During the summer months, beach patrols that operate year round significantly increase the number of lifeguards on the job. Busier times of the year require additional lifeguard staffing. Year round part-time lifeguards can typically add an average of $10,000-$15,000 to their full-time salaries.

REMEMBER

It wouldn't be uncommon in warm weather locations for you to start as a seasonal lifeguard before being considered for a full-time position. In some places, you might even need a specific number of seasons on the job before you can apply for a full-time position.

TIP

Every agency and municipality has different rules and regulations, so be sure to inquire about how it works location by location.

Location Makes a Difference

The one thing you need to take note of is that no single lifeguarding gig is the same. While lifeguards across the globe all have the same mission to protect and save lives, the way lifeguard operations are run waterpark to waterpark, pool to pool, lake to lake, and beach to beach sometimes vary drastically.

Location makes a difference, not just state by state or region by region, but by agency and organization. One quick example is determining how long a lifeguard sits in the chair, stand, or tower during one shift. There is no universal amount of time by law, but we do know that different agencies do different things:

>> On the West Coast, you typically find one beach lifeguard in a tower all alone for a large portion of the day. On busier beaches,

they may have two tower guards, but boats and jet skis help patrol the waterways, while quads and SUVs ride along the shoreline keeping additional eyes on water. See Figure 7-1.

FIGURE 7-1: A lifeguard tower on the beach in Santa Monica, California.

>> On the East Coast, you'll typically see the lifeguard tower look more like a lifeguard stand. You might have one or two guards watching the water. The guards typically rotate every 30, 45, or 60 minutes. See Figure 7-2.

FIGURE 7-2: A lifeguard stand at Jones Beach State Park on Long Island, New York is reminiscent of East Coast lifeguard stands.

Working year-round on the West Coast

If you are looking for the quintessential lifeguard job, the West Coast of California is where it's at. Many of the larger lifeguarding gigs out in California are subdivisions of fire departments. These involve competitive civil service exams.

Lifeguards on the West Coast have been known to have additional responsibilities' including but not limited to cliff rescue, under-water scuba search and rescue, and flood and swift-water rescue. In some places, they even hold peace officer status. Having status as a peace officer allows lifeguards to legally enforce beach ordinances, write tickets, and even make arrests. Southern California is known for its amazing beaches and surfing. It's known to having some of the most fun and dangerous waves for surfing, boogie boarding, and body surfing.

Working at some of these southern California beaches makes you one of the most skilled and professional lifeguards in the world. These are some of the most competitive and difficult lifeguard jobs to get. These jobs are dangerous and lifeguards, like many other first responders, put their lives at risk to save others.

Filling seasonal positions in the Northeast

While the first thing that might come to mind when you think about the Northeast is the cold and snowy weather, let's not forget about the other seasons! Summers in the Northeast are awesome and it gets hot from June through September. Millions of locals and tourists flock to shoreline beaches, lakes, and pools, especially after a cold and long winter. Some of the nation's top beaches are located along the shorelines of New York, New Jersey, Connecticut, Massachusetts, New Hampshire, Rhode Island, Vermont, and Maine.

Many of these water hotspots are staffed with lifeguards who have the opportunity to work full time or part time. There are many professional beach patrols throughout the Northeast.

LOST IN THE LINE OF DUTY

It occurred at the end of a busy 4th of July weekend that was marked by warm conditions, abnormally large and turbulent surf, and giant crowds. Newport Beach lifeguards made 562 rescues that holiday weekend. Many of those were dramatic lifesaving events that resulted in relieved and reunited families, but the next rescue would not. At 5:15 pm, Newport Beach lifeguards Ben Carlson and Gary Conwell were patrolling beyond the large surf in a NBLG rescue boat when they spotted a distressed swimmer. Ben jumped from the boat and after a long swim made contact with the man. As they began to make their way back out to the rescue boat, both were hit by a large wave and taken over the falls.

The distressed swimmer made it to the surface and was rescued, but Ben was missing. A three-hour search ensued that included members from seven agencies including Newport Beach lifeguards, fire, police, Orange County Sheriff's Harbor Patrol, Huntington Beach Lifeguards, Laguna Beach lifeguards, and state parks. Ben was eventually located more than a half a mile away from the original rescue location at 8:00 pm and was transported by Newport Beach paramedics to the hospital, where he was pronounced deceased. He was the first and only Newport Beach lifeguard to die in the line of duty since the service was formed in 1923.

Ben had just turned 32 and had proudly served as a Newport Beach lifeguard for over 15 years. He was a lover of the ocean and an accomplished and dedicated waterman having surfed big waves around the world and explored the beaches on distant shores. Ben was a Division 1 collegiate water polo player at UC Irvine and a strong, competitive swimmer. He gained his love and appreciation of the water from his family, who introduced him to the ocean during a lifetime of beach-going, surfing and sailing. The statue of Ben was gifted to the City of Newport Beach by the Ben Carlson Memorial & Scholarship Foundation, a group of family, fellow lifeguards, and friends who all loved Ben. The funds were provided by many incredible individuals and organizations, some of whom are listed on the plaques surrounding the memorial. The Foundation continues to operate in Ben's name, providing annual scholarships, serving under-resourced children and most importantly working to develop and improve systems to protect lifeguards and the public from a wonderful, but non-forgiving ocean. For more, visit www.bencarlsonfoundation.org.

—Ben Carlson Foundation, 2014

The majority of the outdoor lifeguarding jobs in the Northeast are seasonal (Memorial Day to Labor Day). However, the same opportunities exist for someone to be employed full time as an indoor pool lifeguard. Universities and colleges also hire swim team athletes and students to guard their pools during open swim times for students and staff.

Finding countless opportunities in the South (and South Pacific)

The southern states are typically known for their coastal towns and beaches. While the weather can vary from state to state, warmer weather is typically present year round the further south you go. In places like southern Florida, full-time lifeguards jobs are needed at beaches, pools, lakes, and waterparks. In other places like Virginia Beach and the Carolinas, you might have slightly extended summer seasons since it gets warmer earlier and cools off later compared to the Northeast and other parts of the country.

TIP

If you are looking to head south, you should know that full-time and part-time opportunities both exist! There is a rich lifesaving tradition for down south, similar to other places across the country.

Some of the most challenging beach lifeguard jobs are located in the most southern state of the United States: Hawaii. Oahu's North Shore is home to some of the best breaking waves in the world. There you can find a world class break every 100 yards for seven miles! This seven mile miracle is the holy grail for big wave surf breaks. World class surfing competitions are held here and locals and tourists flock to the most pristine beaches in the world all year round.

TECHNICAL STUFF

In January 2023, one of the most anticipated big wave surf competitions in the world, the Eddie Aikau Big Wave Invitational, was won by Hawaii local and North Shore lifeguard Luke Shepardson — while he was on his break! He took the title over some of the world's most famous and well-paid professionals. Congratulations and way to represent Luke!

WARNING

Even on a calm day, the rip currents pull with immense strength, which means lifeguards typically make dozens and dozens of rescues in one shift. North Shore lifeguards are known to be some of the best and most skilled lifeguards in the world!

Hitting the road to work anywhere in the world

While we just looked at various lifeguarding opportunities around the United States, the reality is that lifeguarding is utilized around the world. Beaches, pool, lakes, and open bodies of water will always be vacation destinations. There are many places around the world that require you to "swim at your own risk," but there are just as many that are staffed with lifeguards with the intention of keeping swimmer safety the number one priority.

VOLUNTEERING AS A LIFESAVER IN AUSTRALIA

Outside of the states, one of the most professional and supported groups of lifesavers and lifeguards come out of Surf Life Saving Australia (SLSA). The SLSA provides both paid and volunteer opportunities. Did you know that volunteer surf lifesaving clubs existed? Yes, that's right. VOLUNTEER! The kind where you do not get paid but do it for the love of doing it! There are actually more volunteer lifesavers then there are paid professional lifeguards in Australia. Fun fact . . . the volunteers are called "lifesavers," while the paid are referred to as "lifeguards." Lifeguarding in Australia is a highly respected job, similar to the ranks of the guards in Hawaii.

You might be asking yourself why would someone choose to volunteer and not get paid? These talented men and women love the ocean, the beach, and saving lives. Many of them participated as "nippers" (junior lifeguards). See Chapter 13 for more information about junior lifeguarding. Some may not have jobs that allow them to lifeguard the beaches full time or part time. If they could join one of the over 300 surf lifesaving clubs and volunteer to be on patrol a few times a month, why not!? At the end of the day, they are making rescues and saving lives!

With 181,572 members and 314 affiliated Surf Life Saving clubs, Surf Life Saving Australia represents the largest volunteer movement of its kind in the world. SLSA has a proud heritage with over 110 years of history and tradition. Check out their site at https://sls.com.au/.

TIP

There is no shortage of lifeguard work available to you, especially if you are willing to travel. You might want to consider certain resort and larger chain hotels. In addition, the cruise line industry recently began hiring lifeguards and aquatic directors for the ships' onboard pools and flow rider surfing attractions!

Choosing a Career that Won't Be Replaced by Technology

If you look back at lifeguarding in its early days and compare it to what it is now, you'll see that not much has changed. Technology has taken over many jobs and careers, but lifeguarding isn't one of them. The question is, what will lifeguarding look like 20, 30, 40, or 50 years from now?

Technology certainly plays a role — for example, lifeguards can use drones to keep an eye on lurking wildlife, identify rip currents, and assist as eyes in the sky during search and rescue missions (see Figure 7-3). But will the human lifeguard ever be replaced with a fully functioning water rescue robot?

Cary Epstein, a veteran lifeguard, is among those being trained to operate a fleet of drones for shark-spotting amid an increase in sightings at Jones Beach, New York, July 1, 2022.

Johnny Milano/The New York Times via Redux

Courtesy of The New York Times Company

FIGURE 7-3: Cary Epstein mans a lifeguard-operated drone over New York State Parks in search of dangerous marine life, circa summer 2022.

No one really knows what the future will bring, but we feel very confident that humans will still need to rescue humans when it comes to the water. There are way too many variables to take into consideration. If we could just drop a life ring out of the sky on every conscious drowning victim in a pool or open body of water such as a lake, river, or ocean, lifeguarding would be easy. But that is not the case! We feel very confident that even with the advancement of technology to help us, lifeguards will never be fully replaced by technology. So, job security is a plus.

3

Training and Preparation

Expand upon your physical fitness traits by building up your strength, stamina, and aerobic/anaerobic base so that you are ready for the lifeguard certification test.

Maintain a well-rounded physical fitness routine by keeping yourself in optimal shape through both consistent diet and exercise.

Remain sharp during the job by reviewing skills in first aid, aquatic rescues, and water equipment with your crew.

Chapter **8**
Diving into Training Workouts

L ifeguarding is a job that does not discriminate. Whether you are 16 or 60, your level of physical fitness needs to be at a high level in order for you to perform well. Lifeguards all across the country take certification and performance exams yearly to make sure that they remain physically fit to do the job.

Regardless of whether you are full time or part time, year-round or seasonal, one of your top priorities throughout the year should be maintaining your physical fitness. That all starts with diving into the pool and stepping onto the track to get into optimal shape.

This chapter describes multiple training workouts that you can use to get into shape and stay there!

Workouts for Strength and Stamina

There is no doubt that having strength and stamina helps any lifeguard on the job. There is a reason that lifeguards are portrayed as very physically fit. Well, let's face it . . . not all lifeguards really look the part, but the bottom line is, the job is physically demanding and you need to be in good shape to perform all the necessary duties.

Because many of these lifesaving measures will naturally take place in the water, it is important that you are prepared to swim. You need to swim, not just yourself, but for your victim too — remember that you will often be swimming for two people!

Getting in the pool

You may find that getting to the pool is more cumbersome. Similar to joining the gym, your first step is to find the local pools in your area. Determine what their hours are for general public swimming. You might also want to ask how many lap lanes they have available at that time. Most pools require some sort of membership. That means you will most likely have to pay a fee. Inquire about membership fees and get registered. Your first lifeguard paycheck will more than cover that expense.

TIP

After you choose a pool, based on the availability of swim lanes and your schedule, make it part of your weekly routine, as shown in Figure 8-1. You need to know ahead of time that you are going swimming. Pack your bag. Put it in your car and go before or after work/class. If you don't do this, just getting to the pool will feel like a chore.

Microgen / Adobe Stock

FIGURE 8-1: A swimmer performs the freestyle stroke and works out on their own.

Now that you've made it through the locker room safely, don't waste all your time on the deck. Swimmers are notorious for standing over their lanes for minutes just avoiding the big jump. Adjust those goggles and get started. Remember, the faster you get in, the quicker you get out!

As we have reiterated time and time again throughout this book, it is important that you get in the water and practice prior to the qualifying procedure or lifeguard test.

Getting in the open water

If you want to be an open water lifeguard, such as at a lake, bay, or ocean, you need experience swimming in that body of water prior to the test. Depending on where you live, the time of year, and the way the seasons change, finding a time to swim in an open body of water can be tricky.

For example, if you're on the Great Lakes and looking to kick-start a career in lifeguarding, your open water training will probably not begin in the middle of February (that's why heated pools exist). However, donning a wet suit in May or June as the water warms up can give you an athletic advantage and a mental head start, especially if you haven't swum in open water much.

REMEMBER

Disclaimer! There are no lane lines in open bodies of water. That means you have to constantly redirect your swimming in a straight line. This takes time and practice. When the time comes, you can easily see who has swum in the open water and who hasn't.

The most important part of any training plan is safety. The questions you should ask include:

>> When do lifeguards get on or off duty?

>> What is the boating traffic like in this area?

>> What is the predicted weather for the day, incorporating all factors such as precipitation, thunder and lighting, high tide and low tide, and wave height?

>> Remember the buddy system. Do you have a workout partner or training group to swim with? This keeps you motivated as well.

>> If you encounter an emergency, what is your course of action?

>> Do you have the necessary equipment to swim? Wetsuit, goggles, flotation device, swim cap, and so on.

>> Are you aware of any marine life activity in the waters?

Swimming in the open water is an entirely different experience compared to swimming in a pool. There's a reason that so many people take up open water swimming as a hobby — it's exhilarating and allows them to commune with nature. However, it is important to remember to approach open water swimming from a safety standpoint. When you're prepared, you minimize the risks involved and make the most out of your training and outdoor experience.

Working Out in Preparation for a Certification Test

Lifeguard certification exams and qualifying procedures vary across the country. A national standard for lifeguard training is published by the American Red Cross. In many cases across the country, before you even inquire about working at a specific location, find out if having this American Red Cross Lifeguard Training course is necessary. Most jobs require it, but some provide their own in-house training certification programs.

Regardless of whether Red Cross certification is required or not, this class is great for learning all about lifesaving. You learn the different types of rescues, with the major focus on pools and still water facilities. The course is approximately 30 hours of basic lifeguard training. Successful participants also get certified in CPR and AED for the Professional Rescuer/Healthcare Provider and First Aid. At the end of the course, there is a written exam that you must get an 80 percent or higher to pass the class.

Training for the prerequisite test

TIP

You must first pass the prerequisite swimming test in order to enroll in the American Red Cross class. This is one reason that working out in preparation for certification is key. This prerequisite test is a 300-yard/meter swim without having to stop, treading water for two minutes, surface diving to the bottom of a 10-12 foot or so pool and pulling yourself up out of the water without using the ladder or stairs. For more information, visit redcross.org.

TIP

To prepare for the American Red Cross prerequisite test, try this training plan:

>> Build your way up to at least a 300-yard swim (12 lengths of a 25-yard lap-lane pool). Don't be afraid to ask the lifeguard on duty the length of the pool (or check the facility's website if you're too embarrassed to ask).

>> Practice treading water. Start at 30 seconds, make your way up to a minute, and try to last for two minutes in the deep end.

>> Throw something heavy into the deep end (10-12 foot depth is good) and retrieve it. Practice this until you're able to do it with comfort.

Doing exercises like these will help you gauge your preparedness and determine which parts of the exam you need to work on. You'll have an edge over the other test takers, who did not take the initiative to jump in the pool.

Anticipating the test topics

Just like with any other test, it certainly helps to know what's covered on the certification exam you'll be taking. You wouldn't walk into a final exam without studying, let alone without knowing what topics are covered. By the same token, you should walk onto the pool deck of your lifeguard qualifying exam knowing exactly what is going to be asked of you.

If you are wondering how to figure out what the test is ahead of time, the answer is a lot easier than you think. Do a quick Google search! If you don't find what you're looking for, call the lifeguard office or reach out to any of their social media accounts. You can also stroll right over to a lifeguard stand and ask them yourself. Most organizations publish the basic requirements on their websites or give interested parties the information when they ask for it.

Distance or sprint: Developing a training plan

If the terms *distance* and *sprint* are foreign to you, think of runners. A marathon runner (26.2 miles) is certainly not a sprinter, and Usain Bolt — who ran 100 and 200-meter races in the Olympics — would probably not consider himself a distance runner. These two types of runners are not on the same training plan. Although training is training, there are many ways to train and work on different aerobic groups. Mixing it up can also make the experience more interesting.

During the lifeguard test, however, you don't get to choose whether you're a sprinter or a distance swimmer. The test chooses that for you.

TECHNICAL STUFF

In the world of competitive swimming, a distance swim is defined as a minimum of 500 yards. Some swimmers consider the 200- and 500-yard swims as mid-distance. That said, someone who did not grow up swimming might find a 200-yard swim, which is eight lengths of the pool, to be rather intimidating. For the sake of this book, we consider a distance swim to be 500 or more yards.

WHAT'S IN A LENGTH?

One length of a standard 25-yard or 25-meter pool (also called a short-course yard pool, or SCY) equals *one* lap. For example, 100 yards/100 meters is four laps or lengths of the pool. Think about a lap as a quarter, or 25¢. If you are swimming 200 yards/meters, how many quarters would you need to make $2? That's right . . . eight. So, 200 yards/meters is eight laps. That said, if you are using an "Olympic-size" pool (or long-course pool), as they are often called, one lap is 50 meters.

Also, 1 meter is 1.09 yards. If you swim in a 25-meter pool, four laps is 100 meters. For the sake of training and using the exercises in this book, you can use yards and meters interchangeably. (As a side benefit, you'll be in a little better shape than you think.)

The bottom line? Make sure you know the length of the pool you're using — whether it's 25 yards, 25 meters, or 50 meters — it makes a difference!

Three Sprint Swimming Workouts

Time to dive into some workouts! These workouts are composed of warmups, the main set, typically a second set, and then cool down. This section maps out a few sprint workouts that we feel are suitable for people who did not grow up swimming every day as part of a competitive team or club. Feel free to try these exactly as written, or use them as a guide and devise a few workouts of your own.

USING SWIMMING DRILLS

As you work through the following workouts, you'll see the word "drill" again and again. There are various types of drills that have proven effective with swimmers around the world and that are utilized by all coaches. These three common drills are used by beginners and professionals alike to develop a better and more efficient stroke:

- **Catchup (often called ketchup).** This drill definitely tops the list of most popular. When alternating strokes, one hand waits extended in front of you while your other hand "catches up" to your opposite one before initiating your next stroke. Great for many reasons, but our favorite is for the elbow, arm, and hand placement. This drill also allows you to focus on what each arm is doing.

- **Six Kicks and a Stroke.** This drill is exactly as it sounds! The main idea behind it is to help swimmers rotate their body as well as fully extend their reaching arm and armpit. It also helps you engage your core while maintaining stability and balance during your six kicks. When performing six kicks and a stroke, start off by kicking almost on your side. Count six kicks then take the stroke and completely rotate to your other side. This should feel exaggerated. With each stroke, focus on extending that arm and feel that stretch in the armpit! The six kicks will come fast. If you find that you need more time to focus, feel free to increase the number of kicks per stroke.

- **Fingertip Drag.** This drill is also exactly as it sounds. When swimming freestyle, purposely drag your fingertips across the surface of the water near your body. By doing this, you are forcing your elbow into a high position, which trains you to keep your elbows higher than your hands. It also reminds you that your fingertips should stay close to (but not touching) the surface of the water when swimming freestyle.

Workout 1: The Express

WARM UP:

200-yard swim

100-yard kick with board

200-yard choice of drill/swim (25 drill down/25 swim back)

REMEMBER

Remember that you can substitute the word *meter* in all these exercises where you see the word *yard* and get pretty much the same results.

The 200-yard swim starts you off with a longer swim (for a sprint set), but it gets your muscles warmed up for the rest of the workout. Concentrate on stretching out and not pushing yourself just yet — the hard part will come!

Maybe you weren't really amping up your legs in that 200-yard swim; the 100-yard kick with a kickboard allows you to activate your legs, which I promise you will be using in the next set. Finally, we mix in some drill into a 200-yard swim so you could emphasize the way that your stroke should come together when you combine arms, legs, and proper technique.

MAIN SET:

$$3 \times \begin{cases} 1 \times 25 \text{ on} : 45 - 1:00 \\ 1 \times 50 \text{ on} : 45 - 1:00 \\ 1 \times 75 \text{ on} : 45 - 1:00 \\ 50 \text{ easy} \end{cases}$$

The goal here is to make the third item in the set, the 75-yard swim, on the interval that is written.

TECHNICAL STUFF

The *interval* is the time between one swim and another. In other words, it is the time it takes for you to complete the total number of laps before starting again. So, for a 1 × 50 on 1:00, you have one minute to push off the wall and swim the 50 before doing the next swim. If you swim the 50 in 45 seconds, you earned yourself 15 seconds of rest!

Of course, you don't have to pick the 1:00 interval. However, it should be something that challenges you. It should be difficult for you to make, but doable. As the distance increases from 25 to

50 to 75, the interval stays the same. Similarly, your effort should be increasing so that you are giving 100 percent at the end of the set before taking that 50-yard swim to stretch back out and catch your breath. As you repeat the set two more times, try to continue making the 75-yard swim on the interval you chose!

SECOND SET:

12 × 50 (1 easy, 1 medium, 1 hard) on 1:00 (or ten-second rest)

Everyone loves a few 50-yard swims! This very straightforward set forces you to differentiate between swimming easy, medium, and hard. The different speeds allow you to build up lactate in your muscle and challenge yourself when you are feeling a bit fatigued. By swimming at three different speeds, you learn what your body can handle at varying efforts.

COOL DOWN:

3 × 100 easy (kick streamline on your back every 4th lap)

15 seconds of rest between each 100 yards

TECHNICAL STUFF

Streamline is a term used in swimming when your arms are extended above your head and held tightly together. Essentially, you are putting your body in its most streamline and hydrodynamic form. Figure 8-2 shows this position.

Total workout: 2,000 yards/meters

Workout 2: Hefty Hundreds

WARM UP:

3× { 50 kick (board optional)
50 swim (freestyle)
50 drill (your choice)
50 stroke (breast stroke, butterfly, or backstroke) }

These 50s will be just enough to get you primed and ready for the main set. Swim each of these 50s at a comfortable pace. It is important that you have a few different options for drills and stroke work during any swimming workout. These drills are great for changing up the muscle groups and adding variety to your laps. Don't be afraid to go outside your comfort zone when it comes to stroke work. Remember, this is the warmup and it should feel as such!

FIGURE 8-2: A swimmer pushes off the wall squeezing their arms tight to their head in streamline position.

MAIN SET:

10 × 100 on 2:00 or :30 seconds rest in between each 100

1 × 100 all out sprint

1 × 100 easy swim/recovery

Welcome to the Hefty Hundreds! 10 × 100s is a classic swimming set for any competitive swimmer. While it might seem daunting at the start, take it one 100-yard swim at a time. You will want to swim these 100s at a moderate pace. They shouldn't be easy but shouldn't be all out sprints either. If you start off too hard, you will never make it through the set. If you start out too slow, you will miss the interval and entire point of the workout.

The idea here is to make all ten 100-yard swims. The interval is on two minutes, but everyone's pace is different. If you aren't able to make the two-minute interval, give yourself 30 seconds of rest between each one. When you complete the main set of ten, give yourself a minute rest and then bang out the sprint! Once that is done, you should feel like a house is sitting on your chest. Take your 100 easy swim recovery and feel proud you just completed Cary and Cameron's Hefty Hundreds!

COOL DOWN:

200 swim easy

Total workout: 2,000 yards/meters

Workout 3: Sprint City

WARM UP:

300 swim

200 kick

100 IM (individual medley)

Another classic warmup here. If you're unfamiliar with IM, it stands for the individual medley, one of Michael Phelps' specialties. (At the time of writing this, he holds the world record in the 400 IM.) This is a medley of the fly, back, breast, and free strokes (in that order). We haven't gone too far into describing the strokes, but this variety allows you to hit other muscle groups and achieve a better feel in the water.

MAIN SET:

$$2 \times \begin{cases} 4 \times 75 \ (25 \ \text{kick} \ / \ 50 \ \text{build}) \\ 3 \times 50 \ \text{fast} \end{cases}$$

The goal is to get faster in speed from the start to the end of the 75 swim. Regardless of how long you are swimming, your speed going into the wall to finish should be reminiscent of a real race.

SECOND SET:

20 × 25 (4 fast/1 easy)

The only way to get fast is to practice swimming fast! Just like any other sport, you get out what you put in. These sprint sets are designed to have your heart rate through your chest. Don't be afraid to push yourself. When the thought of quitting crosses your mind, remind yourself of your goals! When the going gets tough, the tough gets going. Give it everything you got. Recovery is coming! Take the easy swims easy, but really push those hard ones, no matter how tired you feel. This is how legends are made!

COOL DOWN:

3 × 100 choice

TIP

You might be tempted to skip out on the cool down at the end of your swim. Don't do this. It is in your best interest to flush out the lactic acid that has built up in your muscles. You are only doing yourself harm — don't skip out on the cool down.

Three Distance Swimming Workouts

Lifeguard qualifying procedures around the country are all different lengths. As mentioned, when we say distance, we are referring to longer swims that call for a deeper aerobic base.

REMEMBER

One length of a standard 25-yard or 25-meter pool (also called a short-course yard pool, or SCY) equals *one* lap. For example, 100 yards/100 meters is four laps of the pool. Or, if you are using an Olympic-size pool (or long-course pool), as they are often called, one lap is 50 meters.

Workout 1: Going the Distance!

WARM UP:

600 pull (with a pull buoy)

4 × 150 swim

Are you familiar with the Styrofoam pull buoy used in swim training, shown in Figure 8-3? It's the figure-eight shaped buoy that is used to keep your lower body buoyant without the need for flutter kicks. It puts you in a more natural and ideal body position so you can focus more on your stroke and rest your legs. It's also a great way to split up the redundancy of straight swimming.

If you can, get your hands on some paddles to increase the surface area of your stroke. This further helps you emphasize your upper body mechanics. Of course, if you do not have a pull buoy at hand, you can just swim it! We've also seen swimmers hold kickboards between their legs as a substitute for a traditional pull buoy, and it works just the same.

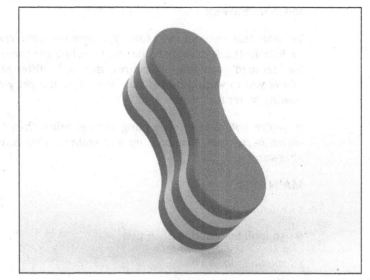

godesignz / Adobe Stock

FIGURE 8-3: This buoyant Styrofoam pull buoy can be placed in between the swimmer's legs to keep their lower body higher on the water and allow the swimmer to focus on pulling, hence, the pull buoy.

MAIN SET:

$$2 \times \begin{cases} 3 \times 200 \text{ on } 3:45 \\ 2:00 \text{ rest} \end{cases}$$

COOL DOWN:

6 × 75 easy

Total workout: 2,650 yards/meters

TECHNICAL
STUFF

In case you're interested, 64 laps (or lengths) in a short-course meter pool (25 meters long) is a mile. If you're swimming in a 25-yard short-course pool, it takes 70 laps (or lengths) to reach a mile. The seemingly small difference between a yard and meter does catch up with you eventually.

Workout 2: The Ladder

WARM UP:

300 swim/100 kick

200 swim/100 kick

100 swim/100 kick

We start this workout with some freestyle (or front-crawl) and backstroke (back-crawl?). While we are technically preparing you for lifeguard qualifying procedures, mixing in different strokes allows you to work different muscle groups and get your blood flowing better for the next set.

If you're not used to swimming strokes other than freestyle, we encourage you to mix it up and embrace that sore feeling afterward!

MAIN SET:

1 × 100 on 2:00

8 × 50 (pull buoy optional) on 1:00

1 × 200 on 4:00

6 × 50 (pull buoy optional) on 1:00

1 × 300 on 6:00

4 × 50 (pull buoy optional) on 1:00

1 × 400 on 8:00

2 × 50 (pull buoy optional) on 1:00

This type of set is known in the swimming world as a *ladder set*, or a variant of one. Technically, it is a one-way ladder because it starts at 100 yards and doesn't go back down. Regardless, it allows you to build up your endurance.

You start with a 100-yard swim and "climb" your way up to a longer, 400-yard swim. Try to keep your effort at a strong pace throughout, so that you are working just as hard swimming 4 laps as when you're swimming 16 laps.

We put everything here on a 2:00 interval base per 100 yard/meter, but feel free to adjust to your skill level.

COOL DOWN:

3 minutes of easy swimming

Total workout: 2,900-3,100 yards/meters

Workout 3: The Bearcat

WARM UP:

600 (150 swim/150 pull/150 kick/150 swim)

MAIN SET:

3 × 400 descend 1-3

Descending is a very common term used in swim workouts, and if you assume it has to do with speed, you are spot on! As you swim these three 400s, your time should descend. In other words, you should be increasing your effort and moving faster. Many times, people get the misconception that these 3 × 400s are easy, a little less easy, then fast. However, my old club coach Rob always reiterated that these should be swam as moderate, strong, and then all out. If you are swimming with others of similar ability, find your competitive side and try to race each other!

These 400-yard swims might initially appear daunting. Approach this set with an open mind. You'll get there!

COOL DOWN:

12 × 50 (25 kick down/25 swim back)

Stepping on the Track

It is worth noting that some lifeguard examinations may not include a running component. Most pool positions likely will not, and it is more common that open water positions will.

As you prepare for a lifeguard examination run, it is important to consider the distance you are training for. Various distances pose different stresses on your body's energy systems.

TECHNICAL STUFF

For example, 800 meter races are run at 120 percent VO_2, the 1600 meter is run at 110 percent, and the 2 mile at 100-102 percent. The VO_2 max is the maximum amount of oxygen your body can use during exercise.

The following workouts provide a guide to the types of workouts you can rotate between as you train for your lifeguard examination.

TIP

We recommend that you get a baseline of your fitness level before you begin training. From there, you can use a comparison effort table (Google the Jack Daniels VDOT table) to determine how fast to run. There are various protocols to test your VO_2 Max (such as the Astrand protocol). If you're a beginning runner, we recommend doing a one-mile time trial. The following workouts work off those times.

The following workouts and information pertaining to "stepping on the track" were provided by veteran Jones Beach ocean lifeguard, Lieutenant DJ Paulson. Coach Paulson is a former Division 1 runner, USA Track & Field Level 2 Endurance Coach, and four-time Nassau County Track Coaches Association Coach of the Year recipient. Coach Paulson has an incredible track record (pun intended) and has proudly coached 36 All-State performances across the New York State Public High School Athletic Association in cross country and indoor/outdoor track.

Stretching prior to running

Before you push yourself on the track or road, it is absolutely crucial that you stretch to avoid injury and allow your muscles and body sufficient time to warm up. Everyone knows that they should stretch, but not everyone takes the time to do it.

There are several types of stretching and drill work you can include in your warmups (see Figure 8-4). We include some stretching drills and warmup examples in this section. If you are unsure what they mean or want to see a demonstration, simply just Google the name of the drill.

Stretching drills

>> Active Hamstring Stretch

>> Walking Straight Leg Kick Up

>> Walking Quadriceps Stretch

>> Walking Leg Cradle

>> Walking In-Step Stretch

>> Walking Single Leg RDL

Rope stretching (static alternative)

>> Hamstring

>> Outer Hamstring

>> Outer Thigh

>> Hamstring and Inner Thigh

>> Calf

>> Quadriceps

Mobility series

>> Jog w/Arms Crossing

>> Backwards Skip

>> High Leg Crossover (L/R)

>> Slide w/Arms Windmilling

Sprint drills

>> A-Run

>> A-Skip

Studio Romantic / Adobe Stock

FIGURE 8-4: The pair stretches their quadriceps (left) and hamstrings (right) on the track before an intense workout.

- » A-Skip Fast Leg
- » B-Skip
- » Butt Kicks
- » Calf Stepover
- » Knee Stepovers
- » Ankling
- » Straight Leg Run
- » Progression Stride

Grasping common track terminology

Before you put those running shoes on, it doesn't hurt to know some basic track terminology. You'll hear others dropping these terms, so it helps to get a clue:

- » **Mileage.** This is the total amount of miles you log during your training program or regimen. You should go in with a plan that includes number of miles and stick to it.

- » **Recovery.** This type of running should always follow high-stress days. The goal for running on recovery days is to get some miles in without pushing your pace. This should be at a pace at which, while not a jog, you can easily carry on a conversation.

- » **VO$_2$ Max.** This is the highest rate of O$_2$ utilization attained during maximal or exhaustive exercise. Research has proven that after endurance running training, more oxygen is delivered to and consumed by the skeletal muscles. Training at this pace provides the benefit of strengthening the heart, by improving its ability to transport blood and oxygen to the muscles.

- » **Lactate Threshold.** This is defined as the breakpoint during exercise at which lactic acid and other waste builds up in muscle cells faster than the aerobic system can remove them. Training around this pace develops more efficient waste removement, ultimately allowing you to run at faster speeds by delaying the onset of anaerobic-only energy production.

- » **Tempo.** A tempo run is designed to push your body, get your heart rate up, and test your stamina. You should be running a bit faster than your regular pace at a shorter duration. Some consider this speed around 30 seconds slower per mile than your current 5K race pace.

>> **Progression Run.** This has also been called "Kenyan runs." The idea here is to get progressively faster each mile of your run (also called *negative splits*). Therefore, you should start at a comfortable pace and aim to get around 15-20 seconds faster each mile of your run. This is a good way to mix up your running workouts and test your stamina.

>> **Hills.** Running on hills changes the feel of your workouts and definitely adds difficulty to your runs. This run should be done at a steady pace. Coach Paulson suggests maintaining your pace as you crest the hill.

Three Distance Running Workouts

In a perfect world, you should know exactly what you are training for, meaning if you are using these workouts to get a leg up on your lifeguard exam, do a little homework and find out what distance(s) you will be required to run.

Anyone can generically be in good running shape; however, knowing on how to train for a specific distance can give you just a little bit more of an edge. Does your lifeguard test include a 100-yard sprint or are you running one mile for time and racing against others in your heat? These require different approaches. The three distance workouts in this section help you build your strength, stamina, and cardiovascular endurance.

Workout 1

8 × 400m with 3 minutes rest between each repetition

TIP

One lap around a standard track is 400 meters. Before jumping into these workouts, make sure you know the length of your track, as some indoor tracks may be smaller!

These 400-meter runs are a fundamental workout for milers. Begin this workout running your date mile pace, minus two seconds. Your *date pace* is your current race pace for a specific distance, as opposed to your goal pace, which is the pace required for your goal time. As the weeks progress, work toward your date mile pace minus five seconds.

TIPS FOR STARTING RUNNERS

- Try a one-mile jog prior to stretching and drills.

- Do not increase your mileage by more than ten percent a week. Doing so risks injury.

- Multiple weeks at the same mileage is not a bad thing! You may need to give your body time to adjust before you add ten percent.

- Do one long run each week consisting of about 25 percent of your total weekly mileage.

- Maintain a strong emphasis on flexibility, mobility, and strength/core work.

It's important to make an individualized training plan for yourself and follow it. Everyone's training plan will be different leading up to the lifeguard procedure, varying by skill, experience, and time you have on hand. For someone with months to prepare, the early months of your training regimen should be designed to help you build a base. Toward the end of month two or three, you should begin adding tempo running, Fartlek training, and progression runs. This will allow you to hit the ground running and intensify your training.

Workout 2

3 × 600m at 1600m (1 mile) pace w/ 200m jog

3 × 300m at 800m (1/2 mile) pace w/ 300m jog

3 × 150m at 400m (1/4 mile) pace w/ 200m jog/50 walk

Note: You can just do these runs can by feel. In other words, imagine you are running a race at that distance and adjust your effort accordingly.

In track and field, these workouts are often referred to as a *blender*. They require you to change your pace as the workout progresses. These are similar to the descending sets in swimming.

Workout 3

This next workout is known as the Fartlek workout, which from Swedish translates to "speed play." The Fartlek workout is great if you do not have access to a track or want to go on a road run.

Here are two examples of a Fartlek workout.

FARTLEK 1

10 minutes moderate running into:

(2 minutes at 5K pace/3 minutes easy) × 3-5 (depending on your goal mileage) into:

10 minutes moderate/cool down running

FARTLEK 2

10 minutes moderate running into:

(30 seconds slightly faster than 5K pace/2 min 30 seconds easy) × 5-8 (depending on your goal mileage) into:

10 minutes moderate/cool down running

Three Sprint Running Workouts

Lifeguards more commonly use their sprinting skills as opposed to distance running skills. More times than not, you will go from 0-100 in sprint mode and maybe go from sprinting to swimming. It is important that your body's muscles get used to this type of physical activity, as it can unfortunately be a great way for you to get hurt if you are not well prepared. Determine what distances you need to run for your lifeguard qualifying procedure and get stepping on the track.

Workout 1

6 × 150m at max effort w/4 minutes of recovery

You can estimate 150m on the track, grass surface, or trail of your choosing. Make sure you have a full, active warmup and then let it rip.

During the recovery portions, try to keep moving so that your body doesn't build up lactic acid and you'll be ready to go for the next one.

Workout 2

$$3 \times \begin{cases} 400 \text{ at 800m pace} \\ :30 \text{ seconds rest} \\ 200 \text{ at hard effort} \\ \text{Full recovery (8–10 minutes) between sets} \end{cases}$$

Workout 3

10 × flying 30m repeats at max effort w/4 minute jog

In terms of speed development, this workout always seems to be a favorite among athletes. The term "flying" comes from starting each rep approximately five meters behind the 30m starting point. Get a good warmup in prior to the workout and gradually decelerate at the end of each repetition. Take four minutes of easy jogging as active recovery.

Chapter **9**

Staying in Shape All Year

I n the famous words of my late grandfather, fitness pioneer, and former Mr. America Dan Lurie, "Health is Your Greatest Wealth!" I (Cary) have lived by that slogan all my life and you should consider doing so too. Your body is the most valuable and precious gift you own. How you treat it and what you fuel it with can make or break you at certain stages of your life. While there are certain things in life you can't control, there are many things that you can! In this chapter, we explore the benefits of staying in shape all year round and discuss how that translates into being a more prepared and better lifeguard!

Maintaining a Healthy Lifestyle

It is hard to believe that what you do to your body now can help you or hurt you in the future. Generally speaking, maintaining a healthy lifestyle goes a long way, not just for how you look, but also how you feel. Choosing the right foods, finding ways to exercise, and maintaining a healthy body weight add significant value to your life!

Maintaining a healthy lifestyle comes with the territory when you're a lifeguard. Whether you work at a pool, lake, ocean, or waterpark, you must be physically fit to do the job. While maintaining your fitness is a very important part of being a lifeguard, let's face it — staying healthy is also key to preventing injuries, staying youthful, and living a long life!

Hitting the gym

There are various ways you can maintain your fitness. One of the best things you can do is hit the gym! While you may not consider yourself a "gym rat," that's okay, because there are plenty of people who don't! Having a gym membership is beneficial, but not everyone is willing or able to do so. Thankfully, there are many creative ways you can "hit the gym" even in the comfort of your own home.

Lifting weights

Regardless of how you may choose to get your workouts in, there are many aspects of working out that all lifeguards should explore. Lifting weights is one of the most important ways to maintain your fitness and build muscle. Not only do you look good, but you also build the physical strength a lifeguard needs in order to perform the job. Let's look at some weightlifting exercises and consider how they benefit you as a lifeguard:

>> The *bicep curl* is a classic weightlifting exercise. Your arms certainly play a large role in your swimming ability and also play a large role in your ability to grab and hold onto a victim in distress. When performing a rear approach rescue with a soft rescue tube, you essentially are performing a double bicep curl when you scoop up the victim. If the victim is unconscious, you rely on momentum and bicep strength in order to roll the victim over from prone to supine and execute the rescue.

>> *Squats* and *lunges* are examples of leg exercises. Having strong legs enables lifeguards to get through the difficult rescues they are expected to perform on a daily basis. Having a strong swimmer's kick is key. Your legs have the largest muscle groups in the human body. Just think about it, your legs are responsible for keeping you standing upright all day. A major part of a lifeguard's responsibility is to provide water rescue to swimmers in distress. When a lifeguard is bringing a swimmer to safety, they often rely on a strong kick to help propel them through the water. Using fins can be essential in some of the toughest conditions. During rescues, lifeguards may have to run before entering

the water. Basic everyday activities, like jumping off the stand, running on the beach, and high stepping through the surf or any open water environment all rely on leg strength. Lifeguards also need to be able to tread water for extended periods of time. This requires additional leg strength, which is why squatting and building up your quadriceps and hamstrings goes a long way in this profession! Figure 9-1 shows two lifeguards building up their legs.

>> The classic *bench press* is designed to help build muscle and strength in the chest, arms, back, and core! A bench press can be done lying flat on your back or on an approximately 60-degree incline. Working these muscle groups builds strength in your chest and arms, which in combination with a good swim stroke, increases your speed and performance.

Photograph by Tim Kanaley

FIGURE 9-1: The lifeguard prepares to squat 385 pounds as his fellow crew member spots him from behind.

As a lifeguard, you learn what to do in the event that a victim grabs you, in an attempt to save themselves. Something called "fight or flight response" takes over when you have to fight for life for survival. Even a small child could get a death grip around your neck and take you down.

WARNING

Unfortunately, many drownings occur when a secondary person who is not trained appropriately attempts to rescue a drowning victim. The process of lifeguard escapes and releases requires quick action (suck, tuck, and duck) and strength. The motion used in these suck, tuck, and duck escapes is similar to the motion of lifting and pushing a weight bar off the rack when you're bench pressing. Being confident with this motion and having the skills and strength to perform this correctly could just be the extra oomph needed to save your life and theirs!

As mentioned in Chapter 6, having solid upper body strength also helps the open water lifeguard get through heavier sets of water during large surf. *Porpoising* through the waves is one of the most common everyday lifeguard skills for open water lifeguards. Even paddling on a rescue board requires significant upper body and back strength. These are essential skills for the open water lifeguard, and bench presses and pushups are just some of the ways to help engage the proper muscle groups.

Upping your cardiovascular fitness

While many people might choose to avoid the cardio section of their gym for one reason or another, it is essential for all lifeguards to be in excellent cardiovascular/aerobic shape.

If you have access to a gym, run on the gym treadmill, use the gym bicycle, try the rowing machine, or use your favorite aerobic machine regularly to train your cardio fitness (see Figure 9-2). Of course, swimming laps is key to maintaining fitness for a lifeguard, and that's covered in the next section.

NDABCREATIVITY / Adobe Stock

FIGURE 9-2: Four runners work on their cardiovascular endurance by running on the treadmill.

Refer to Chapter 8 for some tips on workouts and building your own training regimen. It is important to remember not to start too hard or do too much — start small and work your way up to avoid injuries and get the most out of your training plan.

If you don't belong to a gym, training and maintaining your cardiovascular fitness is still possible. Start running or biking outside, weather permitting, or one of my personal favorites, using the old school jump rope! If you're going to be hitting the trails, it's best to take a workout buddy with you for motivation and safety reasons.

TIP

Another great thing you can do to build on your cardiovascular and endurance training is something called HIIT. *HIIT* stands for *high-intensity interval training* and is an excellent way to push yourself to your best cardiovascular and endurance fitness. These are typically composed of vigorous, fast paced exercises with little rest in a short duration. Create your own HIIT workout by cycling through burpees, mountain climbers, jumping jacks, Russian twists, running sprints, and the like. Sometimes a big part of working out is being creative.

The bottom line is that lifeguards need to be cardiovascular machines! Lifeguard-related duties are fast paced, stressful, and straight up physical in nature. This might include running, swimming, and then performing CPR, all in the span of a few minutes. It might require you to tread water while maintaining head stabilization of a spinal injury victim. The job itself, when it calls for it, is 100 percent physical. While you might picture a lifeguard sitting in a chair most of the time, there are more times than not when they are pushing themselves to the limit and you need to be fit to do that.

Getting in the pool

Swimming is hands down one of the best forms of exercise. It shouldn't surprise you that lifeguards need to be strong swimmers and maintain their swimming shape throughout the year. Whether you are working year-round or seasonally, getting in the pool or swimming in open water should be one of the main ways you maintain your fitness. There are so many different ways you can stay in shape throughout the year, but nothing replaces swimming.

If you want to be a good swimmer, you simply need to swim. Working out in the many other ways will help you be a better, stronger swimmer, but nothing replaces swimming when you're a lifeguard.

At the beginning of all of our lifeguard careers, many of us swam with the main purpose of having to pass a lifeguard qualification test of some kind. Once we achieved that goal, many of us found ourselves continuing to swim to pass our requalification exam, which depending on where you work and what the regulations are, could be as frequent as 1-3 years. Swimming is by far the best exercise for maintaining proper shape and conditioning to do the job well. One of the best ways to gain or maintain your aquatic fitness is to swim laps.

There is no doubt about it that open water lifeguarding is more physically demanding than still water lifeguarding, but that doesn't mean you should train less. To be at your best at all times means training in the pool and out. You should always be running through the worst-case scenarios in your head, "If this were to happen, would I know what to do and would I be physically fit enough to handle it?" You should always be training, keeping your physical fitness in mind, and thinking about how it relates to your job.

If you decide to get an open water swim in, be sure to take a buddy with you! Regardless of your skill level, being out in the open water alone is just asking for trouble. You could suffer a medical condition or accident while in the water. Always swim supervised, no matter how good you think you are!

Swimming like you mean it

There is a big difference between recreational swimming and competitive swimming. Creating a competitive swimming workout helps maintain your swimming shape and most certainly keeps you feeling great. There are many competitive swim teams and clubs around the world for youth and adults. Do a little research in your own community to find the teams and programs available to you. Besides keeping you in great shape, these clubs can become a place to make friends and socialize. Being on a team (even as an adult) makes the hard work a bit more fun. They do say that misery loves company.

TIP

If you are over 18, you can look up United States Masters Swimming and pop in your local ZIP code to find something near you. If you are still in school, consider trying out for the swim team or look for open swim hours at your community or high school pool. Many YMCAs and other community pools offer reduced rates to students and seniors.

Chapter 8 includes some sample sprint and endurance swimming workouts. Give one a try and see how you feel.

Swimming is one of those types of exercises, where if you snooze, you lose. You can be in great swimming shape after months and months of hard work, but if you stop swimming, you lose the fitness. It also takes longer to gain that swim fitness back and it slips away faster. Just like a handful of other sports or sport-related skillsets, with hard work and dedication, you can get your swim fitness back, but it is best to maintain some type of regular swimming routine to keep you at your lifeguarding best! If you find that are you are unmotivated to hit the pool, think about why you are training. Your fitness level could literally save someone's life someday.

Chapter 10
Working on In-Service Training and Drills

It is very important to practice the skills you learn from day one and sharpen them as you grow and develop as a lifeguard. These types of skills range from first aid treatment scenarios to mock water rescues, to specialized drills utilizing various pieces of lifeguard equipment. Your first time dealing with a real emergency shouldn't be the first time you are putting your hands on a piece of equipment or executing a rescue.

Practicing these skills is something every lifeguard should be enthusiastic about, no matter how much experience you have. They don't say "practice makes perfect" for nothing! In fact, they also say "perfect practice makes perfect." Be the lifeguard who takes initiative and leads your coworkers to become a strong, efficient crew.

Running First Aid Drills

One of the many responsibilities of a lifeguard is to respond and provide first aid treatment to patrons in need. It is important to be efficient when responding to these types of emergencies, especially when time is of the essence!

Running these first aid drills with your team is not just important for building your own confidence in the skill, but it's also good for team building. Your fellow coworkers are the ones you will be working alongside in a real emergency.

REMEMBER

Before you begin any drill, make sure you or someone else has pretended to activate the Emergency Action Plan for your facility. Whether that be dialing 911, calling the dispatch office or operations, calling for EMTs, or something entirely else (this depends on your place of employment), this should be the first step of all serious accidents and rescues. It needs to become second nature and for that to happen, it should always be part of every drill (don't actually call 911 during a drill, of course).

The following sections cover these types of first aid-related drills:

>> Spinal injuries

>> Major bleeding incidents

>> Drug/alcohol overdoses

>> Cardiac/respiratory arrests

Managing spinal injuries

Spinal injuries are essentially trauma to the head, neck, or back. These injuries have the potential to be very dangerous and even life threatening. It is not uncommon for spinal injuries to happen in and around the aquatic environment.

Although we hope you never have to treat someone for such an injury, you need to be fully prepared to immobilize someone's spine properly and carefully in order to mitigate any further damage to their spinal column.

This skill takes practice and must be done with precision over speed. Practicing mock spinal injuries in all different types of environments — still water, open water, deep water, and shallow water — will make you prepared and confident to handle the real thing.

TIP

For more on spinal injuries, see Chapter 4.

Create the scenario

In order to properly set up a spinal injury drill, you need one lifeguard to take the lead and create a scenario. Conjure up a story: How did the victim potentially hurt their head, neck, or back? Think of a scenario that is realistic at your facility. Did someone dive into shallow water? Perhaps it was an elderly person who slipped and fell. There are many scenarios you can come up with. It is important to try your best to cycle through all the different possibilities. Challenge yourself and your lifeguards!

TIP

To find realistic scenarios, look through the history of case/call logs and emulate what has happened at your facility in the past.

The lifeguard or supervisor in charge of running the training should designate who will be acting as the first rescuer to arrive on the scene and the second rescuer. As a matter of fact, determine how many rescuers are going to participate in the drill.

You should always be thinking about how this drill applies to a real-life scenario at your facility. For example, if there are 12 lifeguards on duty in the middle of the day, as opposed to 2 lifeguards on duty at the beginning and/or end of the day, you could end up having fewer hands in the mix. There are pros and cons to both sides, which is why you should practice all scenarios.

Recruit your victims

A lifeguard mannequin can often be used to play a victim. These life-sized, waterproof dummies are used to train lifeguards all around the world. As they sit in the water for an extended period of time, they can fill up and get heavier. Most of them even sink right down to the bottom! This isn't to make things harder, but rather to make scenarios and drills realistic to what occurs. Use these mannequins if available to practice spinal injury stabilization and techniques with your crew.

If your facility does not own one of these training tools (and many don't), have no fear — you can just use one another! Real people make great victims too. There is no reason that another lifeguard can't play the role as victim. When this is the case, just make sure you rotate through each position. See Figure 10-1.

There are multiple benefits to using fellow lifeguards as victims, including:

>> The rescuer playing the victim will be sensitized as to how someone might feel on a backboard and being carried.

>> Different guards on your crew can discover and improve on their weaknesses.

Cary Epstein (Author)

FIGURE 10-1: Lifeguards cycle through the roles and drill on head, neck, and back injuries.

Mix it up

In addition to cycling through the members of your lifeguard crew, you should also cycle through the different scenarios that could come up at your facility so you are ready for whatever gets thrown your way. Again, check the log books to see what real incidents have occurred.

Try approaching and rescuing different types of victims with potential spinal injuries:

>> Conscious versus unconscious victims

>> Shallow water, ankle deep water, and deep water situations

>> Still and moving water situations

>> Potential spinal injury on dry land as a result of a slip or fall

These are real scenarios that can occur at your pool, waterpark, lake, or ocean. Remember that you are watching all parts of your facility, not just the wet patrons.

Controlling major bleeding

Did you know that the human body carries approximately four to six liters of blood, and if you lose 40 percent of that, you die? This is why controlling major bleeding is essential in the event of an emergency. Unfortunately, many people have died from massive blood loss. The reality is that with minimal training but a cool, calm demeanor, you can quickly slow down or stop the bleed and save someone's life.

Know what's in your first aid kit

One of the most important things you need as a lifeguard, no matter what type of situation you are responding to, is the first aid equipment. You need to be intimately familiar with your first aid kit or trauma bag. Do you know where to find what you are looking for?

The last thing you want to happen is to have to spend time unzipping each compartment when you need trauma dressing or a tourniquet. This is just one of many reasons why we prepare and train!

TIP

Know what's in your medical bag and/or first aid kit inside and out. Be sure you know where everything is, and understand what each component is for. This might not just save time, but may actually save a life.

Steps for stopping the bleed

There are typically three steps needed to control bleeding. You should practice these motions out loud and role-play on your fellow lifeguards and/or dummies. These motions should come out instinctually, like second nature:

1. Direct pressure with hands (wearing PPE!).

REMEMBER

PPE stands for personal protective equipment. This includes latex gloves and a pocket CPR mask. Remember our simple rule of thumb: "If it's wet and not yours, don't touch it!"

2. Direct pressure using a clean, sterile dressing. Resist the urge to look and apply pressure for several minutes.

3. If there is excessive blood loss and blood is soaking through the bandages, continue to apply more pressure and add more dressings or bandages on top.

4. Apply tourniquet if major bleeding continues. This is a last resort.

Tourniquet use

WARNING

Tourniquets cut off all circulation to the limb in order to save the person's life. In some cases, the limb may need to be amputated. Although this sounds harsh, the alternative could be death.

Using a commercial grade tourniquet is the best and most effective way to stop a major bleed, but the reality is that not every first aid kit comes with one.

Does your facility carry commercial grade tourniquets? Be sure you know the answer to this question, as well as where they are stored. Commercial grade tourniquets are really easy to use. Still, if you have never used one, it will definitely appear to be a foreign object. This is why it is important to practice wrapping it around an arm or leg on your own and then tightening it to the best of your ability.

In order to stop a person's open wound from bleeding using a tourniquet, follow these steps:

1. Apply direct pressure over the wound using a clean towel, T-shirt, or trauma dressing from your first aid kit.

   Make sure you or someone else has already dialed 911 or your local emergency number.

REMEMBER

2. Wrap the tourniquet around the arm or leg just above the bleed.

   No tourniquets on the torso, head, or neck!

REMEMBER

3. Secure the tourniquet as tightly as you can by twisting the rod and securing it in its place (see Figure 10-2).

4. Be sure to write the time you applied the tourniquet on the victim's skin near the tourniquet.

   This should also be documented on the report, but the reports don't always go with the patient.

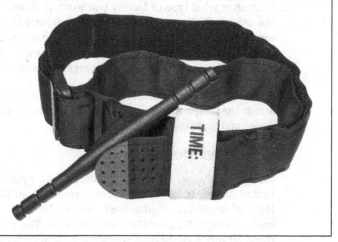

onlooka / Adobe Stock

FIGURE 10-2: This commercial-grade tourniquet is used to control major bleeding.

TIP

In the event that you do not have a commercial grade tourniquet, you can use any item that'll do the job. A belt, T-shirt, rope, and other long, malleable material can be used as a makeshift tourniquet. Simply tie or wrap as tightly as you can around the limb. Do not worry so much about creating a rod for additional pressure if you can't figure out a way to do so.

You should experiment with makeshift tourniquets, like a T-shirt or pant leg. Other items in your first aid kit or trauma bag that can effectively work as tourniquets in a pinch include triangular bandages, rolling bandages, and even cling wrap.

Attending to drug/alcohol overdoses

Drug and alcohol overdoses rank in the top five leading causes of death in the United States. Each year, thousands of people die due to accidental overdoses.

You might think that this is something that lifeguards don't have to deal with, but you would be wrong. In 21st century lifesaving, lifeguards are trained to respond to all different types of emergencies, in the water and on land. Being trained in first aid includes knowing how to properly treat and handle drug overdoses.

No matter what type of facility you work at, your job is to ensure the safety of all people who are in and around the aquatic environment. You will encounter all types of people with all types of stories and backgrounds. It is no longer uncommon for a patron to have a drug- or alcohol-related emergency while you are on duty.

Because of this uncomfortable fact, lifeguard training programs across the nation have begun including how to recognize and treat drug- and alcohol-related incidents.

Opiate overdoses

Unfortunately, we are in the middle of an opioid crisis in the United States. In 2021, the country recorded an all-time record high of overdose deaths (see www.cdc.gov/nchs/pressroom/nchs_press_releases/2022/202205.htm). The main culprits of these fatalities are heroin, fentanyl, and carfentanyl. These specific drugs are considered "narcotic" or "pain-killing" drugs. They are derived from opium and are often referred to as opiate drugs.

The biggest problem with these opiate drugs is that they are heavy central nervous system depressants. A depressant slows down your central nervous system, which eventually slows down your heart rate, decreases your rate of respirations, and drops your blood pressure. Within a short period of time and exacerbated by more drug intake, this can paralyze your diaphragm and cause you to stop breathing.

Signs and symptoms of an opioid overdose include:

>> Shallow or complete lack of breathing

>> Pale or cyanotic (bluish color) skin

>> Lessened alertness or complete loss of consciousness

>> Pinpoint pupils

You might also see track marks/scars on body parts that are frequently injected with needles.

REMEMBER

This goes for all people — bystanders and lifeguards: If you suspect someone might be experiencing an overdose, you should immediately call 911 or your local emergency phone number.

Use of Narcan/naloxone

While pre-hospital care providers such as EMTs and paramedics used to be the only ones who had the means to save someone suffering an opioid overdose, a rollout of training over the last several years now allows lifeguards to administer a lifesaving drug called *Narcan*, who's main active ingredient is *naloxone*.

In a nutshell, Narcan stops an opioid overdose right in its tracks. It essentially blocks the brain receptors that receive the signal from the drug, creating an off switch. By administering this drug to someone who is overdosing on an opioid, you can quickly save their lives.

WARNING

After administering Narcan, there is a possibility that the victim may turn violent and aggressive; essentially, you just turned off their high. Pat yourself on the back though, because you might have just saved a life.

Administering Narcan is not that difficult. It can be delivered intranasally or intramuscularly:

>> The intranasal Narcan comes in a pre-drawn up nasal spray (see Figure 10-3). This has no needle; you simply place it inside the nostril and squeeze. There are a few different styles, but they are all basically the same. Some types require you to put the already prepared Narcan into the syringe, attach what is called an atomizer to help dispense the drug, and then place it in the nose. A mist is released into the nasal passages, and the drug begins to take hold.

>> Intramuscular administration is a little bit different. You'll have three things in your hand: a Narcan vial, syringe, and needle. You will need to assemble the needle and syringe together and carefully withdraw the Narcan out from the vial before injecting the person into their deltoid muscle. Most lifeguards work with the needleless system, which of course is preferred for safety reasons.

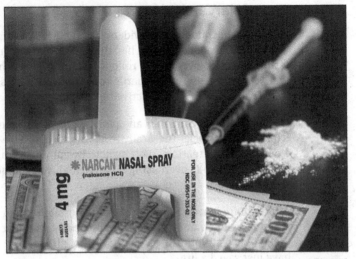

Giovanni Cancemi / Adobe Stock

FIGURE 10-3: This four-milligram dose of naloxone is delivered intranasally to treat and reverse opioid overdoses.

Overdose-related drills

Training and preparing for overdose situations is key. Although it may not happen every day, this even more of a reason why you should be prepared to handle it. Holding drills and performing mock overdose rescues is a great way to make sure you and your crew are fully prepared to handle anything:

» First and foremost, all lifeguards should be fully aware of the signs and symptoms of different kinds of narcotic overdoses.

REMEMBER

The symptoms of an opioid overdose are shallow or complete lack of breathing, pale or cyanotic (bluish color) skin, lessened alertness or complete loss of consciousness, and pinpoint pupils. If you have even the slightest impression that the victim is under the influence of an opioid drug and is experiencing any or all of these signs and symptoms, administer the Narcan.

» Secondly, all lifeguards should be confident administering Narcan. You can practice this by using a Narcan training kit. These are sample Narcan kits that are used for drills. If your agency or organization does not have any of these, get creative.

When doing this during drills, you should verbalize everything you are doing to help yourself and the rest of the team. This will go a long, long way when it happens for real . . . and when it does, it will feel just like training!

>> Lastly, you can't use Narcan if you don't know where it is. We keep bringing up the importance of knowing your equipment. Where do you keep the Narcan? If you don't know the answer to this question, you don't know your equipment well enough.

TIP

If you and the lifeguards at your facility are not trained in Narcan administration, talk to your head lifeguard or administration to learn how to get this additional certification.

Alcohol-related emergencies

Many people go to their local pool, lake, or beach in search of a good time and many bring alcoholic beverages with them. Although this is not always frowned upon (unless they are breaking your facilities' rules), drinking in excess can quickly create an unsafe environment, especially when it is mixed with water. What's so bad about alcohol, you might ask? It's legal and all. Well, consider these points:

>> For starters, drinking and swimming do not mix. Swimmers should never enter any type of body of water with large amounts of alcohol in their system. Many drownings that have resulted in death across the United States have been found to be involved with alcohol-related swimming accidents.

>> Alcohol slows your coordination and depth perception, creating a dangerous situation in deeper water. It also clouds your judgment and thinking, preventing you from making the best or most appropriate decisions. Nearing a pool under the influence of alcohol may cause swimmers to jump or dive into shallow depths of water, which can result in severe spinal injuries. In other instances, excessive alcohol use may lead to erratic behavior and a tendency to engage in risky activities.

>> Alcohol is a depressant, and in large quantities might resemble many of the same symptoms as opiate use does.

>> Alcohol is also a diuretic, so not only will it make you go to the bathroom, but it will force fluids out of your blood through the renal system and dehydrate you.

>> Alcohol in combination with the sun ultimately puts swimmers in the worst form of dehydration the following day, otherwise known as a hangover. Dehydration due to alcohol can have even more severe effects downstream, including heat exhaustion and heat stroke.

TIP

As a lifeguard, your best bet is to get in front of any potential alcohol-related emergencies. First identify any rowdy drinking groups before they get out of hand. You might have to put a stop to these parties if it means maintaining the safest environment for everyone. But don't try this alone. Get sufficient back up. Remember that sometimes being a lifeguard requires you to play the bad cop.

For these drug and alcohol incidents, the bulk of your training will be knowing how to act in these situations. You should be able to identify the symptoms of overdoses quickly and effectively, and as a preventative rescuer, stop potential emergencies before they occur.

Responding to cardiac/respiratory arrests

Lifeguards train for the worst and hope for the best. Our skill set is large and we are ready at all times to deploy whatever means necessary to save a life. If CPR is administered right after sudden cardiac arrest occurs, the survival rate can double or even triple! That said, about 90 percent of people of who experience an out-of-hospital cardiac arrest die. This type of rescue requires all lifeguards to rise to the challenge and put their best skills and training to work.

When a person goes into cardiac arrest, they stop breathing and no longer have a pulse. Life saving measures — such as performing CPR (cardiopulmonary resuscitation), rescue breathing, and defibrillation — are needed.

As professional rescuers, lifeguards are trained to the highest level. This means performing high-quality CPR and early defibrillation.

WARNING

You might find non-emergency personnel who also claim to be trained in CPR, but not as a professional rescuer or first responder. Many organizations teach CPR courses to lay people who are not serving in first responder capacities. You might hear these classes referred to as "hands only CPR" courses. There is a difference in the standard of care when comparing hands-only CPR to CPR for the professional rescuer. All lifeguards must be trained to the highest standard.

REMEMBER

Training together as a crew can make the difference when handling such a chaotic and stressful scene. Working well together doesn't just happen by accident. It takes time and training in order for these types of scenarios to run like a well-oiled machine. We urge you to train with your lifeguard crews, as this will prevent miscommunications and increase the efficiency and communication of the team.

Frankly, your first CPR course and/or CPR refresher at the start of every year is not enough to get these skills down pat. And you will not be doing CPR on a day-to-day basis (at least, we hope not!). The CPR steps should be drilled every now and then throughout the year so that the various rules — 30:2 for an adult, 30:2 for a child, 15:2 for a two-person rescuer, and so on — come naturally.

Running Through Mock Water Rescues

You might hear some people say that a great lifeguard never gets wet. This hints at preventative lifeguarding. While we believe that there is some truth to this good old notion, the reality is that a lifeguard's job is to get wet, and sometimes, no matter how good you are, there is just no avoiding it!

Being a great lifeguard starts with building your confidence that you can perform in any kind of situation or scenario that presents itself. Greatness isn't just given, it is earned and comes with countless hours of practice and training. There is no doubt about it; mock water rescue drills are the best way to stay sharp and learn to think quickly on your feet.

The following sections cover these types of water rescue drills:

>> Active drowning victims

>> Unresponsive victims

>> Search and rescue victims

Saving active drowning victims

Practicing how to rescue an active drowning victim is one of the most basic mock rescues performed by lifeguards all around the world. There are several methods/lifeguard techniques that you can use when rescuing an active drowning victim.

There are also several different types of lifeguard related equipment used to rescue an active drowning victim. When setting up drills/mock water rescues, the head lifeguard in charge or senior guard should oversee the training. These drills can easily be conducted at a pool, waterpark, or open water facility such as a lake, bay, river, and ocean.

Determine your role

Typically, during this type of mock water rescue, one person plays the role of the active drowning victim and one as the rescuer. You can, on the most simplistic level, keep it to a 1:1 ratio.

Assess your victims

If you want to create a more challenging scenario, have a larger number of victims and a smaller number of responding lifeguards. Triaging which victim to rescue first is critical. Some will be struggling and others not. You have to decide how to use your resources.

The lifeguard(s) then simply just swim out to the victim(s) and use the appropriate technique to rescue and tow the victims to safety, based on the type of flotation device they have. Later in this chapter, we talk about rescues that require specialized watercraft such as rescue boards, jet skis, and boats.

Know your equipment

Each municipality could have different equipment, making life-saving at one place different from another! It is important to familiarize yourself with all types, and if you see something that you do not know how to use or have never practiced on before, that's even more of a reason to set up a training and get your hands dirty!

Ring buoy practice rescues

There are various types of buoys that you can use to rescue an active drowning victim. The ring buoy is probably most recognizable to the public. It looks like a giant lifesaver candy. These are great for lifeguards as well as non-lifeguards, as they do not require the lifesaver to get in the water to execute the rescue.

The number one rule for non-lifeguard personnel is to "throw, don't go."

Throwing or tossing the ring buoy to an active drowning victim can be very successful and they aren't just for non-lifeguards. However, there are a few things you should know when practicing:

1. **Take the end of the rope and place it under your foot. Throw or toss the ring buoy along with the rest of the rope underhand, *past* the active drowning victim, and ideally directly over their shoulder or head!**

2. **Pull the rope toward them slowly so that the ring buoy bumps right into them, and then yell for them to grab onto it!**

3. **Make sure that once they grab the rope or buoy, you are not standing too close to the edge of the water.**

4. **Put one foot in front and one foot behind you to support the victim's body weight.**

    If you do not do this and they pull on the rope, they could pull you straight in with them.

5. **Now that you are in control, you can carefully, hand over hand, pull them toward safety.**

One of the best drills you can work on here is practicing the toss! Once you get the hang of it, you will nail it every time . . . but remember, practice makes perfect! Is the ring buoy a regular item in your facility's lifeguard toolbox? Is it in good working order? Make sure you know where it is and that it's in tip-top shape.

Drills for approaching active drowning victims

Mock rescues that practice approaching victims (from the front versus the back) are particularly effective, as there are differences between using a rescue tube (soft and floppy Styrofoam) and a rescue can (hard plastic).

>> Using a rescue tube and approaching from behind, you can simply scoop the victim up under their armpits, lean back, and kick to safety.

>> If you must approach from the front, stop within a safe distance so they can't jump on you before handing them the tube. In a controlled manner, get them into a cross-chest carry, rear rescue, or position to tow them in as long as they are strong enough to hold on.

WARNING

The most dangerous part about rescuing an active drowning victim is when they try to grab you. They will want to grab onto the first solid thing they can, and if that is you, you could have a problem! People who are actively are going through the fight or flight response stage. This means that even the smallest child or adult have superhuman strength if it comes down to a life vs. death situation. That's why it's better to approach victims from behind when at all possible and at least with an arm's distance when approaching from the front.

Escape and release drills: front head-hold escape and rear head-hold escape

One of the drills we frequently train on is escaping an active drowning victim who has grabbed us from either the front or behind. These techniques are referred to as escapes and releases. There are a few different ways to perform this skill, but in a nutshell, you want to do these three simple things: Suck–Tuck–Duck!

1. *Suck* in some air so you have ample time underwater to do what you need to do.

2. *Tuck* your chin down to your chest to prevent the victim from grabbing you around the neck.

This is the worst and most difficult hold to get out of.

3. *Duck . . . start going under water!*

If they do not let go on their own, find their elbows and push up as hard as you can.

Where do you think the last place a drowning victim wants to go? That's right . . . further underwater! Calmly, using a feet first surface dive technique, start working your way down! In most cases, when they realize you are going in the wrong direction, they will let go.

When they do, swim completely away before resurfacing to avoid getting grabbed again. Once you regain your cool, you can approach the victim again, this time from behind or with a buoy at a distance (or, your backup lifeguard can step in).

You can never practice these escape techniques enough. Even seasoned lifeguards can get into trouble this way. The key is not to panic. The more you practice this escape, the less likely you are to panic when it happens to you.

Treating unresponsive victims

On the contrary to active drowning victims, and in more serious circumstances, you and your lifeguard crew may find yourselves dealing with unresponsive victims.

You need to be able to act fast and efficient as a team; in almost all cases, these types of situations cannot be taken care of alone. Several of the exercises that were mentioned in the previous section do not change when the victim is unresponsive. For example, you are still tasked with bringing the correct flotation device with you on the rescue.

Understand your facility's Emergency Action Plan (EAP) and practice putting it into action together with your crew.

TIP

The face down swimmer

Perhaps the first type of unresponsive victim that comes to mind is the face down swimmer. This approach is almost identical to the behind the back approach detailed in the previous section. You need to perform a double scoop beneath both their armpits, turn them facing up toward the air, and swim them back to safety.

The first and most important step in rescuing a face down and unresponsive swimmer is getting their face out of the water so that they can take in fresh air. There are multiple ways to get this type of victim out of the water. With more advanced skill sets, a little personal preference, and repetition and practice, you will find what works best for you and your lifeguard team.

The face up swimmer

The face up swimmer practically sets you up for the ability to grab them by wrapping your arm across their chest and under their armpits for a cross-chest carry. This also puts you in a position to simply submerge the buoy underneath them behind their back and float them to dry land.

REMEMBER

Not all victims remain on the surface of the water. One of the most challenging scenarios is when an unconscious victim becomes submerged. In the event that you can see the submerged victim (in pools, waterparks, or beaches), being familiar with the technique to properly rescue this type of victim goes a long way. In many lifeguard courses, performing this rescue may be a part of the end of class exam. You may then find yourself practicing this submerged rescue even prior to earning your lifeguard certification.

Check the ABCs

When running drills about unresponsive victims, it is crucial that every run through ends the same way: by checking for ABCs. Without getting too deep into this, remember that unconscious victims should be checked for their Airway, Breathing, and Circulation. Vocalize this step during your drills, as well as the proper resources you and your team plan to call.

Submersion: Search and rescue

One of the most difficult parts of this job is participating in a submersion search and rescue. It is mentally and physically taxing. When a submersion is called, it means one of two things:

» There was a witnessed drowning reported by lifeguards or patrons.

» There is a missing person who is suspected (but not witnessed) to be in the water.

All lifeguard team members should run submersions drills, especially those who work at an open water facility with minimal or poor visibility. These real-life scenarios tend to be stressful and chaotic. They often require multiple agencies and organizations, including fire, police, and EMS. The more you practice such scenarios, the more prepared you will feel and be when you participate in the real thing.

There are various submersion protocols that exist. Be sure you know what your agency expects of you when a submersion is called. Typical types of searches include the human chain and dive lines:

>> *The human chain* (see Figure 10-4) is when lifeguards link together, arm in arm, and walk through an area of water no deeper than your chest. The purpose of this is to use your legs to sweep the bottom of the floor for the victim. This technique is only used in open water settings, as you should be able to see straight down to the bottom of a pool.

>> *Dive lines* are a bit more complicated, but essentially lifeguards follow the command of the designated lifeguard in charge. They together create a human grid and dive down simultaneously in an organized fashion toward a particular direction, determined by the officer or head lifeguard in charge. Although this may seem like a simple task, that couldn't be any further from the truth. There are a lot of variables to consider when deciding where and when to start these particular search and rescue patterns.

Cary Epstein (Author)

FIGURE 10-4: Lifeguards begin to enter the water and form a human chain in search of a missing swimmer.

When deciding on where to begin chains and dive lines, some of the most important things to consider as the head lifeguard are:

>> Where was the victim last seen?

>> Is the tide high or low? Is it going out or coming in?

>> Which way is the sweep or water current moving?

>> How many lifeguard personnel do you have on the scene?

>> What direction is the wind blowing?

These factors determine if you dive in one line versus multiple lines, the direction in which you start and finish, and how long the efforts last.

Considering the total moving parts, it is in your best interest to practice and run mock-submersion rescues in a controlled environment. This will allow the crew to feel confident and prepared in the unfortunate circumstance that a real submersion occurs.

Handling Specialized Equipment

Different types of rescues call for different types of equipment. While a standardized water rescue might simply consist of a typical flotation device, there are several circumstances that might warrant specialized equipment.

This section covers the basic types of specialized equipment that you may find at open water bathing facilities. Not every agency has a budget for jet skis and motorized boats, but something as simple as a rescue board is found at nearly every open water bathing facility. Knowing when it is appropriate to use any of these specialized pieces of rescue equipment is the key to a quick and successful rescue:

>> Rescue boards

>> Jet skis and rescue sleds

>> Boats

Rescue boards

The *rescue board* is a classic piece of rescue equipment that you will find at most open water bathing facilities. Rescue boards come in various lengths and sizes, and to your average person, they look very similar to a surf board. Rescue boards are specifically designed to float more than one person, the rescuer and the victim.

A solid rescue board for open water lifeguarding should be in between 9 feet–10'6 feet. (The 10'6 regulation is required for surf lifesaving competitions.) You might see various designs with handles down the side rails to make it easier for a victim(s) to grab and hold on to. Some boards have no handles. Figure 10-5 shows two rescue boards.

Cary Epstein (Author)

FIGURE 10-5: Two rescue boards are positioned alongside the lifeguard stand, ready for deployment.

Some notes about rescue boards:

>> They are excellent for making long-distance rescues. If you have a victim 200 yards offshore and you put someone on a rescue board up against your fastest swimmer, the board is going to get there first, ten times out of ten!

>> The caveat with rescue boards is that they are typically large and dense, and if handled incorrectly, lifeguards can get hurt or hurt someone else. Most lifeguards do not use rescue boards in rescues close to shore for this reason. You must be a very skilled lifeguard to avoid losing the board in the shore break, which is why this is only used for rescues in certain scenarios.

>> Another great reason to use a rescue board is when you have a big rip current with multiple victims. Getting a rescue board into the area basically provides flotation coverage for multiple people to grab onto as individual lifeguards make their way out.

>> It's not uncommon for a lifeguard to assist more than one person at time, but when large groups of people such as families or friend groups find themselves together in trouble, launching a rescue board is a great way to provide flotation when multiple people are struggling out at sea.

>> There are specialized techniques that open water lifeguards employ to make sure they can assist a conscious swimmer onto a rescue board. They must also practice the more challenging task of getting an unconscious victim onto their board and paddling them to shore. These skill sets require lots of training, which is why setting up weekly drills is a great way to stay proficient!

Jet skis and rescue sleds

The jet ski and rescue sled, when used correctly together, are considered one of the most effective pieces of equipment for open water lifeguard agencies around the world. See Figure 10-6.

Adding a jet ski and rescue sled to the lifeguard operation allows lifeguards to respond to marine emergencies farther off shore, as well as assist in large-scale rescues such as boat fires and even plane crashes. Jet skis also allow lifeguards to patrol in larger size surf and during competitions (as seen in the world of professional surfing).

Let's not be confused though, the jet ski/rescue sled is not a toy, and this very specialized piece of equipment is not for everyday use. There are certain conditions and circumstances where launching the jet ski is appropriate and other times where it is dangerous and impractical.

FIGURE 10-6: LA county Lifeguard jet ski with rescue sled.

Lifeguard jet ski operators and rescue swimmers typically go through specialized PWC (personal water craft) training. They learn how to operate the jet ski in all different types of water conditions. The rescue swimmer learns how to scoop up a victim and place them on the back of the sled. While professionals might make it look easy, it is more than just getting your victim onboard. Constant training in all different types of conditions prepares you for the real thing.

You will find that many open water agencies have jet skis. They are expensive, but worth the investment.

Boats (motorized and non-motorized)

Some municipalities even have lifeguard boats. Most full-time or year-round agencies on the West Coast, for example, have a fleet of lifeguard boats that have a wide variety of responsibilities. These boats are often operated by lifeguards who also certified Emergency Medical Technicians (EMTs) or paramedics. The lifeguard boats essentially respond to all sorts of situations on the water:

>> They might back up the tower guard on a rescue that is occurring on the beach or provide medical assistance to a victim on a boat.

>> They might assist a vessel in distress that is in immediate danger of sinking or is out of control due to a mechanical failure.

>> They might provide search and rescue services during a submersion and assist the United States Coast Guard.

>> They essentially provide a full range of services that combine law enforcement, scuba diving incidents, marine firefighting, and marine mammal rescue.

Typically, these boats are specialized units that require many hours of training and certification that not every lifeguard is willing to get. See Figure 10-7.

Photograph by Joel Gitelson

FIGURE 10-7: LA county Lifeguard baywatch rescue boat.

Non-motorized row boats are used up and down the East and West Coasts and, for some agencies, are primarily used for working out. However, the old school surf dory boats or Van Duyne boats (pictured in Figure 10-8) can be used to rescue victims if the scenario is right. Just like anything else, they are another tool in the toolbox. The downside of the non-motorized rescue boat is that on land, it weighs between 500-800 pounds and needs to be launched though the surf! If conditions aren't suitable or the execution is poor, lifeguards and patrons could both get hurt launching the boat or bringing it into shore.

FIGURE 10-8: A traditional Van Duyne rescue boat is launched through the surf zone.

TIP

Rowing is a challenging skill that requires practice. There is no doubt about it — rowing a boat can be one of the faster ways to get out to someone or something in the distance, but you must weigh all the variables (the lifeguards' ability, crew members on backup, water conditions, and the situation on the water) before choosing this particular piece of equipment as your rescue device of choice.

4

Exploring Other Lifeguarding Activities

Explore the different lifeguarding opportunities outside the traditional pool, waterpark, still water, and ocean settings.

Find a way to embrace your competitive spirit and put your skills to the test against lifeguards around the region, nation, and world.

Learn all about what it takes to be a junior lifeguard and why you should take the plunge.

Learn how to support professional organizations and get to know the groups that give structure to the career and make lifeguarding possible.

» Exploring the various industries where lifeguards are needed

» Taking your talent and passion for lifesaving and making it a business

Chapter **11**

Working Outside of Your Lifeguard Facility

The purpose of this chapter is to fill you in on the opportunities for certified lifeguards outside of your primary workplace. In 2022, there was a national lifeguard shortage across the United States.

As the summer of 2022 began, all across the country we saw facility closures and limited swimming hours as waterparks, pools, and ocean bathing facilities struggled to hire certified professional lifeguards. The good news is that there is no shortage of work! If you want to work seven days a week and make a decent competitive wage, it is yours for the taking.

Lifeguarding and Water Safety in the Private and Public Sectors

There are lots of different work opportunities for water safety professionals. Typically, when most people think of lifeguarding jobs, they think about their local beach, pool, or waterpark. Many of these are public service jobs, where the employer is a local government, city, or municipality. You might even work for the parks department or a division of the fire department.

The private sector, on the other hand, is typically made up of privately owned business and companies. Companies hire lifeguards for facilities that they own and operate. Some examples of private companies that hire lifeguards are camps, waterparks, hotels, condominium pools, and private businesses that offer swimming lessons. There are many opportunities for work in both the public and private sectors in the field of water safety.

REMEMBER

While the responsibilities of your job as a lifeguard will always stay the same, there may be some differences when it comes to additional roles you might play. For example, lifeguards who work on campuses are expected to provide swimming instruction. Lifeguards who may work at a private country club may be responsible for handing out or collecting towels and setting up chairs when not in stand. *If you feel that the additional responsibilities are not for you, you do not have to take the job. Make sure to ask what is expected of you when you are not lifeguarding.* See what job postings are available in your town and figure out what might be the best fit for you!

As a trained and certified lifeguard, your professional skill set is valuable. Whether it is your first day on the job or you are a seasoned professional with decades of experience, lifeguards understand water safety and have knowledge that an average person does not have. These specialized skills give you the upper hand, especially during a national lifeguard shortage!

Lifeguard salaries vary across the country, but recently, we have seen starting salaries move well above minimum wage and closer to $22–$25 hourly, with some West Coast salaries starting at $29–$32 per hour, depending on your certifications. Facilities are trying to attract more people to hit the water and get certified.

As an example of this demand affecting pay, in June 2022, New York State Governor Kathy Hochul directed a pay increase for state lifeguards to help address the staffing shortage at New York State Park beaches and pools, as well as at the Department of Environmental Conservation campgrounds and day-use beaches. Starting pay rates for lifeguards at upstate facilities increased 34 percent, from $14.95 per hour to $20 per hour, and 21 percent for lifeguards at downstate facilities, from $18.15 per hour to $22 per hour.

"All New Yorkers deserve the opportunity to safely enjoy our public beaches and pools this summer," Governor Hochul said. "With a lifeguard shortage threatening access to swimming facilities, we are aggressively recruiting more lifeguards to ensure safe access to outdoor recreation during the summer months."

The point is, if you want to work and have the skills, there is no shortage of opportunities out there, and the pay is better than ever.

TIP

Although it's great to busy all the time, you can easily lose track of your commitments if you are working various jobs. It is important to keep a calendar of when you are working and where. Double-booking yourself or calling in sick when it comes to lifesaving services can become a very serious problem and jeopardize not just your crew but overall public safety. Take the job offers that you accept seriously and stay organized!

Checking Out the Types of Gigs You Can Get

Let's take a look at some of the most common types of side gigs you can get as lifeguard. There are many circumstances in which lifeguards are required. In fact, in many circumstances, without lifeguards, it would be illegal for the pool, beach, or waterpark to operate.

Here are just a few scenarios in which lifeguards are employed to keep people safe:

» Ready for this one? You're watching your favorite TV show or movie and there is a water scene and some of the actors are swimming. Guess what? There is a lifeguard on set! That could be you!

» You're watching the Olympics on TV and the 4x100 swim relay is about to take off. But first . . . a wide shot of the pool and there sits . . . the professional lifeguard! Yup. Who else actually gets paid to watch the Olympics and have a front row seat no less.

» You are heading to the beach one Sunday morning and you get diverted due to a road closure because of a local triathlon or charity swim event happening in your town.

While these athletic events are fun and exciting for all of their participants, safety is the most important factor. Someone has to lifeguard these events and someone needs to be organizing water safety. In most if not all cases, you get paid for your professional service!

>> It is a beautiful summer afternoon, and you are heading to a backyard birthday pool party for a family friend. There will be 50 guests both adults and children. When you arrive, there are two lifeguards walking around the pool with rescue tubes. This can be you!

The next sections look deeper into various opportunities, depending on your level of lifeguard training.

Working open water swims and triathlons

One of the biggest areas where lifeguard work is needed is in the open water swimming community. There is an entire worldwide circuit of open water swims and triathlons (see Figure 11-1). For years, race directors have relied on lifeguard volunteers for water safety support. In recent years, a lot of negative attention has focused around triathlon-related drownings, which have happened more often as the sport has grown.

Floored Media / Epi+Center RESCUE

FIGURE 11-1: Epi+Center Rescue lifeguards watch over competitors in the Hudson River during the swimming leg of the annual New York City Triathlon.

THE BIRTH OF EPI+CENTER WATER RESCUE

As an avid triathlete, ocean lifeguard, and EMT, author Cary Epstein couldn't help but to find himself thinking about other people's safety during his own swims while racing. It was in 2008, while participating in a triathlon, that he stopped his swim to assist another triathlete who was having a panic attack. When he looked around for official water safety help, there was no one to be found. He was able to calm the swimmer down and get her to a point where she was okay. He stayed with her until he was finally able to find a volunteer in a kayak and asked him to keep an eye on her. From that moment on, he found himself looking at the lifeguard and water safety operations at the triathlons he participated in and came to the realization that they were severely under-resourced. Coincidentally, around the same time, one of his good friends invited him to have lunch with him and a race director whom he had just met. He tagged along to NYC and made small talk over some food and drinks. It was after hearing about his triathlon experience combined with his expertise and passion for lifeguarding and EMS that the race director asked him if he might be able to help him better increase water safety for his event. That meeting led to the birth of his own side hustle, a business he named Epi+Center Rescue.

Floored Media / Epi+Center RESCUE

Epi+Center Rescue is a private, full-scale water safety business, owned and operated by author Cary Epstein.

(continued)

(continued)

Epi+Center Rescue is a full-scale water safety staffing and aquatics consultation business (see the image). At the time of this publication, Epi+Center Rescue has been operating successfully for 11 years. Over the years, Cary has learned that actually putting safety first and just "saying" you put safety first are two very different things. Our clients truly put safety at the top of their lists and because they do, the likelihood of a tragedy during one of their open water swims decreases drastically. It is true, however, that no matter how prepared the safety team is and regardless of how good they are, no one can prevent someone from suffering a sudden cardiac arrest while swimming. With that said, the most important question Cary asks his potential clients is, "when it happens, will you and your team be prepared?" If there is any hesitation whatsoever in their thinking, or they just aren't sure, the answer is no. Although they hope it never happens, clients know unfortunately these things do occur. Without trained professionals standing by who have the ability to react quickly when something does happen, the outcome would be poor.

In the past, race directors used to cross their fingers and hope something bad didn't happen, but in this day and age, it's become unacceptable to be unprepared if something does go wrong at an event. Cary's company fills a gap in the market by providing lifeguards and safety coordinators for any events that involve swimming and or/water, and their presence makes them safer by tenfold. Epi+Center Rescue sits down with clients and draws up full-scale Emergency Action Plans based on individual needs. From there, they determine the number of lifeguards needed to guard each swim appropriately. They coordinate both pre- and post-race briefings with their open water certified lifeguards and any other water safety personnel. They also coordinate with local public safety assets, such as the U.S. Coast Guard and local fire, EMS, and police departments.

Additionally, one of the most important tools his service provides is the use of their jet ski/personal water craft (PWC) and rescue sled. In the event of a swimmer emergency, these tools have become invaluable for extricating swimmers in a safe and timely manner. Their water craft is driven by a trained and certified rescue operator and staffed with a lifeguard. Depending on the size of the event, more than one PWC may be recommended.

A swimmer in distress is assisted by the water rescue team and catches his breath on the rescue sled.

These professional services are more expensive than relying on lifeguard volunteers, which are nearly impossible to find these days, but it is an insurance policy. It provides peace of mind to know that everyone who goes into the water will come out of the water, and if something does goes awry, a trained team is there ready and able to handle it. While some race organizers still choose not to spend extra money to hire professional safety teams, Cary has sadly seen that in many cases it' just a matter of time until something happens at these races. Races and special events involving water happen regularly around the world, and Cary has found that niche services for lifeguards are only becoming more and more in demand as the popularity of these events grows. Visit the website at epicenterrescue.com.

The days of volunteering for a bagel and T-shirt are almost behind us, as event organizers and public entities are recognizing the need for professional water safety services and full-scale emergency actions plans. While this can be quite expensive and not every organization is able or willing to afford it, having good lifeguards is an insurance policy that is undeniably worth it! No one wants to "Monday morning quarterback" your safety plan, after tragedy strikes.

Backyard pool parties and other events

You're celebrating your cousins' tenth birthday party and she is having 25 friends over to the backyard pool. While you are not required by law to have a lifeguard on duty, it certainly wouldn't be safe if you didn't! Why not grab the gig as a backyard pool party lifeguard! There are pool parties going on all summer long or even all year long if you live in a warm climate.

Backyard pool parties are a great, fun way to have family and friends over to celebrate joyous occasions. While many people are safety conscious and might think about having a guard ahead of time, unfortunately all too many don't consider one until it's too late. It's all fun and games until tragedy strikes and they are completely ill prepared to handle it.

The bottom line is, it is *not* illegal to have people over your own home and not have a professional lifeguard on duty. However, adult "water watchers" are not professionals and have been known to get caught up talking to guests and sometimes even drinking alcoholic beverages. When it comes to water safety, there is zero room for error and the risk just isn't worth it.

We've seen and heard all too many times, one too many stories where both adults and children get seriously hurt or killed. Having a professional lifeguard to handle all things is well worth the investment.

There is a big market for these types of lifeguard gigs and if you are really good at networking and making a name for yourself, you can find jobs weekend after weekend working private parties.

TIP

People have found success landing lifeguard roles at private parties by posting advertisements in the newspaper or posting flyers around town and on public billboards. Social media and/or Facebook groups put you in contact with big networks of people in and around your area. After one successful event, remember that people will be more likely to recommend you to their friends and family.

Although in most cases it is not required, it is not a bad idea to look into securing a small insurance policy. This is an extra layer of protection should you get named in a lawsuit of any kind somewhere down the road. It is not required but not a bad idea.

Also, make sure you have the appropriate equipment you need to do the job. This starts with the basics: a rescue tube and first aid kit. Rescue tubes like the Styrofoam Peterson tube are perfect for these types of gigs (as opposed to a Burnside buoy, the plastic can). These can be purchased easily online. A first aid kit can also be purchased stocked and ready to go from your local convenience stores. Your first aid kit should include:

>> Band-aids

>> Gauze pads

>> Roller cling

>> Peroxide/bacitracin

>> Trauma shears

>> Tourniquet

>> Gloves

>> CPR pocket face mask

>> Bag-valve mask

Prior to committing to any job, it is important to understand what you are getting yourself into. Ask the appropriate questions beforehand. The answers to these questions may change what you bring, how many people you staff, your calendar, and the pay. Some of the questions you should ask include:

>> How big is the swimming area?

>> How many swimmers do you expect to be swimming?

>> What is the age range of these swimmers?

>> What is their swimming ability?

>> What is the deepest depth of the pool or body of water?

>> Is alcohol being served in any capacity?

>> If this is a kid's party, will the parents be present?

TIP

While accepting one of these private gigs alone might seem like a great idea, it is much better to work in pairs. Having two lifeguards on duty allows for bathroom and/or snack breaks without jeopardizing the safety of those in attendance. In addition, if something catastrophic were to happen, two working professionals is always better than one. Let your client know that you require a minimum of two lifeguards on duty at all times. Also be sure that all the lifeguards are properly briefed on the conditions and expectations, as shown in Figure 11-2.

Cary Epstein (Author)

FIGURE 11-2: Water Safety Director Cary Epstein goes through the pre-race briefing with lifeguards prior to the start of the event.

In terms of compensation, a good ballpark for someone with abundant experience can be from $50 to $100 an hour. Many consider twice their hourly rate at their full-time place of employment to be appropriate. The truth is, only you are in control of how much you are paid for your services.

Teaching others as a lifeguard training instructor

Did you know that once you are certified as a lifeguard, you can take a class to be a lifeguard training instructor? Doing so allows you to teach and certify future lifeguards. Think about who provided you with your training. Maybe you can see yourself as a lifeguard training instructor one day. There are great opportunities for you to make some additional money by hosting your own lifeguard training courses.

TIP

The American Red Cross allows individuals and businesses to become Licensed Training Providers or third-party instructors. They work directly with the Red Cross to provide cost-effective programs that meet their quality, compliance, and budget needs. Courses are easy to start up and administer, providing flexibility for training. What an awesome way to give back and a great way to make a few extra dollars.

The following qualifications are needed to become a lifeguard training instructor for the American Red Cross:

>> You must be minimum age of 17 years old.

>> You must possess a current Red Cross certificate in Lifeguarding/First Aid/CPR/AED.

>> At the time of signing up for the instructor's course, you must complete an online training session for the Lifeguarding Instructor class.

>> To teach waterfront skills, lifeguarding instructors must possess a basic-level Waterfront Skills certificate (which may or may not have been included in your original American Red Cross Lifeguard Training class). Once you complete this, you will go through 24 hours of rigorous instructor training and learn all of the tools needed to teach the lifeguard training course.

As long as you are following the guidelines required as an instructor, you can set up your own lifeguard training classes and make some extra money!

There are an unlimited number of places you can take your lifeguard training instructor skills too — from camps, to YMCAs, to beach clubs and youth swim teams. The best time to run a lifeguard training class or refresher course is the winter and spring, leading up to a hot summer season. In areas that are hot year-round, there is no peak lifeguard training season.

When you became an instructor, you determine the overhead costs to run a class, and based on this, you can decide how much you should charge per student. One of the most expensive parts of running a class is renting an area for your classroom and pool space, so be sure to take this into consideration before starting. On average, you might be looking at approximately $350-$500 a head.

Movie, TV, and film sets

Another popular area that is often overlooked is movie, TV, and film sets. This is a more difficult industry to get involved in, but there are private companies out there that provide all sorts of services to the TV and film industry.

In many cases lifeguards are hired through stunt companies. Reach out to local stunt agencies and ask about their water safety divisions. In addition, private companies that work in TV and film may also have aquatics or safety divisions. Do a Google search for your area and type in keywords such as lifeguard, water safety, TV, film, stunts, and so on.

TIP

If you know a movie is in the works or in production, try searching for the movie title accompanied by the buzzwords "casting call for real lifeguards."

Every production that is putting actors in or near the water is required to have a lifeguard on set. There are dozens of private companies out there that are staffing lifeguards for movie, TV, and film sets — you just have to find them. If you have never worked in this industry before, keep this in mind. The money is good, but the shoots are long. It is not uncommon to be on set for 10–12 hours, sometimes even longer. Even if they are done using the pool or body of water, if the production is still shooting near it, the lifeguard might need to be present. There are a lot of very serious rules when it comes to the TV/film industry when on set, and someone has to oversee water safety. Will it be you behind the scenes next time?

>> **Fun Fact #1: Season 3 of Netflix's** *Stranger Things*. There is a pool scene at the Hawkins Community Pool when they introduce Max's brother Billy. In the show, his character actually plays a lifeguard, but a real lifeguard had to watch all of those swimmers in the pool. I (Cary) was blessed to fly out to Atlanta and got paid visit the upside down! As the real lifeguard on set, I even ended up getting used as an extra and you can see me in the pool on the opening shot. See Figure 11-3.

>> **Fun Fact #2:** *Baywatch* **reboot with Dwayne the Rock Johnson and Zac Efron.** If you didn't watch this reboot, what are you waiting for? During the lifeguard tryout scene, where Zac Efron is competing to make it to *Baywatch*, there are

about 30 lifeguard recruits attempting as well. Here's an insider secret . . . everyone single one of them (including myself, lifeguard cadet #24 in the blue speedo) are certified lifeguards! Yes, that's right. The casting company set out to find and hire certified lifeguards for this one scene, which was filmed in Tybee Island, Georgia.

The majority of the faces you see in this scene are professional lifeguards from across the Southeast, and I believe mainly, Florida. I was definitely the only New Yorker! We swam and ran through the obstacle course for hours, and despite it looking 90 degrees and sunny, it was actually April and pretty cold (you would never know it!). Several of us also swam alongside some of the other A-list actors and kept an extra eye on them as they swam in the ocean. This was a pretty cool experience. Getting paid to be the real lifeguard on the set of the *Baywatch* movie was something I will never forget!

🎬 "Stranger Things"

⭐ Real Lifeguards

Must have lifeguarding experience / be trained in CPR

- Males + Females
- Any Ethnicity
- Ages : 30 - 55 yrs
- Rate : $150 / 12hrs *higher rate special skill* you must be able to present you current certification at your fitting & on the day you work - we will actually be using you as lifeguard types for our BG in addition to other Lifeguards that will be working the scene :)
- Location : Atlanta, GA

Credit: Casting TaylorMade

FIGURE 11-3: Casting call for real lifeguards on the set of "Stranger Things."

TIP

It's all about being friendly, personable, and doing a great job. Once you get the first gig, it oftentimes leads to the others. That's what happened to me. Leave a good impression with the casting director and maybe they will reach out to directly next time they are looking for a lifeguard. It's all about networking.

KNOW THE GOOD SAMARITAN LAWS

The Good Samaritan laws were enacted to protect first responders and helpful citizens from frivolous lawsuits and encourage them to step up and act in times of crisis. In a nutshell, when you are working your job, you have what they call a "duty to act." That means no matter what the circumstances are, you must respond and do what you can within your scope of training to save lives. When you punch out and are off the clock, you no longer have that "duty to act," but you still have the skills and knowledge necessary to save a life. These laws protect everybody, regardless of your level of training.

Many professionals who carry this skill set — such as doctors, nurses, police, firefighters, lifeguards, and EMS personal — were fearful of getting involved in emergency situations off the clock because they were not protected by employee-related liability insurance. In a world where everyone sues for everything, it is a legitimate thing to be fearful of! The Good Samaritan laws changed all of this, and because of it, more lives are being saved. To be clear, Good Samaritan laws don't stop someone from suing you, it just adds a layer of protection for the "Good Samaritan" who was simply trying to do the right thing. To date, there has never been a successful lawsuit where someone who decided to help was sued and lost.

Balancing Your Full-Time Job and Side Gigs

When taking on extra opportunities and putting your lifeguarding skills to good use outside of your regular facility, it is important that you keep your priorities and other commitments straight. Do not undertake roles that will cause conflicts with your other jobs, especially as it relates to scheduling.

Here are some tips that we have picked up along the way (or maybe have learned from personal experiences). They can help you stay out trouble, keep organized, and make a few bucks on the side:

- >> Don't take lifeguarding equipment from your home facility, at least not without asking for permission.

- >> Don't wear lifeguard uniforms from your full-time job to your private gig — know who you are representing! You do not, for example, want to get accused of "impersonating" public state lifeguards.

- >> Make sure your full-time employer is aware of your other commitments.

- >> Don't blow off your full-time work for your part-time work. Of course, there is a way to manage your vacation time and time off to properly juggle both.

- >> Don't double dip! You should not be getting paid to be at two places at once.

REMEMBER

Regardless of whether you are representing your full-time pool or working a birthday pool at a private residence, your lifeguard training remains true. Always think before you act. Being confronted with a life-threatening emergency causes many stressors on the body. If your team of lifeguards is a little bit more scarce (you won't have a full crew behind you), you might need to be more resourceful with the numbers you have.

Stop, breathe, and think clearly before you act. This small practice will help you make the best decisions possible in every lifeguarding scenario.

Chapter **12**

The Sport of Surf Lifesaving

I f you aren't doing it yourself, you might never know it. . . but there is an entire world of lifeguards who dedicate themselves to local, regional, national, and even worldwide competitions! These competitions mean so much more than winning a medal and finishing at the top of the playing field; they are about homing in on the lifeguard skill set and improving the job skills you will be performing on the most challenging days. This is one very important piece of what it takes to be a great lifeguard.

Competing for Lifeguarding Excellence

There is no doubt that a large part of lifeguarding calls upon the ability to be efficient in the water and on land. The best lifeguards can perform and execute a rescue in any type of condition. This requires leadership qualities and sharp decision-making skills, as well as the physical ability to perform specific rescue-related functions. Surveillance — the ability to spot a rescue or problem — is just one of many characteristics all great lifeguards possess. The best lifeguards can spot a struggling swimmer, sometimes even moments before the swimmer is in trouble, as well as make rescues in the most demanding situations.

Facing off against guards from near and far

There is no definitive list or ranking of all the lifeguard agencies across the country. So how do we measure which group of lifeguards reign superior over their peers? Their number of rescues in a given period of time? Or the number of rescues they *didn't* go on, as a result of their preventative lifeguarding skills? The fewest number of drownings that occurred during lifeguarded hours?

To raise competitive spirit in the heart of lifesaving, beach patrols across the country and around the world created the sport of *surf lifesaving*. When a group of lifeguards returned to the United States from a trip to Australia in 1962 where they competed against other professionals, they decided to form what is now known as the *United States Lifesaving Association* (USLA). The goal was to replicate the camaraderie and patrol-to-patrol exchange generated during that lifeguard competition.

It is very common to find beach patrols and lifeguard agencies hosting inter-beach or intra-crew competitions throughout peak season. Lifeguard agencies split up based on where they are staffed that season. Lifeguard municipalities that are formed based on beach towns may divide themselves into geographic regions, such as East, West, and Central teams. Even larger lifeguard groups comprised of different towns sometimes compete against one another to assert their dominance as the best lifeguard competitors in their respective county.

In addition, there is a long-standing tradition made interesting by rivalries among beach patrols in the same local or regional areas. For example, on Long Island, all the patrols that make up the ocean lifeguards on Long Island compete at the highly esteemed Long Island Lifeguard Championship, hosted at Smith Point County Park in New York.

On a larger stage, any USLA dues-paying member can choose to compete in any open events at their Regional Lifeguard Championship as well as the National Lifeguard Championships. At Regionals, you compete with other municipalities in your designated region.

There are nine regions in the USLA: New England, Mid-Atlantic, South Atlantic, Southeast, Great Lakes, Gulf Coast, Southwest, Northwest, and the Pacific Islands.

At Nationals, all the regions compete against professionals from around the country. You can only imagine the level of skill that shows up here!

On the largest scale, lifeguards from around the globe congregate on the world stage at the World Championships, also known as the *Rescue* series, which is hosted by the International Life Saving Federation. This Rescue series takes place every other year. Every four years, the *World Games* are held in different venues. It is from the results of the United States Nationals Championship that a world team is scouted and eventually formed to compete at these world events. Age group categories are also created in five-year increments for those interested in competing over the age of 30. The eldest age group represents those over 75!

Benefits to competition

There are many benefits to getting involved in the lifeguard competition circuit of your local beach patrol beyond fulfilling your competitive itch:

» One of the best things about it is that you get an opportunity to meet other guards in your own lifeguard corps whom you might not normally work with or had the opportunity to know. The lifelong friendships, bonds, and memories created from within your own team will blow you away when you look back years down the road.

» These competitions build lifeguard agency camaraderie when you're back on home turf patrolling the public. Lifeguards take a lot of pride in trying to be the best at what they do, and competition is no exception. The rivalries from one beach to another are often passed down from generation to generation.

» You also get a chance to meet other lifeguard competitors from the beach patrols that you are competing against. It is because of the lifeguard competition circuit that we can travel to any major beach patrol in the country and strike up a conversation with a familiar face or recognize a lifeguard competitor.

> ❯❯ In this world, there is an understood, mutual respect that is earned in the profession, which makes competition such a worthwhile "extracurricular."

Demonstrating Your Skills in Different Relays and Events

In total, there are 15 events at the USLA National Lifeguard Championships. Each one is specific to a certain skill set that is eventually used on the job. The following sections highlight some of the races to give you an idea as to what takes place at these competitions.

TIP

You can check out this video montage of the 2022 United States Lifesaving Association National Championships in Hermosa Beach, California to get a little taste of the grit and competition at www.instagram.com/reel/ChXAqyiKqBe/?igshid=YmMyMTA2M 2Y%3D. Figure 12-1 shows the flyer from the 2022 championship.

Surf race

In this event, competitors in heats of 30 or so begin on the sand. At the official's start, they run into the water and swim a 400-meter course designated by buoys, which the swimmers typically perform right shoulder turns around. At the end of the swim, the competitors run out of the water and up the beach for a quick dash through the finish line.

Board rescue race

The *board rescue race*, as the name suggests, requires a competition regulation rescue board, not to exceed 10'6. This event, with teams of two, is designed to replicate a board rescue that takes place on the job for farther distance saves. The first competitor on the team, acting as the victim, races to a flag line floating about 100 meters off shore when the race begins. When they reach their flag, they knock it down to signal to the rescuer to paddle out with the rescue board and pick them up. For this reason, this event is sometimes called the *paddle pick-up*. The two must paddle back to the shoreline together and cross the finish line with both competitors in contact with the board. See Figure 12-2.

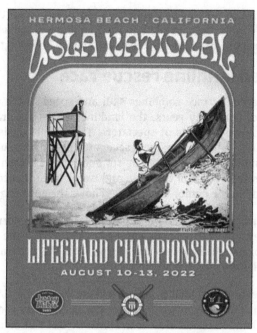

Credit: United States Lifesaving Association

FIGURE 12-1: The highly anticipated 2022 USLA National Lifeguard Championship.

SuperStock / Adobe Stock

FIGURE 12-2: Surf lifesaving competitors charge the water with their competition boards in hand.

There is also a rescue race with the same rules, except the rescuer swims (rather than paddles) to the flag line and pulls the victim back to shore attached to a lifeguard buoy or Peterson tube.

Mixed landline rescue race

This particular race combines skill and speed in the water and on land. For many years, the landline rescue has drawn some of the largest crowds of spectators. This event consists of four lifeguards — the victim, the rescuer attached to a rescue line, and two landline pullers. As of the summer of 2022, each team had to be evenly mixed of two men and two women (hence the word "mixed" in the name). Figure 12-3 shows the 2022 champions.

This has changed over the last few years and is currently still being examined to determine if it should go back to the prior open field format. At the publishing of this book, the 2022 mixed landline rules are still in place.

Each team is assigned to a lane and corresponding flag buoy by random draw immediately before the heat. Heats consist of no more than ten teams. Here is the basic flow of this competition:

1. Prior to the start of the race, the victim casually swims out to their assigned buoy on the flag line.

2. At the sound of the start, landline swimmers run to the shore, put on their rescue fins, and race out to their victim.

3. Once contact is made between the victim and their rescuer, the swimmer signals by raising their hand to the lifeguard pullers on the beach, who begin to tandemly pull them toward the shoreline.

4. Once the rescuer and victim make it to shallow enough water, the victim must be picked up and carried across the finish line with all four competitors in contact and the victim still holding the buoy.

The victim cannot drop the buoy — many, many teams have been disqualified for this seemingly trivial rule.

FIGURE 12-3: Mixed Landline Rescue National Champions at the 2022 USLA National Championships in Hermosa Beach, CA.

Beach flags

Often the most anticipated event in every lifeguard tournament, *beach flags* is a lifeguard's version of musical chairs on the sand. Competitors gather into a 20-meter long beach flag pit and draw for lanes. The lifeguards lay lined up on their stomachs at one end of the beach flag pit. They lie facing away from the other side of the pit, where batons (beach flags) are positioned (see Figure 12-4).

At the starter's whistle, the competitors rise, turn, and race across the pit to snag one of these coveted beach flags buried upright in the sand. There are always fewer beach flags in the sand than competitors in the beach flag pit. Those who fail to grab a baton are immediately eliminated from the following round. This continues until there is one lifeguard left, crowned the champion.

Beach relay

The *beach relay* is the lifeguarding's equivalent to track and field's 4x100. However, in the lifeguarding world, this four-person 90-meter sprint happens on soft sand! Each competitor has to pass a baton to the waiting runner. Two competitors wait on either end of the groomed sand track. At the sound of the start, the lifeguard leading off runs across the track, handing the baton to the second runner, and so on.

MediaNews Group/Torrance Daily Breeze / Getty Images

FIGURE 12-4: Lifeguard competitors race to the beach flags located on the opposite side of the flag pit.

WARNING

Don't drop the baton; otherwise you will wind up holding up your team to find it, pick it back up, and finish your run!

Blink on this particular event and you just might miss it, as these lifeguards are usually the quickest across the field! There's no diving allowed on this land event; competitors must complete their leg of the event on their feet in an upright position.

Surfboat race

Surfboat racing goes back to the original roots of lifeguarding. This is often one of the most exciting events to watch, especially when there is shore break or big surf. Hands down, this is the most dangerous event at any lifeguard competition, as these boats weigh several hundred pounds. It is not uncommon for competitors to lose contact and control of their surfboat without necessarily becoming disqualified.

Surfboat racing usually involves two or three laps, depending on if you are racing in the open category or in your age group. Three lap races are approximately 2,000 meters; two laps are approximately 1,300 meters; one lap is approximately 665 meters.

Two-person surfboat teams row around the three outside buoy courses, returning to shore where one member disembarks from the boat and runs up to the touch line. Once across the touchline, the member can return to their surfboat for a second lap, repeating the touch line run. After they finish the third lap, one member must leave the boat and run up to cross the finish line.

Table 12-1 includes a comprehensive list of the USLA National Championship individual and team events. For the most updated information, visit their website at www.usla.org/page/NATIONALRULES.

TABLE 12-1 USLA National Championship Events

Individual-Based Events
Surf Race
Run-Swim-Run
Board Race
Surfski Race
Ironman/Ironwoman
American Ironman/American Ironwoman
Beach Flags
Beach Run – 2 km

Team-Based Events
Surfboat Race
Board Rescue Race
Rescue Tube Rescue Race
Landline Rescue Race
Beach Relay
Taplin Relay (swim/paddle/surf ski/run)
Paddleboard Relay

Entering Competitions

If you have never participated in a lifeguard competition, you don't know what you are missing! It's one of those things that gets you hooked and sucks you right in. The majority of beach and open water lifeguards around the world have some sort of athletic background, and for most, the drive and power to be the best feels like home during lifeguard tournaments — sometimes we all just need something to satisfy our competitive itch! Figure 12-5 shows one such competition.

Photograph by Andrew Presta

FIGURE 12-5: Rescue swimmer, victim, and tender emerge from the shore toward the finish line.

Not every competitor on the field comes from a traditional athletic background. Once you find an event that appeals to you, you will only want to improve. It is practice, practice, and practice that helps you rise within the ranks to the top of your competition field.

Finding competitions (local, regional, and national)

As mentioned, there are opportunities to compete on all stages. There is no shortage of lifeguard competitions to partake in, in and out of your state. One of the biggest problems you might face is choosing which ones to go to! For many agencies, it is somewhat of a tradition to continue to attend the same line ups year after year, but new lifeguard tournaments and competitions emerge on the scene all the time.

For seasonal agencies, this gets tricky because there are only so many dates within the full 8-12 weeks of summer, and you can't go to everything! Agencies that work year-round can spread out their attendance to various tournaments. You must also be conscientious about staffing and make sure there are enough guards to stay back and protect the public.

REMEMBER

You are a lifeguard first and lifeguard competitor second. If your crew can't cover you on a given day, you have an obligation to stay back and protect the public.

It is always enticing to travel out of town to compete, but to get the most bang for your buck, consider these issues:

>> Does your beach patrol have adequate coverage while you are gone?

>> Are you taking additional days off or are you getting paid for the time? Being in pay status could just mean you are getting paid to compete on that one day of competition but not on a travel days.

>> What other expenses will you incur?

Knowing what you'll pay

The majority of the time, these competitions come with some sort of cost (but from someone who is constantly being persuaded to go, it is always worth it!). The cost of competing comes from multiple sources:

>> The direct costs of competing include the entrance fee and possibly membership fees. Entrance fees may be assessed on an individual basis or a team basis, depending on the competition you are entering. Competitions run by the USLA — such as Nationals and Regionals — require you to be a member of the association (which has a fee to join), as well as pay the entrance fee to compete. A local competition such as a distance swim might only incur an entrance fee to race.

>> The indirect costs of competition are more variable. Depending on whether you are staying nearby or venturing out far, the cost of travel changes. A flight across the country to compete against the nation's best may be pricey compared to a drive along the coast to a local rival beach, after factoring in gas mileage and tolls. Farther trips call for hotel arrangements, and most lifeguards will probably recommend piling as many people into your hotel room as possible!

>> Some pieces of racing equipment can be fairly expensive too, especially for the higher end and fancier options on the market. Watercraft such as USLA-regulation size rescue boards, surf skis, and surfboats are no small investment. To get these precious toys from your home beach to the competition field will also cost you.

Seeking sponsorships

While the costs of competing may not be astronomical for the casual competitor, they can grow higher when you find yourself signing up and participating in many events and tournaments. Also, flights nowadays are rarely on the economical side. How can you offset these expenses? Sponsorships!

Sponsorships allow lifeguard agencies and teams to raise money so that lifeguards don't have to pay for everything out of pocket. There are many ways you can fundraise, and every agency and beach patrol does something different. Here are just some ideas:

>> Lifeguard T-shirt sponsors, which put forth some money to have their names on the back of team uniforms.

>> Sporting events, such as group ticket sales for professional hockey, baseball, and basketball games.

>> Donations from organizations or individuals like parents, alumni, retirees, and other long-time supporters of the team.

>> Fundraising parties, such as holiday gatherings and union race celebrations that occur throughout the year.

It is hard work to make these special events happen, but the lifeguard competitors certainly appreciate the support. For some smaller beach patrols and lifeguard agencies, it's the only way they can afford to compete.

Prepping to Compete

Once you choose your team or decide you are going to compete as an individual, you must prepare physically and mentally. As high school basketball coach Tim Notke was known for saying, "Hard work beats talent, when talent fails to work hard."

Just like preparing for a marathon or Ironman, you can't show up on race day without putting in the time. What do the months, weeks, or even the year prior to competition look like? What are you doing to prepare yourself for success? Take the time to think about your individual and team goals and map out what you need to do to achieve them.

Team workouts and preparation

In the same way that every qualification exam can be different, the procedure for getting involved in competition for every agency is unique as well. In some organizations, no such procedure may exist at all. For example, attending and competing at open water swim events only requires you to pay the preliminary fees.

Assemble the dream team

For the more elite teams or for team-based tournaments with a set timeline of events and scoring system, you may have to try out. These competitions put the best lifeguards from each patrol up against each other, and only one group can represent the agency to come out on top.

The first step, naturally, is to assemble your team. Ask yourself these questions:

>> Is there a team captain?

>> Do you have the appropriate number of swimmers? Paddlers? Land animals (to pull lines and run!)?

>> Do you need an alternate in case someone gets hurt on race day?

Train, train, train

Whether you are competing on a team or gunning for gold on your own, the next step is always training — setting yourself up for success. Getting faster in the ocean is a completely different beast than swimming in a pool. Your endurance on land does not perfectly translate to your capabilities on watercraft.

TIP

If you want to be an efficient paddler, you need to practice on the rescue board in all surf conditions, including your exits and entries into the water (which can make or break your race!). If you want to be a strong rower, you have to get in the boat and get those reps in.

No champions are born overnight!

As a member of a relay team, you must be sure to practice together. We have seen some of the greatest races go south very quickly all too many times. Taking four of your best teammates and putting them together in a relay doesn't necessarily equal success, especially when they haven't practiced together.

Most of these events have very technical rules that require you to pay very close attention. It is important that together you practice every move and have excellent communication skills. Without practicing the little things, lack of attention to detail can derail the top contenders. Know the rulebook and know what each team member is responsible for doing. As silly as it sounds, taking this for granted might cost you the gold or, even worse, get you disqualified.

REMEMBER

The USLA surf lifesaving rulebook is very technical; it is important to have a good grasp of the rules so you don't get disqualified on race day!

Getting the equipment

You can't compete at a lifeguard tournament without lifeguard equipment. Some of the most common things you need to bring include:

>> Rescue cans/tubes

>> Rescue board

>> Rescue line

>> Caps, goggles, and fins

>> Surf ski

>> Surfboat and oars

>> 10x10 E-Z UP canopy and umbrellas (because it gets hot!)

It is crucial that you practice with all of these pieces of equipment during your training regimens so you are comfortable using them during the real thing. Something as minimal as practicing with the pair of goggles you plan to use on race day or the surfboat you will be rowing in on Day 3 of Nationals (with your partner!) can make a world of a difference when the competition arrives.

So, how does it all get from your home beach to your destination? In some cases, your agencies might have designated lifeguard vehicles with trailers that can transport these pieces of equipment. In other circumstances, members of the team will have to stow away certain items in their own personal cars.

In the event that the competition is not local and you are flying out to the venue, you might consider checking your equipment as luggage. Check with your airline in advance, as you might incur some additional fees for traveling with oversized items.

TIP

If you are putting your rescue board on the plane as checked oversized luggage, consider packing the board in a board bag wrapped with lots of towels to prevent dings and cracks in the fiberglass!

In some cases, some regions rent 18-wheeler trucks and then each agency splits the cost depending on how much equipment they are putting on the truck. For the larger and more expensive items like surfboats, surf skis, and paddle boards, this is a far better way to prevent damage than typical commercial airline travel.

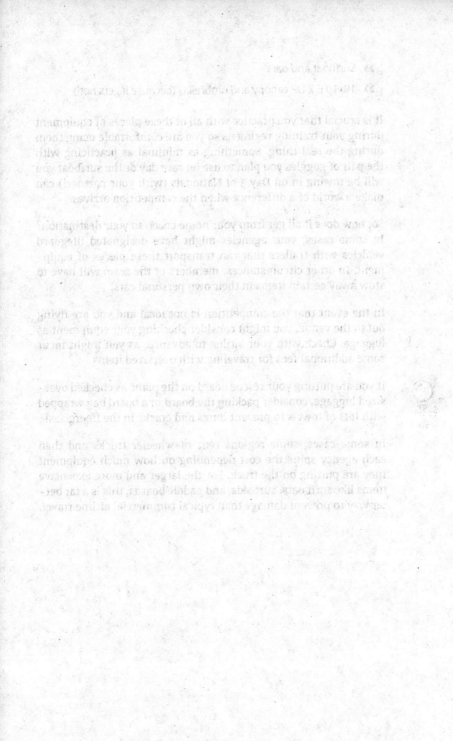

Chapter **13**

Starting Early: Junior Lifeguard Programs

f you've ever been to a beach, pool, or lake as a kid, I would bet the five-year-old-you took a nice, long look up at the lifeguard chair and reveled in its glory.

Maybe your mother caught you gazing, and she nudged you, explaining that the lifeguard would come get you if you started to drown. Perhaps you gave a friendly wave toward the lifeguard, who caught you in the corner of their eye and snuck a wave back. Oh, how starstruck you must have been, before going on to tell yourself that you want to be a lifeguard one day, perched up on that chair with a birds-eye view of the entire area.

Or maybe that was just how we felt as children. But we hope not. Many lifeguards can tell stories like this one as the initial itch that nudged them toward a job in lifesaving.

One great way to enjoy the lifeguarding experience is through a junior lifeguard program. This chapter explains how starstruck teens and preteens can take part in junior lifeguard programs, the purpose they serve, and the benefits these young stars gain from a young age.

Introducing Junior Lifeguard Programs

Today, junior lifeguarding is commonplace in lifeguard agencies around the world, with Australia leading the way. They are famous for nicknaming their junior lifeguards *nippers*. The numbers are only growing; see for yourself:

>> United States: 35,000 Junior Lifeguards

>> Australia: 50,000 Nippers

>> Canada: 3,000 Juniors

>> Mexico: 300 Jr. Salvavidas

>> New Zealand: 15,000 Nippers

>> Ceylon: 900 Juniors

>> Great Britain: 10,000 Juniors/Nippers

>> South Africa: 25,000 Juniors

The following sections explain what kids and teenagers can expect when they join a junior lifeguard program. We also talk about all of the great ways junior lifeguards can develop new skills and mature as a result of participating in these programs.

Creating future lifeguards

These junior lifeguard programs persist around the world today for the very reason that "Sam's Boys" was created almost a century ago (see the nearby sidebar seven or eight) — to help aspiring lifeguards gain the necessary skills at a young age so that they are prepared to ace the real lifeguard test. Most junior lifeguard programs are open to children as early as 7 or 8 years old.

Junior lifeguard "curricula" does, of course, vary from one organization to another. By its nature, these programs are designed to emulate the eventual lifeguard test that the aspiring lifeguard can take once they reach the eligible age. The final age group will therefore be exactly one year younger than the required age to take the test. Since these tests differ from one patrol to another, so will the week-to-week (and day-to-day) activities.

As an example, one of the most important portions of our own organization's lifeguard exam was a cross-chest carry from one end of the pool to the other. On multiple junior lifeguard sessions — especially the final summer preceding the year our age group would become eligible to take the exam — the lifeguard instructors took the class to the pool with plastic dummies — the same ones used on the real exam. We practiced lugging these heavy, bulky dummies 25 yards across the pool. If it weren't for these sessions, our classes (many of whom would go on to take the lifeguard exam and pass with flying colors that following year) would not have been as prepared.

THE FIRST JUNIOR LIFEGUARD PROGRAMS

In more recent years, junior lifeguard programs have swelled in popularity, popping up around the Atlantic and Pacific Coasts and exposing aspiring lifeguards to Mother Nature's beautiful seas years before the minimum age of employment. To what organization can we attribute the first junior lifeguard program?

The earliest junior lifeguard program appears to have originated on the shores of Chicago, patrolling Lake Michigan, which borders it. In the 1910s, with the onset of World War I and outbreak of the great influenza, the area began to struggle finding lifeguard coverage. In 1919, the City Lifeguard Service in Chicago began to recruit "junior lifeguards" to aid the scarce number of lifeguards. Their job was to alert lifeguards of struggling patrons. Their compensation? The opportunity to take advantage of all lifeguard equipment for supplementary training.

As this practice of the young lifeguards aiding the full-time lifeguards started to spread further along the shores of Chicago's coastline, one lifeguard, Sam Leone, declared that there needed to be more structure. He worked to establish a better program for training and gave these young people the chance to lifeguard full time once they became of age. And so began what appears to be the first official junior lifeguard program, titled "Sam's Boys." At that time, this program, and lifeguarding in general, was open only to males.

California's first junior lifeguard program was created in 1927 by the Los Angeles City Beach Lifeguards. In the early 1970s, the East Coast started seeing similar programs with the United States Lifesaving Association extending into the Atlantic coastline.

TIP

If you made the early decision to become a lifeguard with a particular eye for a specific lifeguard organization, find out if they offer a junior lifeguard program. It will give you an upper hand, even compared to someone who may be more athletically fit, but is unfamiliar with the dynamics of the test.

Regardless of their specific curricula, these programs do have many aspects in common. Junior lifeguards learn many important skills:

>> Learn confidence while swimming in a body of water, whether that be the nearby ocean, Great Lake, or local pool.

>> Learn and understand beach and water safety.

>> Become incredibly skilled in the open water. It goes without saying that maneuvering around in the ocean is a completely different animal compared to treading water in a pool.

Swimming hundreds of yards out into the vast ocean is a daunting task that most adults wouldn't take a chance on. To be able to dive into the ocean with confidence at a preteen age is certainly something to be proud of.

>> Under the guidance and surveillance of professional lifeguards, learn to use real life-saving equipment.

FACING THE DANGER OF RIP CURRENTS

Whether you like it or not, there will be many days as a junior lifeguard that you will arrive at the beach with rough waters facing you. With rip currents being one of the lead causes of drowning, you can expect to learn about these water-sucking phenomena during your junior lifeguarding program. In fact, junior lifeguards gain extensive experience, not just spotting these rip currents, but intentionally entering them to learn about their mechanisms, how it feels to swim in them, and with the challenge of making it out on their own.

This is intimidating, especially for younger swimmers. However, these programs, especially the most elite ones, must be certain that their juniors can make it in and out of a rip current with their troubled swimmer back on dry sand.

> As a former junior lifeguard myself (Cameron here!), I speak from experience that growing comfortable with rescue cans, buckets, and boards made my first summer on the ocean a lot easier. I could then focus on other aspects of the job.

This chapter would be incomplete without including how uniquely fun of an experience these junior lifeguarding programs truly are. We speak for the majority of all Nippers when we say that the next summer of junior lifeguarding is something to look forward to, from the second the season ends, through the cold winter, and until the moment you are back in the water with your fellow junior lifeguard group. Many of these junior lifeguards meet their friends for life through this program — no joke.

What to expect from a typical junior lifeguard program

Many junior lifeguard programs are offered around the country for young, aspiring lifeguards. One well-known course is the American Red Cross Jr Lifeguarding Program, designed to introduce the ambitious youth between the ages of 11-14 to the actual American Red Cross Lifeguarding course.

This junior course is intended to build a strong foundation in the knowledge, attitude, and skills required of future lifeguards. It typically spans 10 weeks, totaling a little over 30 hours, and is comprehensive in that it takes place in the classroom, on dry land, and in the water.

The program develops skills in swimming, treading water, and executing in-water rescues. Students are introduced to first aid techniques, as well as the proper ways to deliver CPR and use an AED. It is a well-rounded program for those looking to dive into a career in lifeguarding regardless of the venue: traditional pools, multi-use facilities, waterparks, and lakes and rivers.

The goal is for students to have the knowledge and skills needed when they enroll in the full American Red Cross Lifeguarding course once they reach the required age of 15. See Figure 13-1.

These courses typically conclude with a ceremony and certificate of completion. While these certificates do not signify the student is ready to take to the lifeguard stand, they demonstrate that they possess a firm understanding, knowledge, and skill set to be prepared for a career in lifeguarding.

MediaNews Group / Orange County Register via Getty Images / Getty Images

FIGURE 13-1: An aspiring lifeguard learns to jump into the water equipped with a rescue tube.

An average day in the life of an open-water junior lifeguard

This section goes through a normal day of a junior lifeguard who is training to be an ocean lifeguard. Don't expect that this will be an everyday sequence of events, though. One of the best parts of being a lifeguard is the excitement of not knowing what the day will bring.

1. Arrive on time to practice. This is particularly important because you don't want to miss any minute.

2. Stretch with your age group. You have quite a session ahead of you; prepare to activate just about every muscle in your body.

3. Participate in a nice, aerobic exercise to get your blood flowing. This is typically a longer ocean swim, relaxed run, or — our favorite — a mix of both: a run-swim-run. See Figure 13-2.

4. Listen to a quick lecture by the lifeguard instructors, in which they will either introduce or review an important lifesaving technique, such as a line rescue or board rescue.

FIGURE 13-2: A junior lifeguard group braces the brisk, morning sea together for an aerobic, open-water paddle.

5. It's your turn! After breaking out into groups, you practice what you were just taught. As your instructors observe closely and offer comments, you repeat and repeat until your technique is pristine and the motions become muscle memory.

6. Next, the instructors might teach or review another rescue technique. Or, you might learn how to set up an area of the beach, such as the lifeguard area or a lifeguard satellite chair with the necessary equipment: floatation devices, line buckets, surfboard, and so on. In doing so, you help set up the beach for the incoming full-time crew (that is, assuming the junior lifeguard session is in the morning).

7. At times, you'll have some time leftover at the end of the day, in which case the instructors may allow you some time to play. Go surf. Splash around. Frolic in the water. Get salty!

Growing as a person

Junior lifeguard organizations are intended to be an instructive program, but in many ways, you learn so much more than how the ocean works, or how to paddle on a surfboard, or pull someone out of rough waters. Just like joining your little league team or middle school drama club, there is so much more to gain than just the physical skills.

Junior lifeguards:

>> **Grow more confident in themselves as people.** Diving down to the ocean floor hundreds of yards off the coast and not coming back up without a hand full of sand? Jumping off the pier at the end of a great summer season? These are core memories that undoubtedly build self-confidence in young, aspiring lifeguards.

>> **Develop a respect for the water.** They will see the many ways that the ocean will humble you, your friends, and everyday beachgoers. A common saying around here is that Mother Nature is merciless, and while most days will be calm, you learn that you should not mess around with an angry ocean.

>> **Are more equipped for emergencies.** Most junior lifeguard programs incorporate a First Aid, CPR, and AED portion into their courses. It is no secret that these are important skills to have as a professional lifeguard. At the bare minimum, knowing how to act and deliver chest compressions in these high-stress situations can save a life.

>> **Stay active in the summer.** Of course, most kids will be enjoying the weather in the summer. Doing so on the beach and working out, legitimately every muscle of your body, ensures that you return to school fit and healthy.

>> **Learn how to be competitive.** We touch on this more in the next section, but in these types of programs, competitive exercises arise at least once, if not multiple times, a day!

>> **Build camaraderie.** Working with your group in the water and coming together in competition builds serious camaraderie.

Working with Junior Lifeguards as an Instructor

Considering that many lifeguard patrols' future crew members come from these junior lifeguard programs, the best people to instruct and coach these juniors are full-time lifeguards. After all, they know best how their facilities should be run. They took the test themselves to earn a spot in their lifeguard organization.

Being a junior lifeguard instructor/coach is just another of the many opportunities to undertake as a full-time lifeguard professional. Of course, the way that various junior lifeguard programs operate differs from one organization to another. Some instructor positions are volunteer, while others are paid. One thing to be certain of, however, is that the instructors were once lifeguards. This adds to the list of (exciting!) ways they can be more involved in their organizations, in addition to their unending surveillance of the ocean. See Figure 13-3.

Photograph by Andy Eng

FIGURE 13-3: Lifeguard instructors demonstrate how to properly swim with a rescue can on the way to a victim in the water.

TIP

Instructors should always be conscious of their attitude, as these juniors are emulating them. In essence, they are striving to be like their instructor a few years down the line. It is imperative that instructors leave a great impression on them and act like the person they want them to be. As an instructor, you are likely their utmost role models. In addition to looking forward to the next practice, these kids look forward to seeing you just as energized to push them.

Entering Competitions at the Junior Level

There seems to be no shortage of competition in this job. Competition among others is natural, instinctual. So why not throw youngins into it, and help them tap into their competitive sides?

As mentioned in Chapter 12, surf lifesaving is one heck of a sport — loved by many and taken seriously by all! At the junior level, competition is split up by age. Table 13-1 details the official age groups designated by the United States Lifesaving Association (USLA).

TABLE 13-1 Age Categories for Junior Competition

Division	Age Range
U19	16-17 year old Junior Guards and 16-18 year old Professional Guards
A	14-15 years old
B	12-13 years old
C	9-11 years old

These programs — or teams, rather — are not instructional or meant to prepare you for the day-to-day life of a full-time, professional lifeguard. Being on these teams means that you are dedicated to improving as a competitor and are extracurricular to the actual junior lifeguard program.

If you want to be a stand-out athlete, you've got to have the same drive, determination, and aggressiveness as the older competitors mentioned in Chapter 12. Age only changes who you are up against; the talent and aggressiveness remains true. After all, their coaches are, as you probably assumed, also competitors (or past-successful competitors) in the Open events. And just like them, as a junior lifeguard, you have the opportunity to compete on the local, regional, and national levels. See Figure 13-4.

Fewer events are offered by age group than compared to the Open level. For example, the surf boat and taplin relays are not included in U19 events. A complete list of the age group events are listed here (pulled from the USLA National Junior Lifeguard Championships website):

>> Beach Flags

>> Distance Run

>> Surf Swim

>> Ironguard

- Board Race
- Swim-Run
- Surf Ski
- Beach Sprint
- Ironperson
- Rescue Race
- Board Rescue
- Swim Relay

Photograph by Andy Eng

FIGURE 13-4: Junior lifeguard instructor Cary Epstein reviews the rules for the rescue race at the starting line.

TIP

For the most updated information about these events, visit the website at www.usla.org/page/NATIONALRULES.

In most cases, programs have tryouts. There may only be a certain number of spots available in each age group, and the competition just to get on the team is pretty intense. Typically, only the best make it. If you don't make it one year, train harder and come back the following season.

REMEMBER

If you make the cut, you need to be able to keep up with the rigorous workouts and practices so that you can show up on the day of competition and rank among the best. Competition teams take only the best of the best, so train your tail off independently, get your hands on the equipment when you can, and earn your stripes at the tryout!

Chapter **14**

Joining a Professional Organization

There are many benefits to joining professional groups and organizations in every line of work. With that said, there is no shortage of groups and organizations on the local, regional, national and worldwide stage that you may be eligible to join. This chapter looks at some of the most common professional lifeguarding organizations and shares some of the benefits of membership.

Enjoying the Benefits of Professional Organizations

So, what are the benefits of joining a professional organization and how do you qualify? In most cases, there is a set of qualifications that you need to meet in order to be eligible, and each is a bit different. Most professionals associate themselves with these types of organizations because of the advantages they carry. While the benefits of membership might not be anything too lavish, for starters it is nice to receive discounted car rentals, hotels, and professional related merchandise.

More importantly, however, it is your membership card and professional affiliation with the organization that usually holds the prestige. While every fee structure is different, membership fees and fundraising keep these entities in business. Money collected from their members and other events help fund professional development, conferences, and other career initiatives.

Seeing What Professional Organizations Are Available

Many lifeguards join professional organizations for the added benefit of being part of an entity larger than just their local patrol. It allows them to network with other members and spread their influence over a bigger area in the world of lifeguarding.

TIP

Whichever professional lifeguarding organization you join, be sure to read up on their mission, values, and interests and make sure they line up with your own.

The United States Lifesaving Association

The United States Lifesaving Association (see Figure 14-1) is a nonprofit, professional organization comprised of lifeguards from beach and open water facilities. Commonly known as the USLA, their efforts primarily focus on minimizing the incidence of death and injury through public education, national lifeguard standards, training programs, promotion of high levels of lifeguard readiness, and other means.

The USLA is composed of over 100 chapters around the country, which are organized further into nine regions: New England, Mid-Atlantic, Great Lakes, Northwest, South Atlantic, Gulf Coast, Southeast, Southwest, and the Pacific Islands.

The most common type of members in the USLA are known as *professional members*. To qualify as a professional member, you must meet these requirements:

Credit: United States Lifesaving Association

FIGURE 14-1: The official logo of the United States Lifesaving Association.

» Be a direct, active, seasonal, or retired individual, including a chief, director, or equivalent, who has worked in the capacity of a lifeguard of an ocean, bay, lake, river, or open water lifesaving or rescue service.

» Worked a minimum of eight hours annually for a respective service, or be retired from the service, having worked in the service 15 years or more and maintained membership in good standing in the USLA.

» Be a member of a local chapter.

» Pay annual dues to the chapter, region, and national organization, as prescribed by the board of directors of each.

There are additional membership categories for alumni, those who just want to support the organization, and even junior lifeguards. Find the category that best describes you and consider supporting the largest and most professional organization of open water lifeguards in the United States!

Consider this list of benefits gained from being a part of the United States Lifesaving Association, which are pulled from their membership page at www.usla.org/page/BENEFITS:

» Membership in America's professional beach lifeguard and open water rescuers association

» Discounts on sunglasses, swim fins, and many other items

- >> The BenefitHub Marketplace provides negotiated discounts on many brands

- >> USLA membership card

- >> *American Lifeguard Magazine* subscription (for members with United States addresses)

- >> Lifeguard educational conferences

- >> Local, regional, and national board of directors meetings

- >> Public education materials

- >> USLA decal and other items

- >> The latest information on open water rescue

- >> Networking with other open water rescuers

- >> And much, much, more

Special benefits for professional, junior, and alumnus members include:

- >> Participation in USLA-sanctioned competitions

- >> Regional, national, and international lifeguard exchanges

- >> Affiliation with junior lifeguard programs and competitions

- >> And much, much, more

The International Life Saving Federation

The International Life Saving Federation (ILS) is made up of the various lifesaving organizations that exist around the world (in fact, the other groups mentioned in this section are all part of the ILS). Each entity within the International Life Saving Federation is known as a *member federation*. Together, the hundred or so member federations work to ensure the highest level of safety in, on, and around the water.

The different member federations accomplish these goals by transmitting helpful information from one group to another. Conversations about drowning prevention practices and efficient ways of making rescues are exchanged across the different groups and nations. Efforts are also made to create even more lifesaving organizations to ensure the highest level of safety in every corner of the world.

The International Life Saving Federation (see Figure 14-2) also helps facilitate and organize lifesaving sport on the worldwide stage, where competitors from all around the globe congregate to display their skills in the water.

Credit: International Life Saving Federation

FIGURE 14-2: The official logo of the International Life Saving Federation.

Similar to the USLA, the International Life Saving Federation offers various options for membership, ranging from two-year memberships to lifetime status. Benefits include your name listed in the Life Saving Hall of Fame, a discount in the shop, a subscription to the *ILS Newsletter*, invitations to ILS official dinners, and many other promotional items.

The American Red Cross

Hands down the most notable organization in this realm, and one that you are probably familiar with, is the American Red Cross. This organization differs slightly in mission from the USLA and ILS, which are professional lifeguard organizations.

The American Red Cross (see Figure 14-3) serves various functions, including being one of the leading organizations that trains and supports lifeguards around the United States, in addition to officers, firefighters, clinicians, emergency medical technicians, paramedics, and babysitters. There are many, many ways you can support the American Red Cross and its mission. However, unlike the USLA and ILS, there is no individual membership.

FIGURE 14-3: The official logo of the American Red Cross.

This mission of the American Red Cross is to minimize all types of human injury when emergency situations arise by training volunteer caregivers and with the generosity of donors. While there are many divisions in the American Red Cross, the one that the majority of lifeguards are most familiar with is the lifesaving training and certification they provide. Other avenues that the American Red Cross encompasses include blood donation services, disaster/emergency response, and training and certifications in a variety of other domains.

REMEMBER

CPR/AED and first aid training have been conducted by the Red Cross for decades. This is the most common type of training for lifeguards. While there are other organizations that offer these courses, the American Red Cross has proven to be the leading provider in the aquatic industry. In addition, the basic lifeguard training course offered by American Red Cross is taken by most starting lifeguards. Although this class may not be required, depending on where you plan on working, it is a solid start to understanding the professional responsibilities of a lifeguard.

The American Red Cross is recognized as one of the member federations in the International Life Saving Federation.

The Young Men's Christian Association (YMCA) of the USA

Although many Americans have heard of the YMCA, most do not realize the historical significance it played in teaching swimming and promoting water safety over the years. Also a member federation of the ILS, the YMCA has been an undisputed leader in water safety in the United States for well over a century. See Figure 14-4.

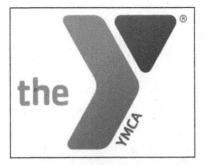

FIGURE 14-4: The official logo of the YMCA.

Sometimes nicknamed "America's swim instructor," the YMCA emphasizes that the aquatic environment is a place for everyone. It should be fun and recreational, not frightening, when you are aware of your surroundings and familiar with most water safety guidelines.

REMEMBER

Chapter 3 mentions how the YMCA constructed the first public pools in the United States.

Since the organization's conception, the YMCA continues to teach millions of children around the United States invaluable skills in water safety and swimming. It has grown to be a massive professional organization, reaching communities wherever pools and recreational bodies of water exist. Their mission persists to this day, which is to bridge the gap between swim lessons and water safety education.

5

The Part of Tens

Learn the lifeguards' top ten commandments that we live by to ensure a safe environment for all who visit.

Mark these down as the things you don't want to forget before you head out for a busy day lifeguarding.

Be aware of the tell-tale signs that a struggling swimmer is in need of rescue and it is your time to get wet!

Learn our top reasons why you should get certified and jump in on the best job you will ever have in your life.

Benefit from the words of wisdom of other professional lifeguards.

Chapter **15**

The Lifeguard's Ten Commandments

The Lifeguard's Ten Commandments truly are biblical! This is hands down one of the more important chapters in this book in terms of how you should carry yourself, perform your duties, and ultimately keep your facility safe. No one ever plans to end their day by visiting the emergency room or planning a funeral, but it unfortunately does happen, and you don't want to be the reason these mistakes occurred. By following these lifeguard laws, you ensure that you and your lifeguard crew perform as expected.

Watch the Water

Water levels in pools and beaches can go from ankle deep to overhead in a matter of steps. A particularly strong undertow can sweep a person off their feet and take them to a deeper part of the water in just seconds. A swimmer can suffer a medical emergency and slip under the water.

WARNING

Regarding children, their parents can turn around for a fleeting moment, and in that second a wave with a mind of its own can sweep their child out to sea. Never assume that parents are keeping a close eye on their kids. While children love to venture out past their comfort zone, this is where trouble waits. Warn parents of any present dangers and be aware of those who pay less attention than maybe they should, so you're ready to spring into action if need be.

Watching the water is more than just being cognizant the moment an emergency occurs. It also includes knowing how your body of water is acting that particular morning or afternoon. It means knowing the characteristics of the people entering your water and making judgments or assumptions about swimmers who might need help in the near future. It means *always* watching the water (see Figure 15-1).

Cary Epstein (Author)

FIGURE 15-1: On-duty lifeguard lieutenant overlooks the entire beachfront on a busy afternoon.

TIP

The best approach? Identify all high-risk swimmers and remain alert to their presence.

Well-seasoned lifeguards know it is good practice to be facing the water at all times, even when you are not sitting up in the stand or tower. Even when you are digging flags into the ground, shoveling sand, setting up equipment, or sitting on dry land, you should make it a habit to constantly face the water.

Educate the Public

While preventative actions are a key component to keeping all who visit your beach, park, or pool safe, we know that sometimes accidents cannot be avoided.

The most effective way that you can prevent emergencies from occurring is by educating the public of present dangers in and around your facility. The best practice is to not just enforce the rules, but explain them as well.

For example, rather than just telling someone that they can't swim in a certain area, you should explain the reasons why: There is no lifeguard present. A rip current continues to open up there. And the right place where you can swim is just over there, between the green flags.

WARNING

When on duty in a lifeguard chair, stand, or tower, you shouldn't be having full-on conversations with patrons. Your main focus should be doing your job and concentrating on the water. Long discussions with patrons can draw your attention away from what's important and put your area of responsibility at risk. A simple, friendly response should do.

If necessary, don't be afraid to explain to someone that they could be distracting you from your job responsibilities. If their question requires a more complex answer, it might be best to point them to the direction of another lifeguard who is not on duty for more information.

Protect Yourself from the Sun

One of many reasons people flock to the beach or pool is not just for swimming, but for sunbathing! While you could argue that everyone looks better with a tan, too much exposure to the sun can cause real deal, very serious health consequences. Take it in small doses and most importantly, protect yourself!

Would you jump out of an airplane without a parachute? Probably not, right? So why lay in the sun without sunscreen? You can still tan through sunblock; you are just blocking out the dangerous ultraviolet rays that increase the likelihood for getting skin cancer.

TIP

Apply water-resistant sunscreen with an SPF of 15 or greater at least every two hours and after going into the water; make sure you cover all your exposed skin. Be smart . . . find the right potion and grab your lotion!

In addition to getting burned, the sun is the culprit for dangerous heat stroke and heat exhaustion. Be sure to take some shade when temperatures exceed 90, even 80 degrees! Lifeguards must often tend to these medical emergencies before higher-trained professionals are called in. These heat-related emergencies are no joking matter.

TIP

Wear a lifeguard straw hat or visor, or sit under an umbrella. The sun can be draining, and the public and its swimmers need your complete attention. Nobody is stronger than the sun.

Enforce the Rules

Remember who is in charge — don't be afraid to enforce all rules, even to someone your elder. You may find it to be awkward as a 17-year-old to tell a father that they cannot throw their child, but that is your job.

Be respectful and kindly remind patrons about the rules. These regulations are designed for the safety and well-being of all.

Here are some common rules at public swimming facilities:

>> NO running

>> NO lifejackets or flotation devices in the water

>> NO glass bottles on the pool deck

>> NO ball playing in the water

>> NO roughhousing (chicken fights, dunking, and so on)

>> NO loud music (or music at all)

>> NO diving

>> NO sitting directly in front of the lifeguard stand or tower

>> NO swimming in unprotected waters

>> NO surfing

>> NO fishing

>> NO swimming while fully clothed

Know Your Facility

As the lifeguard, you are the expert at your facility. But even life-guards must be constantly cognizant of their surroundings. There is much you need to know before climbing onto your stand or perching up in your lifeguard tower.

Here are some of the most important things you should know to ensure a fun and safe day for the swimmers at your facility and an efficient work environment for your lifeguard crew:

>> The current water conditions

>> The water depth

>> The weather (current and future)

>> The rules of the beach, pool, or lake

>> Your Emergency Action Plan (EAP)

>> Who and where your backup is

>> Where the designated swimming area is

>> Your communication and whistle signals

>> Where to find and how to use the equipment

>> How to deal with lost children/family members

Practice Makes Perfect

The lessons you learn in lifeguard class and during rookie training teach you crucial skills you will carry into the rest of your life-guarding career. And — newsflash — you will continue to learn and grow day by day, season after season with every experience.

You will adopt skills in first aid, mock water rescues, and handling equipment. We've all heard the saying time and time again, that "practice makes perfect." And the only way you improve from Day 1 is through time and diligent practice.

Take turns with your crew, going over mock rescues. Cycle through the different roles and try being the victim every now and then. Run through a few head, neck, and back injury scenarios so that when the real time comes, your crew will be prepared.

Practice using the various rescue equipment: tubes, cans, first-aid tools, BVM, AED, boards, boats, and other watercraft. Know when and how to use these specialized pieces of equipment, as no two rescues will ever be the same. Figure 15-2 shows three hand-carved rescue buoys.

FIGURE 15-2: Three hand-carved, Styrofoam rescue buoys are set up in the sand, ready for action.

And finally, train! Get in the water. Swim laps. Run. Row the boat. The list goes on.

When in Doubt, Go!

There is no reason you should ever get in trouble for attempting to rescue a person you thought needed help. The worst that can happen is you jump off the stand, swim to the victim, but by the time you've made it to them, they have made it to shallow water. No — rather, the worst thing that can happen is that you choose not to go on the rescue, hesitate for too long, and the swimmer begins to drown.

We touch on the dangers of hesitating many times throughout this book. If you ever find yourself in the moment simply asking the question, "Should I go?" the answer is YES! and you should've already been in the water!

When Thunder Roars, Stay Indoors

We bet if you ask most beachgoers what scares them more — getting eaten by a shark or getting struck by lightning — most would choose the shark! But did you know that swimmers are so much more likely to be struck or killed by lightning than they are to even be attacked by a shark!? Poor sharks have a bad reputation.

REMEMBER

With thunder comes lightning, even if you can't see it. Storms along the water tend to roll in quickly and can pack a very powerful punch. If you hear thunder, you should assume there is lightning. It is best to blow the whistle and bring all the swimmers out of the water.

Have everyone seek shelter immediately and wait for the storm to pass. Lightning is known to strike in open fields, water, and the tallest objects it can find, which in some cases could be you or your swimmers!

TECHNICAL STUFF

According to the National Weather Service, lightning strikes the United States about 25 million times a year. Although most lightning occurs in the summer, people can be struck at any time of year. Lightning kills about 20 people in the United States annually, and hundreds more are severely injured.

Be Professional

When you are in pay status, you are expected to look and act like a professional. That means wearing your uniform and carrying yourself in a way that your employer expects to be represented. Your uniform should be clean and free of any holes or stains. Tattered uniforms do not convey a sense of professionalism. Being a professional rescuer means acting and dressing like one. Be proud of the uniform you put on at the start of every day and be sure to consistently be the best version of yourself.

Acting childish while on the job gives off the impression that you do not know what you are doing and you are not taking your job seriously. A large part of your job is enforcing rules, so it is important that the public sees you as a person of authority; otherwise, your words are useless.

Talk to Your Senior Guards and Heed Their Advice

There is something to appreciate about someone who has been working the same job for 20, 30, or 40+ years. That real-life experience is irreplaceable. Talking to your senior lifeguards provides you with insight that only someone with decades of experience can share. Don't pass up these moments, as they have learned some of the most valuable lessons from those before them.

In a career like lifeguarding — where the essential skills like reading body language and the ocean's mechanisms cannot be easily explained in a textbook — wisdom from older and experienced guards is priceless. Only they can put into words and show you firsthand from the lifeguard stand what to look out for. It is testament that being out on the field is truly the best type of classroom, and these older guards are the best types of teachers.

Chapter 16

Ten Tools You Need in Your Backpack

There are a handful of things that every lifeguard needs in their bag before heading out to work. Whether you work at a pool, waterpark, or open water facility, we think you will find all these items relevant and crucial. Some of them are important for getting the job done, and others are just convenient to have.

There might be other things you personally need to bring, but we have no doubt you will be happy to have tossed these ten items in your bag before walking out the front door.

A Pair of Sunglasses

We have mentioned that lifeguards might as well just be known as professional people watchers. At all times of the day, you should have a clear sight of the swimmers in your area. Not only should you be able to see them, but it is important that you can make out their body movements and at least a little bit of their facial expressions.

A good pair of sunglasses on a sunny day works miracles, prefer-ably a pair of polarized sunglasses (see Figure 16-1). Try on a pair of polarized lenses before throwing on a pair of non-polarized lenses. The difference between the two is truly night and day.

Credit: Hobie Eyewear

FIGURE 16-1: A lifeguard sports his Mojo Float polarized sunglasses from Hobie Eyewear, the official sunglass partner of the USLA.

WARNING

Not having a pair of sunglasses will lead to a very bad day. The brutal glare of the sun off the water has the power to completely obstruct your vision and cause serious eye damage.

In fact, you really should have *two* pairs of sunglasses. Sometimes you leave your main or favorite pair of sunglasses at home or in the car or something, so it is good to have an extra one on deck. We always do! Or maybe you can hold onto an extra one in case one of your crew members happened to have forgotten a pair. Leave it in the eyeglass case somewhere in your bag to protect those frames and lenses too. You'll be surprised what kind of things can crush your delicate eyeglasses — it's happened to the best of us.

TIP

Best advice for not losing or breaking your sunglasses? They are either on your face or in the case!

You don't need to splurge on the most expensive or snazzy pair of sunglasses. A simple polarized pair will do. Though we will say, we are firm believers of "look good, feel good," especially at work.

The bottom line is: If you can't see your swimmers, you cannot do your job.

A Bottle of Sunscreen

You saw this one coming! Sunscreen is an absolute must. Neglecting to put on sunscreen only causes harm. Unprotected skin leads to sunburn. Constant exposure to the sun's harmful rays can escalate to skin cancer. If you are going to be outside and exposed to the elements, there is no reason to not wear sunscreen.

TIP

Carry a sufficient amount of at least 30 SPF sunscreen, with enough to reapply every two hours throughout the day. If you jump in the water and dry off, it is recommended that you reapply then too, even if it does say water resistant! Get a bottle that is labeled broad spectrum.

Cover all parts of your body with sunscreen. Don't forget the tops of your feet and the tips of your ears! Perhaps get yourself a tube of zinc for your nose and cheekbones, the most elevated parts of your face and very prone to getting burned first. Then you can really pull off the lifeguard look! Sunscreen lip balms exist for protecting your lips from burns and blisters. Let's also not forget the top of your head.

Wearing a hat is great, but those with thinner hair can also get spray sunscreen designed for your scalp.

A Whistle

TIP

What was it that we said earlier about this particular piece of equipment? Oh yes — a lifeguard without a whistle is like a firefighter without a hose! Now, we understand that this may be a little exaggerated. And we are aware that some lifeguards may not even use whistles.

For those lifeguards who blow whistles to get swimmers' attention or signal to your lifeguard crew that something is wrong, you will definitely find yourself in a pickle if you are whistle-less in an emergency situation. Not only is this dangerous for the swimmer whose attention you need to grab, but it also puts the rest of the swimmers in the area in danger and possibly even yourself if you're without backup. Simply put, you do not want to be caught in this situation.

Like the other items on this list, it doesn't hurt to have one or two extra whistles in your bag. These small items don't take up much room to begin with. Because of their smaller size, they can get misplaced pretty easily. And it is not entirely out of the question for them to fall off and slip from your arm or neck (however way you are wearing it) while jumping in for a rescue.

Our favorite whistle? The classic Fox 40, shown in Figure 16-2.

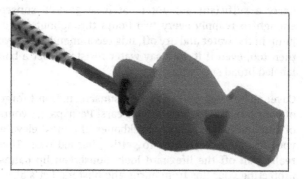

Cary Epstein (Author)

FIGURE 16-2: Don't be fooled by the small size of this whistle: The Fox 40 can be heard clearly from hundreds of yards away.

Your Bathing Suit

Now this goes without saying! If you aren't going into work already changed, you better have your lifeguard uniform packed in your bag. There is no way you are going in the water to guard lives without a bathing suit! Whether you wear swim trunks or a bathing suit, make sure it's ready to go when your shift starts.

This item in your bag is more than just what you need to go into the water. It's your uniform. It helps the rest of the people on the pool deck or at your park, swimmers, and your fellow lifeguards alike identify you as a lifeguard and employee at your facility. Being identifiable fosters a safer environment where people know who they can reach out to and ask for help if any sort of situation arises.

In most cases, the municipality that you are working for will provide you with a lifeguard bathing suit. If you prefer to wear a different style (jammer vs. speedo or one-piece vs. two-piece), make sure that it is approved by your head lifeguard or direct supervisor.

TIP

It doesn't hurt to pack an extra bathing suit (or two!) as well. Changing into a dry suit after going in the water for a rescue can be lifesaving. Although you might not always have the opportunity to change into something dry afterward, it never hurts to have an extra suit!

A Trusty Water Bottle

You've got to stay hydrated when you're out in the sun for hours at a time. Sweating is great and all, as it cools you down. But you have to replenish those fluids after sweating them out.

Essentially, you should be sipping water throughout the day. Make an investment in a good bottle that stays cold all day. Yeti, Hydro Flask, RTIC, Swell, and many more brands make phenomenal insulators.

TIP

Take a good look at the color of your urine. It should run almost clear, with a slight yellow tinge. If you are peeing golden, you've got to drink more water, my friend.

Dehydration causes you to lose focus and prevents you from scanning the water in the most efficient manner. The last thing you want to do is pass out from heat exhaustion while you're sitting in the lifeguard chair trying to ensure other people's safety. You can't take care of others if you don't take care of yourself.

A CPR Pocket Face Mask

At the end of all CPR classes, recertification procedures, and refresher courses, you get to keep the pocket face mask that you used during the hands-on drills (see Figure 16-3). The set should come with an adult mask and pediatric-sized mask. There is also a convenient keychain version that fits anywhere. It's always best to be prepared no matter what!

FIGURE 16-3: This pocket face mask compacts easily into its case and takes up minimal room in your bag.

So just throw the pocket face mask in your bag and take it to you work every day. You won't even notice that it is in there taking up nearly no room! Another option is to clip it onto a zipper or hook on your bag. You can say otherwise, but we personally think it's a pretty sweet fashion statement.

These pocket masks are super important because they work as breathing barriers to prevent disease transmission when giving rescue breaths or ventilations. Who wants to give mouth to mouth to a stranger? Not me — who knows what types of diseases they may carry.

A Towel

Don't be that lifeguard who constantly has to ask their coworkers to borrow their towel. You don't want to be that person!

But seriously, it will never do you harm to pack a towel, no matter how often you wind up going on rescues. There will certainly be days when you might not even step in the water. But learning from personal experience, the days that we have forgotten to pack a towel are always the days we wind up needing one. Yes, we have asked a crew member to borrow their used towel. We grow close to one another in this job.

New microfiber towels are compact and dry fast! These are great for lifeguards who are constantly going in and out of the water.

A Warm Sweatshirt

Yes, we made the whole spiel earlier about packing a water bottle because of the heat and dehydration. And it's true! The sun is no joke. But there will certainly be days on the opposite side of the spectrum. Personally, we like to have a sweatshirt, raincoat, or some sort of outerwear in our backpacks at all times to shield ourselves from the elements if they do turn south and the temperatures drop.

For many instances of unfavorable weather, pools, beaches, waterparks, and swimming facilities will remain open. Try your best to remain comfortable and adjust accordingly as the weather changes. What you don't want to happen is you wake up the following morning with a cold, forcing you to call out of work.

A Hat

A light hat that keeps the sun out of your face is surely something you'll want in your backpack. Some of you might be telling yourself that you're not a hat person. We hate to break it to you, but sometimes we have to be hat people. If the sun is beating on your face, you'll be happy that you threw that hat into your bag or hooked it onto the handle of your backpack. Baseball caps, trucker hats, bucket hats, lifeguard hats, visors; the list goes on. Figure 16-4 shows the traditional lifeguard hat flaunted by life-savers around the world.

Cary Epstein (Author)

FIGURE 16-4: The lifeguard shields herself from the sun's rays beneath her straw hat while reading the day's schedule.

A Tasty Lunch or Snack

One of our colleagues and best friends John never leaves his house for work without a lunchbox packed with snacks. And it is never just one or two; his backpack looks like your buddy's kitchen cabinet whose mom always kept the shelves stocked with the best stuff: goldfish, granola bars, pretzels, bagels, and so on.

Lifeguarding can get tiring! Whether you are running rescues and can't seem to stay dry or you're mentally drained from watching the water, a packed lunch or snack can make a world of a difference and turn your day back around, taking you back to 100 percent again.

Recharge and refuel with a PB&J made at home or stop at the deli on the way to work for a cold cut sandwich. During an eight-hour shift, your stomach will certainly start to growl, and your fellow lifeguards may not be as generous as our John, who always (but reluctantly) shared his snacks with us.

Chapter **17**

Ten Reasons to Dive into Lifeguarding

For many chapters, we have discussed the ins-and-outs of this career and what lifeguarding by the beach, at the pool, and on the ocean entails. There is no beating around the bush that we love what we do during the few months in the year we spend as lifeguards.

Lifeguarding is a one-of-a-kind career that anyone can pick up if they truly want to, and we encourage you to do so! Here we compiled our top ten reasons that you will have no regrets diving into a career in lifeguarding.

You'll Learn How to Save Lives

Just look at the title of the profession: lifeguard. This job will help you adopt water rescue capabilities and develop lifesaving skills.

Lifeguarding teaches you simple skills in first aid and how to respond to emergencies, big and small. You will learn how to react appropriately to victims with a small cut, someone choking, or an unresponsive person not breathing on the ground.

You'll always know how to save someone's life, even after your lifeguarding days are long behind you. Once a lifeguard, always a lifeguard! In the professional lifeguard community, we use this phrase "lifeguards for life." Whether you are a career guard, seasonal guard, or only worked a few years . . . you will remember many of the skills you learned even decades later.

You Will Build Lifelong Skills and Character Traits

Lifeguarding teaches you so much more than water rescue. For starters, a great lifeguard is a leader and works remarkably well with others. They have very strong communication skills and are confident in all aspects of their job. These lifelong character traits will often times translate into skills off the beach or pool deck. Some of the other character traits you take with you apply for the entirety of your life, such as confidence, responsibility, and self-esteem.

TIP

Turn back to Chapter 1, where we talk about the various characteristics that lifeguarding inadvertently develops in its rescuers.

Each of these skills will ultimately shape your future. You will be surprised how you can use them in every part of your life, even outside of the aquatic environment.

You Will Serve the Public

We argue that there are only a handful of other jobs as rewarding as lifeguarding. It might take a few rescues for it to click, but you really are saving lives in this job. Lifeguarding gives you the ability to give back to your community and serve the public.

Not to mention that in this career, people around you are watching you do your job will look up to you . . . literally!

You'll Make Lifelong Friendships

The friendships you make on the job often last forever. It is not uncommon to bond with your coworkers very quickly. You will laugh with these people, cry with these people, and share a few libations with them (at the legal age, of course!). They will be there to back you up when you need it the most, in the most critical of situations.

The lifeguard community is strong, and your fellow lifeguards will end up being some of your closest friends. Don't be surprised if you end up being a bridesmaid or even a best man at a lifeguard wedding. We have even seen and been to countless lifeguard weddings, where both the bride and the groom "started out as friends" and then ... well you know what happens next! ☺

It's the Fountain of Youth

There aren't too many jobs in the world that keep you young. As a matter of fact, most people say that their jobs bring on the gray hairs early and a few extra pounds from sitting at their desks and in their offices all day.

As a lifeguard, you have endless opportunities to stay in shape, both on and off the job. Not to mention, if you work outdoors, there is undeniably something about being in the elements (sun, wind, water, and sand) that keeps you grounded with nature. This is all healthy for your mind, body, and soul, which keeps you feeling and looking youthful.

As you age, you will find yourself trying to keep up with the younger lifeguards, which will only make you challenge yourself more. Some might argue that too much exposure to the sun causes wrinkles and spurs the aging process; we have found that most professional lifeguards look younger and find themselves in the top percentage of their age group when it comes to overall health and physical fitness (as long as sunscreen is religiously applied, of course).

You Get Paid To Do This

Sometimes we forget that this is a real, paying job! In between the day-to-day routine and those tasks we refer to as maintenance work, we truly do find time to have fun and take advantage of the playground around us.

Think about any other job where, in one day, you could potentially:

>> Work out during daily or weekly training sessions

>> Row one of the surf boats or squeeze some laps in the lap lane or in the ocean during your break and between sits

>> Catch a few waves on your boogie board, surfboard, or just plain enjoy body surfing

>> Pick up a book to kill some time on a rainy day during your break (but *never* while on duty)

If you're clocked in on a work day, you are getting paid to do these things.

It's a Never-Ending Challenge

While some days on the job might seem similar to the last, when it really comes down to it, no two days are the same. Perhaps a few rainy days in a row may seem like a drag, but once in a while, you will get that stretch of days where the ocean is not letting up or the pool is packed with swimmers during a heatwave, and from the second you sign in until you initial out for the day, you are charging the water and running rescues.

These are the most challenging days, and lifeguards are always up for the task. There is no monotonous end to lifeguarding; it never turns into what we sometimes might call the "same old."

Lifeguarding is a constant challenge. Whether it be day to day on the job or in lifeguard competitions, lifeguarding presents physical, mental, and emotional challenges. It's okay to get outside of your comfort zone!

It's an Adrenaline Rush

If you like a good adrenaline rush, you will love lifeguarding! While the job certainly has its relaxing moments up in the stand or tower, in a matter of seconds that all can completely change. The adrenaline that you experience when going out for a rescue or performing lifesaving skills such as CPR or rescue breathing will have your blood circulating at levels equivalent to your favorite rollercoaster!

While this shouldn't be the only reason you become a lifeguard, it's a pretty intense feeling that you eventually get better at controlling with time and experience.

You'll Have a Different Type of Office

What we often say is "A bad day at the beach is better than the best day in the office!" While this concept can be easily applied to any beach, pool, lake, waterpark, or aquatic setting, it should be no surprise that you'll have a different type of office as a lifeguard that we promise you will love.

Despite the non-traditional setting, some guidelines in all professional workplaces are still to be followed, including, but not limited to, sexual harassment, discrimination, and workplace violence. In this job, you won't be required to show up in suits, or at least the uncomfortable kind! A bathing suit, on the other hand, will do the job just fine.

You Don't Have to Quit Your Day Job

One of the best perks about this job, which we cover in depth in Chapter 7, is the flexibility that most lifeguard municipalities offer to its employees in terms of work. Many lifeguard agencies will not force you to quit your day job, unless of course you want lifeguarding to become your day job.

The fact that lifeguarding presents the opportunity to work full-time year-round, full-time seasonally, or part-time entirely is a game changer for many. For careers with both flexible and standard schedules, those who insist that lifeguarding remain a part of their lives (like us!) make it work with their trade with ease.

Chapter **18**
Ten Reasons To GO (On the Rescue!)

Once you're a full-fledged lifeguard, you will find many of your non-lifeguard friends asking you, "Have you ever made a rescue?" And because you have been asked this question a million times over, you will probably exclaim "YES!" in response.

When you start as a lifeguard, you will likely be pretty tense up on that chair for the first few weeks. In every situation, it could be your call whether you take off from the stand and go for the rescue. Sometimes it's obvious that someone needs help, and other times it's not.

This chapter covers some of the most common reasons that you should take your dry clothes off if you're wearing them. *It's going down!*

You Hear "HELP!"

It doesn't get much clearer than this. "HELP!" is the most common word used by people in distress. Unfortunately, it will not always be as obvious as this. Most people do not have the ability to shout for help when they are actively drowning. They are using all of their effort to stay above water and conserving their air as they brace for the unthinkable: slipping underwater.

WARNING

Even when someone does yell, many factors can contribute to you not hearing them. Windy conditions and large surf might make it impossible to hear someone yelling for help, as can the overall din at a busy pool or waterpark. This is why it's important to keep your eyes on your swimmers at all times.

If someone is yelling for help, or even if you just think they are yelling for help, do not hesitate! Get off the stand and jump in the water! #DummiesOnTheRescue

Climb the Ladder

Ah, yes — climbing the ladder. When we talk about climbing the ladder here, we are certainly not talking about a painter's ladder used to get to hard-to-reach places. Nor are we talking about the ladder that we you use to get in and out of the pool. We are talking about the invisible ladder. The imaginary ladder that a drowning swimmer appears to be climbing when they are in distress!

Picture this: They are grabbing for the invisible rungs above the water in an attempt to hoist themselves up and out of the water. You might not be able to see their legs perfectly underwater, but it is almost like they are doing a weird scissor kick and trying to step up out of the water (see Figure 18-1). Behold, in your mind you are picturing a very poor and inefficient swimmer. These efforts are futile. This is not how you tread water!

If it looks like someone is climbing an invisible ladder, and despite their efforts, they are beginning to slip beneath the surface of the water, they are probably drowning and need your help. Blow your whistle, sound the alarm, and activate the EAP! Whatever it is that your facility does, let the rest of your lifeguard crew know you are making a rescue and GO!

FIGURE 18-1: The drowning victim is climbing the invisible ladder to the surface: One hand holds an imaginary ladder rung while the other reaches up for the next.

This motion can happen rather quickly. Perhaps your distressed swimmer accidentally finds themselves in deep water, which could sometimes be only feet from the shallow end. Maybe their parent turns around for a split second and misses them wander into treacherous territory, and they begin to slip underwater. Do not hesitate; when this catches your eye, make the rescue! #DummiesOnTheRescue

Bad Hair Day

Who knew having a bad hair day could be a sign that you might be in trouble! Just kidding, no one cares about your hair when you're at the pool or beach. But in all seriousness, people with long hair and who are struggling often have their hair all tangled up and draped across their faces.

Their hands and arms are primarily occupied with keeping them afloat — maybe they are climbing the invisible ladder. Or maybe they are just poor swimmers and can't efficiently tread water. As they continue their efforts to stay above the water, they cannot push their hair from across their face and over their eyes.

TIP

One of the best ways to assess any drowning situation is by looking at a person's face. Their facial expression and the undeniable look of terror is a good way to tell if someone is in trouble. In circumstances where their hair is covering their faces, sometimes the only thing you can make out is the whites of their eyes bulging as big as saucepans. This indication of fear and their inability to brush the hair out from their eyes means it's your turn and time to save a life. #DummiesOnTheRescue

Mom Tells You To Go

There are some people you don't fight with; simply put, you'll never win. One of these people are moms — you shouldn't fight with your own mother, and you shouldn't fight with other moms. You will not win! As the old saying goes, "Don't mess with mama bear." A mother will defend their cubs until the very end, and sometimes their mechanism of action will be to yell at the lifeguard to do their job and help their child.

If they tell you to go, don't question it. You might know what a drowning victim looks like better than they do, but they know their own children better than anyone. When a mom says to go, you go! Sometimes it's not worth the argument. #DummiesOnTheRescue

Face Down and Motionless

Now, this one goes without saying. There are many reasons that someone might lay face down or motionless in the water. The biggest question you need to ask yourself is whether or not they are just playing around. Are they seeing how long they can hold their breath? Or is that the furthest thing from what they are doing? Be sure to watch them and their friends' body language closely. Is it different from how they have been acting all day? This is why it is important to assess every patron swimming while you are scanning the water.

It doesn't take much for someone to suffer a medical emergency like a stroke, heart attack, or seizure. In a matter of seconds, a recreational bather or lap swimmer can suddenly stop in their tracks, and before you know it, your victim is face down, motionless in the water. Once you recognize this, act immediately. If you are not sure if they need assistance, you are better off going in any way! #DummiesOnTheRescue

Concussed!

Head injuries are some of the most common types of injuries in the aquatic environment. If you suspect that someone slammed their noggin against the side of the pool, hit the diving board on the way down, or even cracked skulls with another swimmer's head, there is a very good chance you might be getting wet. Do not hesitate to activate your facility's Emergency Action Plan (EAP). Blow the appropriate number of whistles and make the rest of your crew aware that there is a situation at hand. #DummiesOnTheRescue

REMEMBER

Your first instinct should be to assume a head, neck, or back injury. Take the appropriate measures to restrict spinal motion while the other lifeguards respond with the backboard.

Into the Deep End

All pools should have written depths on the deck that specify how deep the bottom is. More often than we like, however, swimmers fail to notice the depth marked there and will jump in without realizing it is far past their comfort zone.

One day, if you are working at a pool with a diving well, you will be assigned to the diving board chair and will find yourself thoroughly surprised the first time someone jumps off the board and begins to drown because they did not know that the depth reaches 12 feet deep. Believe it or not, this happens more times than we like to admit!

In these circumstances, you have to jump off the stand and scoop them up before they slip deeper underwater. Non-swimmers might make no effort to swim up toward the surface. For those that jump in by the edge of the pool without realizing how deep it is, they will grab for the wall if they can reach it and call out for help. A simple lifesaving assist is all that is needed to get them out of the deep end and back on dry land. #DummiesOnTheRescue

The Grip of the Rip

If it looks like your swimmer is not making any forward progress, resembling a runner on a treadmill or moving backward in the water while facing the shore, they are most likely caught in the grip of a rip. This is no joking matter as these types of ocean rescues can grow more serious rather quickly. Rip currents are one of the main causes of drowning victims because swimmers get caught in a rip current, grow tired, and then struggle to stay afloat before beginning to sink.

Don't assume that the swimmer will be able to pull themselves out of the rip current and swim back to shore. Pull the trigger and go! The worst thing that can happen is that you get there and they don't need your assistance. Big deal . . . you get paid to get wet! #DummiesOnTheRescue

TIP

For more about rip currents, how they form, and the best practices for escaping them, turn to Chapter 6 to learn about this biggest danger on the ocean.

Points for Assist

There is no "I" in team! Some of the most fundamental characteristics about lifeguarding comes down to teamwork and communication. A lifeguard on your crew going in for a rescue might benefit from or need your help. Rack up those assist points and go back that coworker up!

There are many ways you might assist your fellow lifeguards. Maybe you can grab a second buoy, rescue board, or even a rescue line. There are many cases where lifeguards cannot successfully execute a rescue by themselves. This could be a particularly heavy swimmer, a multi-victim rescue, a cardiac arrest, or head, neck, or back injury. In these cases, you can provide an extra hand, another buoy, an AED, or a backboard. Nothing beats the feeling of knowing that everyone on the lifeguard team played a role in the success of a rescue.

In non-rescue-related situations, a lifeguard on your crew might find themselves in a heated conversation with an unhappy patron. In these times, an extra lifeguard or two could help deescalate the situation. #DummiesOnTheRescue

A Gut Feeling

"Always trust your gut. Your brain can be fooled, your heart is an idiot, but your gut doesn't know how to lie." —Unknown

We are saving the best for last. It is important to remember that you will never get in trouble for going on a rescue, even when it turns out the person did not need your help. We understand that there is a lot of gray area when making a rescue. We might have just listed nine reasons to go on the rescue, but even then, you might find yourself hesitating. In this type of career, however, it is always better to be safe than sorry. A mistake in this field can result in the worst consequence: death. If you think that someone needs your help, just go! #DummiesOnTheRescue

REMEMBER

When in doubt, go out!

Chapter 19

Words of Wisdom from Ten Lifeguards Near and Far

I t's safe to say that if you've made it this far, you've probably spent a lot of time reading about how we feel about lifeguarding as a profession. We thought it was important for you to hear what other lifeguards from near and far have to say about it too.

"Being a North Shore lifeguard to me is a big responsibility. Gotta be up for the test 'cause it does get dangerous. The way I was raised is to always help out when you can and do what you can to help others.

The most rewarding thing is seeing people be able to go back to their families alive at the end of the day. Seeing them still here and being able to be with them still makes me love what I do even more."

Luke Shepardson

2023 Eddie Aikau Big Wave Invitational Champion

City and County of Honolulu Ocean Safety, Hawaii

Four Years Lifeguarding Experience

"Minute for minute, the professional ocean lifeguard prevents more loss of life than any other emergency services professional. Fast paced and highly demanding, this job will take you to your limit and beyond. The ultimate reward — that unmatched feeling of accomplishment — when you have snatched a life from the jaws of certain death."

Daren Jenner

International Surf Lifesaving Association, Phuket, Thailand

Nine Years Lifeguarding Experience

"Ocean life guarding or 'surf lifesaving' as it's known in Australia, is more than keeping the beaches safe or staying fit and strong; it's a community of like-minded people. The skills I have developed from training day in and day out in the ocean have not only empowered me with the capability to perform a rescue and save a life, they have given me the personal challenge and enjoyment from competing at an elite level in events that are based on rescue skills. I have travelled the world competing in ocean events, become a world champion, met some incredible people, and taught these skills to many so they can enjoy the ocean in the same way I do."

Harriet Brown

BMD Northcliffe Surf Life Saving Club, Queensland, Australia

World Surf Ironwoman Champion, 2x Nutri-Grain Surf Ironwoman Series Champion, 3x Molokai to Oahu Paddleboard Champion & Record Holder

17 Years Lifesaving Experience

"Ocean rescue lifeguarding is more than being a guard on a stand. Dedication, hard work, and accountability. That is what it takes. 'When in doubt, go out.' I learned that my rookie year. It has not only taught me to be a better waterman but to never be afraid to go for it. A true waterman is a skill that is honed through time and not easily given. You must accept the failure in training to be better than the day before. These skills have not only taught me to push past limits but have lead me to take greater chances in life, which has put me toward a career path as a paramedic/firefighter in Florida."

Shannon Snell

Fort Lauderdale Fire Department Ocean Rescue Division, City of Deerfield Beach Ocean Rescue & Seasonal California State Parks

Nine Years Lifeguarding Experience and Junior Lifeguard since age eight

"Everything you learn on this job will carry through to other areas of your life. The training is hard because the job is hard. Train like you mean it. Work hard for yourself, your teammates, and the people you will help. Lifeguarding is a team sport. Always aim to enhance your own skills so that you can have confidence in your abilities and be a stronger member of your team. Don't underestimate the power of consistency. If you can look in the mirror and say with certainty that you gave your best efforts each day, you will go far and continue to improve. I am now a doctor doing my residency in general surgery. My years of surf rescue training built foundations that enabled me to feel confident in my ability to take on challenges in all areas of life, and to know the reward of achieving long-term goals, learning each day, and helping others."

Alexandra Shapiro

Ocean Beach Lifeguards, Fire Island, New York

11 Years Lifeguarding Experience

"Being an ocean lifeguard is one life best jobs in the world. You will make lifelong friendships and carry the experiences with you forever. It's also a very serious job. Unlike any other emergency response job, we are tasked with anticipating and preventing emergencies before they happen, as well as responding to them when they do occur. The keys to success are to trust your instincts, effectively communicate with the public, and respect the ocean. If you think someone is in trouble, go check on them. If you see a group of people engaging in a potentially dangerous situation, have a brief, courteous conversation with them. If the ocean is cranking, educate and protect the novice bathers. Lastly, always watch the water."

Scott Blutstein

Rockaway Beach Lifeguards, NYC

22 Years Lifeguarding Experience

"It's a career of a lifetime. Fulfilling in so many ways. It's an almost imperceptible job that means so much at the right time. Every action you do or don't take can be a matter of life or death."

Andrew Krupa

Spring Lake Beach Patrol & Neptune Aquatic Center, New Jersey

47 Years Lifeguarding Experience

"Understand just what you are getting into. Most people assume that we are just sitting there tanning, but don't understand the seriousness of the job. Also, not everyone will say thanks for saving them. You work long hours, tired and exhausted at the end of every shift, but I wouldn't trade it for the world."

Braeden Boyle

Bethany Beach Patrol, Delaware

Three Years Lifeguarding Experience

"Strive to become a waterman, and lifeguarding will become second nature. All the great leaders this world has known had one common trait. An undeniable communication skill set. Their ability to sell an idea, to motivate, and clearly express their orders. Lifeguards get to practice this skill 100+ times a day. You want to educate the public in such a way that they make an informed decision on their own safety. Lifeguard crews are a family. The crew you work with will become an integral part of your life forever."

Austin Turnbull

Navarre Beach Fire Rescue–Beach Safety Division, Florida

20 Years Lifeguarding Experience

"You could not make a better decision. The people you meet, the things you learn, and the experiences you have will change your life. It will certainly change the way you sit at a beach. Working or not, home or on vacation, once you start, you will never stop scanning the water."

Cameron Burton

Town of Southampton Lifeguards, New York

Nine Years Lifeguarding Experience

Index

D

Dead Sea, 35–36

death, 21–22

decision-making, 20

deep water rescue, 285

demonstrating skills, in relays and events, 224–229

digital pool testers, 84

distance
  about, 152
  running workouts, 165–167
  swimming workouts, 152, 158–161

dive lines, 195

diving board, whistling for, 92–93

dolphins, 57

doubt, 264, 287

drills. *See also* in-service training and drills
  for approaching active drowning victims, 192
  escape and release, 192–193
  first aid, 177–189
  overdose-related, 186–187
  sprint, 163–164
  stretching, 162

drone, 143

drowning, science of, 39–42

drug overdoses, managing, 183–188

dry drowning, 41–42

dry period, 104

E

eating habits, 14

Eddie Aikau Big Wave Invitational, 141

educating the public, 261

Emergec, 285

Emergency Action Plan (EAP), 82, 178, 193

Emergency Medical Technician (EMT), 124

endurance test, 76–77

enforcing rules, 262

entering
  competitions, 230–233
  competitions at junior level, 245–248

environmental concerns, stillwater facilities and, 107–108

Epi+Center Rescue, 209–211

Epstein, Cary (lifeguard), 143, 209

equipment
  about, 42, 196
  bathing suit, 43
  boats, 199–201
  checklist for, 86–87
  for competitions, 234–235
  jet skis, 198–199
  lifeguard stand/tower, 44–46
  for mock water rescues, 190–191
  for ocean rescue lifeguards, 121–126
  rescue, 47–49
  rescue boards, 197–198
  rescue sleds, 198–199
  specialized, 196–201
  sunglasses, 46–47
  whistle, 44

escape and release drills, 192–193

events
  demonstrating skills in, 224–229
  working at, 212–214

The Express workout, 154–155

F

face down swimmer, 193–194, 284–285

face mask, 271–272

face up swimmer, 194